# NEW
# LIGHT

*Discovering the Psalms*
*in the Prayer of the Church*

Richard Atherton

a redemptorist publication

Published by Redemptorist Publications

Copyright © The Congregation of the Most Holy Redeemer.
A Registered Charity

Cover: Orchid Design
Design: Rosemarie Pink
Maps: Bernard Atherton

First Printed January 1993
Second Printing June 1995
Redesigned Edition December 2002

ISBN 0 85231 138 9

Printed by Estudios Gráficos Zure Spain

# Redemptorist
## P U B L I C A T I O N S

Alphonsus House Chawton Hampshire GU34 3HQ
Telephone 01420 88222 Fax 01420 88805
rp@ShineOnline.net www.ShineOnline.net

# CONTENTS

# FOREWORD

In his Apostolic Letter 'At the Beginning of the New Millennium'[1], Pope John Paul II raised the rallying cry: 'Launch into the deep', as he urged the Church to move forward into a new era with confidence in the Lord. But in that new era, he argued, the Church must be "distinguished in the 'art of prayer', 'Christian communities must become genuine "schools of prayer"' and 'education in prayer should become ... a key-point of all pastoral planning'. Then came the surprise. He explained that he himself would make his own contribution to the education in prayer by dedicating his Wednesday general audiences to reflections on the psalms. And since then, week after week, he has been exploring the psalms that are used in the Church's Morning Prayer and Evening Prayer.

When 'New Light' was first published some ten years ago, it was an attempt to do much the same as the Holy Father has been doing recently, but to do it for the whole of the Office, not only for Morning and Evening Prayer. And so its aim was – and still is – to open up the treasures of the Psalter to those who wish to make the Divine Office part of their daily prayer. It was also hoped that it might help those who have long been acquainted with the breviary to deepen their love and appreciation of the Prayer of the Church, and in particular of the psalms, those ancient prayers that have been on the lips of countless men and women, Jewish and Christian alike, in all parts of the world for the past three thousand years and more.

The 17th century cleric and poet, George Herbert, was a diligent pastor to his people in the parish of Bemerton, near Salisbury. At the centre of his ministry were the offices of Morning and Evening Prayer which he recited daily with many of his parishioners in the tiny parish church. And even labourers in the field would interrupt their work to join in prayer from afar. In one of his poems Herbert wrote:

4

*The church with psalms must shout,*
*No door can keep them out:*
*But above all the heart*
*Must bear the longest part.*

This book is addressed primarily to the heart; it is not intended to provide a detailed commentary on the psalms but rather to show how these psalms, written so long ago and in circumstances so different from our own, can become rich and rewarding prayers for us today. However, prayer involves the raising of the *mind*, as well as the heart, to God. We can hardly do justice to any prayer unless we take the trouble to understand its meaning and how it might apply to our situation, and this is particularly so when we are dealing with the prayers of another age and another culture. Vatican II's *Constitution on the Sacred Liturgy* tells us that: "All who take part in the Divine Office are earnestly exhorted in the Lord to attune their minds to their voices when praying it. The better to achieve this idea, let them take steps to improve their understanding of the liturgy and of the Bible, especially the psalms".

That is why the first part of the book might be described as a kind of *Teach yourself the Psalms*: it offers a brief general introduction, designed to enable us to use the Psalter intelligently. One advantage of this arrangement is that from the outset it presents us with certain basic ideas about the psalms (e.g. how to 'spot' the different types, how to use the 'difficult' psalms and so on), so that we are able to approach them with greater confidence. It also means that material covered in this part can be taken for granted in the rest of the book, and so repetition will be reduced to a minimum.

The second part of the book deals with the individual psalms, as they occur day by day in the four-weekly cycle of the breviary. Ideally, this book should be read with the Prayer of the Church at hand. Sometimes it will explain a difficult idea, or a geographical location, or an allusion not readily understandable; at other times it will highlight a word or phrase that has special relevance for today, or indicate the way in which ideas in the psalms are re-echoed, and given a new depth of meaning, in the New Testament.

Finally, to repeat the call of John Paul, may I encourage readers of this book to 'launch out' with confidence into the Prayer of the Church, and like the apostles who responded to a similar call long ago, may they too in the end be 'amazed at the catch they (have) taken' (see Luke 5:1-9).

\*\*\*\*\*\*\*\*\*\*\*

The reprinting of "New Light" gives me the opportunity to thank once again all who helped in any way to make this book possible. In particular I wish to express my gratitude to the many experts – such as Arthur Weiser, Claus Westermann, Walter Brueggeman, Derek Kidner, John Graghan, whose scholarship underlies much of what is written in the following pages.

---

[1] Published on the feast of the Epiphany, January 6th, 2001

# Introducing
# the Psalms

*NOTE: This book is not a substitute for the Prayer of the Church but meant to be read in conjunction with it. The verses of the psalms are not numbered in the Prayer of the Church, though they are printed in stanzas. Throughout this book reference will be made to the stanza and, where the psalm is divided into two or more sections, to the section also. Thus, st 3 means the third stanza, while §II st 4 means the fourth stanza in the second section of the psalm.*

# THE BIRTH OF THE PSALMS

The psalms are deeply rooted in the history of the Hebrew people; but for them, the history was not simply *their* story; it was in a sense God's story, too; for he had intervened in their affairs, had rescued them and made them his own people, and in doing so had revealed something of himself. At the heart of their response to that revelation was prayer and worship.

Thus, in briefly tracing Israel's history not only do we discover the context in which the psalms came to be born; we also meet people and ideas that surface time and again in the psalter. The history can be summarized in three phases:

**Abraham to David, David to the Exile and Exile to Jesus Christ.**

### PHASE ONE: Abraham to David

| | | |
|---|---|---|
| 1850 | Abraham to Canaan, the Patriarchs | A FAMILY |
| 1700 | Patriarchs in Egypt<br>* *Psalm 103* (14th cent) | |
| 1250 | Exodus, Covenant and Law | A NATION |
| 1220-1200 | Entry into Canaan, slow progress<br>* *Psalm 28* | |
| 1200-1020 | Judges | |
| 1030 | King Saul | A KINGDOM |

The story begins almost 4,000 years ago with Abraham, who lived in Mesopatamia, 'the land between the two rivers' (Tigris and Euphrates), in what is now Iraq. Like other nomadic shepherds, he was used to moving from place to place to find water and pasturage for his flocks. But one day he set out on the most momentous journey of his life. In answer to God's call, he left his own country and people and made his way to Canaan, later to be called Palestine. Locked in his heart there was a great secret: God had entered into a covenant, a solemn alliance, with him, which carried with it the promise of a land, numerous descendants who would become a great nation, and a blessing that would extend to all people. The promise began to be fulfilled with the birth of his son, Isaac; then with that of his grandson, Jacob. Having proved his faithfulness to God, Jacob was given the new name Israel, a name later to be passed on to the whole people who were descended from him through his twelve sons.

When we take up the story again, some 500 years after the call of Abraham, the Israelites are a sizable colony settled in Egypt, but they are in a desperate situation. Their growth in numbers seems to pose a threat to new Egyptian authorities. And so they are oppressed, reduced to slavery, and, worst of all, a pogrom is launched against their children: every male child is to be killed at birth. It is in these circumstances that we meet the most outstanding leader and the most decisive event in the Old Testament. The leader is Moses and the event the Exodus, which comprises the escape from Egypt, the renewal of the covenant at Mount Sinai, the years of wandering in the desert where the group of runaway slaves begin to be welded into a nation and their arrival on the borders of Canaan, the Promised Land. These events were seen not only as the story of a people but even more truly as God's story. It was God who had led them to freedom 'with mighty hand and outstretched arm'; and so they became the heart of Israel's religion, just as the life, death and resurrection of Jesus were to become the heart of Christianity.

Gradually Israel's tribes took possession of Canaan, but their hold on the land was precarious. They were attacked from without, undermined by pagan Canaanite influences from within and isolated from each other. Though God raised up Judges (war-leaders, we might call them) who saved them from complete disaster, what they needed was a central authority, they needed a king. Saul, the first to assume that role, was little more than an old-style Judge, but his successor David was among the most charismatic leaders the people ever had.

## PHASE TWO: David to the Exile

| | | |
|---|---|---|
| 1000 | David king, Jerusalem captured, ark installed on Mount Sion<br>*Most of Psalms* from now on | |
| 961 | Solomon king – first Temple | |
| 931 | Two kingdoms | DIVIDED KINGDOM |
| 9th Cent. | Appearance of Prophets (Elijah,Elisha) | |
| 721 | Fall of Samaria to Assyrians end of Northern kingdom | |
| 701 | Jerusalem besieged by Assyrians | |
| 587 | Fall of Jerusalem, Temple destroyed Babylonian Captivity. | A CHURCH – community of worship, religion no longer identifiable with Temple or Jerusalem or kingdom or nation. |

David was a real king, like the kings of the surrounding nations, and his reign was a golden age for Israel. He showed his astuteness, as well as his military prowess, by capturing the virtually impregnable city of Jerusalem, which was perched on a mountain range, and making it his capital. Its fairly central position and its neutrality, in the sense that it had no associations with the tribes in the north or those in the south, helped to unite the whole people in a way that had never before been possible. Moreover, in a tent shrine within the city walls, he installed the ark of the covenant, the portable box with the ten Commandments, which had accompanied the people in their desert wanderings and was the symbol of God's presence among them. Jerusalem was not merely the political but also the religious centre of the nation; it was Sion, the City of God.

It was now possible to centralise the three great feasts, which had once been agricultural festivals but later became the occasions for celebrating Israel's deliverance from slavery. The spring **feast of Passover** commemorated the departure from Egypt; the feast of the wheat harvest, occurring fifty days later and known as the **festival of Weeks (Pentecost)**, commemorated the making of the Covenant; and the autumn fruit harvest **feast of Tabernacles**, lasting for seven days, during which the pilgrims lived in shelters made of branches, commemorated the forty years of tent-dwelling in the wilderness which preceded the entry into the Promised Land. On these occasions the people – including, in later times, many who lived outside Canaan – would come on pilgrimage to Jerusalem. They were times of great jubilation, especially the feast of Tabernacles, and the setting for many of the psalms.

David's son Solomon consolidated his father's work and built a magnificent Temple, with a special room to receive the Ark; now God had his permanent home among them. The Temple was to win renown for its liturgy in which the singing of the psalms played a prominent role. But the glory was short-lived: on the death of Solomon a split, which was never to be healed, divided north and south. The southern kingdom, Judah, retained Jerusalem as its capital, while the northern kingdom, Israel, made a new capital for itself at Samaria. The prophets, who arose in both Judah and Israel, strove to draw the wayward people back to faithful service of God, but a terrible fate awaited both kingdoms. First, Israel fell to the mighty power of Assyria and its people were marched off – into historical oblivion. One hundred and fifty years later Jerusalem fell to the new super-power of Babylon; city and Temple were destroyed. The people were carried off into exile and we are left with the haunting picture of the psalm-singers, unwilling to be parted from their harps, who sit mourning by the streams of Babylon, while their captors taunt them to 'sing to us one of Sion's songs'.

## PHASE THREE: Exile to Jesus Christ

| | |
|---|---|
| 538-333 | Persian period – Return from Exile<br>*Wisdom Psalms* |
| 520-515 | Second Temple |
| 333-63 | Greek period |
| 3rd Cent | The Septuagint – first Greek translation of Old Testament<br>*Psalms* in finalized form |
| 166-135 | The Machabees |
| 63 | Pompey captures Jerusalem |

Judah languished in far-away Babylon for the next 50 years, but though robbed of political independence and deprived of land and Temple, king and priestly services, they remained faithful to their religious calling. Each Sabbath day they would gather to listen to God's word and to recite the psalms: it marked the birth of the Liturgy of the Word and the rebirth of the people as a Church, a worshipping people of God. It was the Persian king, Cyrus, who eventually captured Babylon and allowed the exiles to return home. They rebuilt their Temple in Jerusalem, but with none of the splendour of its predecessor. The High Priest became both civil and religious leader. God's law became the law of the tiny state and the Jews (the people of Judah) involved themselves in the immense task of gathering and editing the books of the Bible. However, there were still difficult times ahead.

The spread of the Greek empire and its culture in the 4th century endangered the purity of their faith and eventually led to bloody persecution and a rebellion by pious Jews, whose forceful deeds won them the nickname Maccabees (the hammers). When peace returned, the Jewish boundaries slowly extended until they virtually matched those of King David's day. Then, in 63, the Romans invaded the land. Once again city and Temple were devastated (though the latter was re-built, beginning in 19 BC, on more lavish scale than ever, by Herod the Great), and Palestine became a Roman province.

It was in that province, some 60 years later, that a Child was born who was to be the fulfilment of all the Old Testament dreams; 'son of David, son of Abraham' (Matthew 1:1), he would gather a new people of God and forge a new and eternal covenant for all peoples, and his 'kingdom would have no end' (Luke 1: 33); he would be Emmanuel, God-with-us, and his parents 'named him Jesus' (Matthew 1: 25).

# THE AUTHOR OF THE PSALMS

Traditionally, David has been credited with the authorship of the psalms. That is not surprising: he was a poet-musician who served as lyre-player to king Saul, he is credited with the making of musical instruments and the setting up of guilds of psalm singers and there is even a poem in which he is described as "sweetest singer of Israel". It seems indisputable that he played an important role in bringing the Psalter to birth. However, no-one today seriously contends that David composed all or even most of the one hundred and fifty psalms.They reflect the spectrum of Israel's piety and belief over the whole course of its history. Psalms – the word simply means songs sung to a stringed instrument – were not unique to the Bible: they are already to be found in the writings of many ancient near-eastern nations and they have left their mark on Israel. It seems that at least one or two psalms originated in other nations during the first phase of Hebrew history (cf diagram p.8 ) and were later re-edited to become part of Israel's own collection of sacred songs.

Just as some psalms were in existence before David's birth, so others were composed long after his death, in the third phase of Hebrew history. The post-exilic period was particularly fruitful not only in the composition of new psalms but also in the re-editing of those already in existence.

The fact is that the Psalter came to birth only after a long period of gestation. It has sometimes been called the 'Prayer Book of the Second Temple' (the temple built after the Babylonian exile), but perhaps it could more accurately be described as the "Hymns Ancient and Modern of the Second Temple": a collection, and selection, of one hundred and fifty of the most popular hymns of Israel, composed by different people at different times in the long history of God's people and now brought together for the liturgy of the Jerusalem sanctuary. And even that is not the end of the story: it was perhaps not until the third/second century that the psalter was finally born in the form in which we know it today, a book of psalms, long in the making, but destined to become the most widely-used and best-loved prayer book in the world.

# FAMILY TRAITS IN THE PSALMS

Since it is almost impossible to identify either the date or the author of a particular psalm, the question that naturally comes to mind is: do we, then, have to take each psalm on its own, treating it as quite different from any other? Modern scholarship suggests what we have to do is to find the characteristics that certain psalms have in common, their 'family traits', if you like: their similarity in style and language and content. Then, they can be gathered together in groups or families. The psalter is largely made up of three main families. There are the **hymns** of praise, the **laments** or petitions, both of which have their own sub-groups, and the **didactic** or teaching psalms.

## The Hymns

The original setting for these psalms seems to have been one of the great liturgical festivals: they contain many references to gestures of prayer – raising of hands, rhythmic clapping, dancing, singing, bowing, bending low; to musical instruments of every kind; to incense and sacrifice; to priests and processions; to sanctuary and altar. The hymns usually consist of three parts:

*Introduction*: a summons to praise: "Praise the Lord, all you nations".

*Main Body*: usually introduced by 'because' or 'for', and giving the motives for praise: what God is or what he has done, especially creation and redemption.

*Conclusion*: a renewed call to praise or a request for a blessing or a simple 'Alleluia'.

In St Luke's story of the healing of the ten lepers, "one of them turned back praising God at the top of his voice, and threw himself at the feet of Jesus and thanked him" (17:15-16). Thanks and praise go together; indeed, the Hebrew word often translated as 'thanksgiving' is more accurately rendered 'praise'. And so it is appropriate that after the psalms which make up the family of hymns, we should turn to those which belong to the sub-group of thanksgiving.

**Psalms of Thanksgiving**: most seem to be prayers of individuals, though a few are undoubtedly community prayers. Their usual structure is not unlike that of the hymns:

*Introduction:* usually an expression of thanks or praise.

*Main Body:* a description of the danger or affliction experienced, followed by the anguished prayer.

*Conclusion:* an account of the Lord's intervention.

Two other sub-groups, linked by their style to the hymns of praise, are those of God's Kingship and those known as the Songs of Sion.

**Psalms of God's Kingship or Enthronement Psalms**: what distinguishes them from all others is the fact that they proclaim the reign of God and praise him as king. He is king because of his creative power, king because of the Exodus events, and king of all the earth. Some incorporate the formula "God is king". This has led scholars to believe that their original setting may have been a special feast, perhaps the great festival of Tabernacles, during which God's enthronement was somehow actualized through the liturgy, rather as our own Sacraments make present the mighty acts of Jesus.

**The Songs of Sion:** there are half a dozen psalms in this sub-group, and their prayer of praise focuses upon Jerusalem, or Sion, the holy city where God dwells in his Temple and where the tribes go up to worship at the great feasts. They love that city; they long for it as they long for God himself; they 'love her very stones' (Psalm 101:15). Praise and thanksgiving come naturally to those who believe in the all-powerful, all-loving and all-knowing God. They certainly filled the prayers of the Hebrew people.

## The Laments

These are prayers of petition and they make up the largest family of psalms. Like the Hymns of praise, these psalms have their own peculiar mood and form of words and manner of expression. They normally fall into three sections:

*Introduction:* almost always this is an anguished cry to God for help, an appeal which may surface time and again throughout the psalm, and sometimes it will be reinforced by questions – when will God take action? how long must the anguish continue? why does he not intervene?

*Main Body:* this is the lament proper, a description, often in colourful language, of the distress caused by sickness, enemies, exile, or desertion by friends. Despite the vividness of the description, the language used is so stereotyped that it is seldom possible to discover the precise nature of the problem. However, this is not without its advantage; it means that we can take these psalms on our lips and apply them to our own particular needs. Often the psalmist cites motives for God's intervention. More importantly, he frequently includes an expression of complete trust and confidence in God. The word 'lament' can be misleading: it might suggest someone ringing their hands in despair; in fact, it is a complaint or a pleading suffused with hope.

*Conclusion:* the spirit of confidence often spills over into the conclusion. The psalmist anticipates a positive response; indeed, in some cases the conviction of being heard is expressed with such certainty that it sounds like a psalm of thanksgiving for a favour already received. It may be that in these psalms the author is re-living his past trials and then giving thanks to God for his escape from them, so that the psalm in fact is not a 'pure' lament at all, but a straightforward thanksgiving. Or it may be that at the point of transition the person at prayer received a response (or oracle) from God by means of a Temple priest or prophet, so that at once his 'mourning was changed into dancing' (Psalm 29:12). Finally, on the principle that the darkest hour of the night is the hour before dawn, it may be that it was when the psalmist touched rock bottom in his misery that he found himself raised up by such conviction that God would intervene that he is ready even now to thank him for his help.      Closely linked to the family of laments is a small sub-group, which takes the element of confidence, a characteristic trait of so many of the laments, and develops that motif on its own.

**The Psalms of Confidence:** they are amongst the most attractive compositions in the psalter and their structure is extremely simple: an opening expression of trust which is then developed throughout the rest of the psalm.


## The Didactic Psalms

Their purpose and specific family trait, as their name implies, is to teach and instruct, but they do so in various ways. Some (the historical psalms) use Israel's history to point up the lesson that is to be imparted. Some (the wisdom psalms), which owe their origin to literary work after the exile, contain admonitions and practical advice: they trace the road to 'beatitude' (true happiness), stress the importance of the Law and deal with the great issues which have always occupied the minds of thoughtful people: suffering, God's providence, and the trials of the good contrasted with the prosperity of the evil. Some didactic psalms adopt a style reminiscent of the great prophets, who spoke in God's name and called the people to conversion and a practical concern for justice. Some (the Liturgies) are centred upon the dispositions of those who come to worship the Lord and the blessing that descends upon those who have worshipped in the Temple.

It might be useful to complete this section with two points to remember: First, not every psalm is a perfect fit for any of the families mentioned: one type of prayer will often overflow into another; Second, the value of being able to spot a psalm's characteristic traits and so place it in its appropriate family is that it enables us to tune in to the psalmist's wave-length from the start. We know what to expect, our hearts are ready for praise or petition or thanksgiving.

# THE PSALMS ARE POETRY

The psalms have a distinctive quality. They are not prose but poetry – Hebrew poetry, a poetry that has a life and rhythm of its own. It's not the kind of poetry we are used to because it doesn't rhyme or have an obvious metre. Its most characteristic feature is known as 'parallelism': the psalmist constantly repeats himself by saying the same thing in slightly different ways, for example, "give thanks to the Lord upon the lyre,/ with ten-stringed harp sing him songs". The parallelism gives a lilt and rhythm to his words. It has been likened to the steps of a ballroom dance, and, just as the basic steps allow for endless variation, so too does parallelism.

The three common forms it assumes in the psalter are:

> *synonymous*, where the thought of one line is taken up again with
> a slight variation of words in the next: "When Israel came forth

from Egypt,/ Jacob's sons from an alien people";

*antithetic*, where two lines express the same thought but by means of contrast rather than repetition: "For the Lord guards the way of the just/ but the way of the wicked leads to doom";

*synthetic*, where the second line completes or develops the sense of the first: "A mighty God is the Lord,/ a great king above all gods".

The psalmists use other poetic devices to make their words dance, some of which will be mentioned in dealing with individual psalms. However, the all-pervasive one is parallelism.

If poetry is "words that dance", it is also "words that paint pictures". The psalms are full of them, poetic images derived from their authors' own culture and background and often expressed in the colourful and hyperbolic language one expects of a poet. While some of them may seem strange and even uncongenial to our way of thinking – like the God who is depicted as a mighty warrior, fully-armed and ready to annihilate his enemies – most can be readily understood and appreciated. We know that the psalmist is struggling with the limitations of human language when he visualizes God as laughing, or covering us with the shadow of his wings, or stretching out his hand to hold on to us or even seeming to be asleep when we pray; we are one with him when he describes man as being, in comparison with the everlasting Lord, like a dream, or grass which springs up in the morning and withers by evening time. We know from personal experience what the psalmist means when he cries out that he is longing for God like a piece of arid ground longing for rain. And many thousands of people choose the shepherd psalm ("The Lord is my Shepherd") to comfort them at a funeral or to express their confidence and joy at a wedding. The fact is that most of the imagery of the psalms can be brought to life for us if we are prepared to try and understand the mind and heart of the psalmist-poet.

If we are to understand the psalms and allow them to give warmth and colour to our prayer, we need to see them as an anthology of religious poems. They are poems which welled up from the depths of a people filled with faith in God, and poems that continue to have a power and a beauty to captivate.

# THE PSALMS – OUR PRAYERS

We cannot always be on spiritual tip-toe, yet perhaps there are times when we feel a thrill of excitement as we take up the Psalter, for what we hold in our hands was our Lord's own prayer book. It was from this collection of psalms that he learned to pray at his mother's knee. They were prayers that had been honed by his people over the course of many centuries of extraordinary history, in response to the covenant God had made with them. They had been used by prophets and kings and by a countless multitude of poor and pious people and they had been sung to the accompaniment of musical instruments and elaborate dancing in the august setting of the temple. But, above all, these psalms, given by God to his people and inspired by his Holy Spirit, were the raw material of the prayer of his Son. Jesus was, as Augustine put it, 'this marvellous singer of the psalms'.

At the age of twelve, religious adulthood, Jesus went up to Jerusalem and, no doubt as on the other occasions throughout his life when he approached the Temple to celebrate the great Jewish festivals, he would have sung the **Songs of Ascent** [Psalms 119-133 (120-134)] with the other pilgrims. Each year at Passover he would have joined in the Great Hallel, meaning Praise, [Psalm 135 (136)], which tells of God's glorious deeds in rescuing his people from Egypt. At the Last Supper, he quoted the line of a psalm in reference to Judas' forthcoming betrayal: "Thus even my friend... who ate my bread, has turned against me" (Psalm 40:10); and when the gospels report that he and his companions sang a hymn after the supper, they are doubtless referring to the Egyptian Hallel [Psalms 112-117(113-

118)] which was the traditional conclusion to the Passover meal. And so Jesus and his disciples left the Upper Room singing triumphant psalms which proclaim the redemptive power of God and his utter faithfulness. But a terrible ordeal awaits him and in the agony of dying it is to the psalms that he turns again: "My God, my God, why have you forsaken me?"[Psalm 21(22)]. He was quoting from a psalm of lament. Like others of the same family, it may begin with an dreadful cry of distress but it ends on a note of complete trust and even of triumph. According to Luke his final word from the Cross, again taken from a psalm (30:6), is one of filial confidence: "Father, into your hands I commend my spirit".

If all Christian prayer is in fact a sharing in the continuing prayer of Jesus Christ, then the Prayer of the Church should have a privileged place in our prayer, using as it does the words he used during his earthly life.

As we have seen, the psalms belong to one of three 'extended' families – the Hymns, the Laments and the Didactic Psalms. There should be no difficulty in joining Jesus in praying the hymns of praise, or the psalms which offer thanks to God, or those which celebrate his kingship. Similarly, we can join him in the laments, the psalms of petition, and the psalms of confidence. We have noted how Jesus prayed Laments in his Passion; we too, as disciples, have to take up the Cross and follow him, and be united with him in crying out to the Father in the midst of our trials. We may not know the precise problem that the psalmist was facing as he called out for help: the language is stereotyped and often exaggerated. But that means that we can the more easily apply it to our own situation, which is what Jesus did in his death agony.

There is another point to note: when our Lord prayed "My God, my God, why hast thou forsaken me?" was he not gathering up all the anguished cries and petitions of the whole human race, all the bewilderment and distress that men and women experience when pain and suffering enter their lives? Like Jesus, we are called to the mission of prayer for all peoples, especially the poor, the suffering, the deserted ones. In times when we enjoy sound health of mind and body it may seem incongruous to be praying: "Have mercy on me, Lord, I have no strength; Lord, heal me, my body is racked; my soul is racked with pain"(Psalm 6:2-4). But if we take seriously St Paul's words: "If one member (of the Body) suffers, all suffer with it" (1 Corinthians 12:26), then we shall realise that in union with Jesus we are linked up with all our suffering brothers and sisters, and can reach out and help them with our prayers. If we are to make good use of the psalms, we must learn not to be too self-centred in the way we pray.

There are some Laments which are concerned with sorrow for sin: for that reason seven psalms are traditionally known as the **Penitential Psalms** (6, 31, 37, 50, 101, 129 and 142). Naturally, we have no difficulty in reciting them, but we might wonder how they could ever be the prayer of Jesus, the Sinless One. The answer, which was given by the early Christian Fathers is that the 'whole Christ' consists of Head and members, and he who made himself so intimately one with us that he was, in the bewildering phrase of Paul,'made into sin', also accepted words of contrition on our behalf.

Finally there is the family of didactic psalms which more easily lend themselves to meditative prayer. Here we find reflection on the lessons of salvation history, pondering on the Law which our Lord summed up in the great commandment of love. Here also is consideration of the deep issues, such as the problem of evil, which are seen in a new light thanks to the death and resurrection of Jesus.

However, in praying the psalms not only are we one with Jesus in his prayer to the Father; we are also brought to a deeper understanding of Jesus himself. As St Irenaeus expresses it: "Christ is the treasure hidden in the field of the Old Testament." We have the assurance of our Lord himself that that is as true of the psalms as it is of any other part of Old Testament. Within hours of his resurrection he was comforting his disheartened friends. "Everything written about me in the law of Moses and the prophets and the psalms must be fulfilled", he told them, and "Then he opened their minds to understand the scriptures" (Luke 24: 44-45). Gently he showed them that the psalms have depths and richness of meaning that even their original authors could never have guessed.

There is one group of psalms called the Royal Psalms. They do not belong to any particular family – they may be laments, for example, or thanksgivings – but they form a group because they all deal with an event involving the king: it may be his enthronement or his marriage: it may be a plea for his victory or thanksgiving for his success in battle; some are spoken by him, others dedicated to him, and still others addressed to God on his behalf. However, there are two remarkable features about them, which are of particular significance for our prayer. The first is that they use language of such extravagance that, even allowing for the conventional court style of a middle-east potentate, it is hard to believe that they refer to a mere human being. And the second is that, though composed in the era of Israel's monarchy (the second phase of its history) between the 11th and 6th centuries, they continued to be used even when there was no longer a king on the throne (the third phase of Israel's history). This was possible only because they were reinterpreted and given a future orientation. Those who prayed them did not simply look forward to an anointed king (the Aramaic term for anointed gives us the word 'Messiah', just as its Greek equivalent, *Christos*, gives us the word 'Christ'). They looked to *the* anointed king, the Messiah, the Christ, the one who fulfils Nathan's prophecy that through David's dynasty God's kingdom would be realized. In the simple statement of St Jerome:"Our (King) David is Christ". And of course in this context the exalted language becomes perfectly appropriate.

However, the New Testament sees Jesus not only as the Messiah but also, through his resurrection, revealed as Lord, ( a word reserved in the Old Testament for God alone). And so each time 'Lord' appears in the psalms it directs our attention to Jesus himself, the God man. We read "The Lord is my shepherd" and remember that Jesus said:

"I am the good Shepherd" (John 10,11), we hear "The Lord is my light" and recall that Jesus claimed: "I am the Light of the world"(John 8,12). As Augustine contended, in praying the psalms we do not merely pray *with* Jesus (as our Head), but sometimes *through* him (as our High Priest), and at other times we pray *to* him (as our God).

It is the advent of Christ which has transposed many of the psalms into a new key, given them a freshness of meaning. The glorious triumph of the exodus becomes the still more glorious triumph of the paschal mystery: the Lord has drawn to himself a new pilgrim people, marching through the desert of this world towards the promised land not of Palestine but of heaven. And the Songs of Sion which once celebrated the city of Jerusalem, now celebrate the Church on earth, as well as the glorious new Jerusalem of heaven, where everyone is a first-born child of God. They can even be used of ourselves: "Know you not that you are the Temple of God and the Spirit of God dwells within you?" The "Glory be to the Father..." recited at the end of each psalm is in itself a reminder of the transformation that has taken place in our understanding of the psalms. Jesus has opened our minds to their fuller meaning, just as he opened the minds of his friends on the Emmaus journey.

The Psalter provides not only a wealth of 'complete' prayers, but also a rich quarry of 'arrow' prayers which we can send speeding up to God at any moment of day or night: "Your love reaches to the heavens and your truth to the skies" (Psalm 56:11), "If you, O Lord, should mark our guilt, Lord, who would survive?" (Psalm 129:3), "It is your face, O Lord, that I seek; hide not your face" (Psalm 26:8), "My heart is ready, O God" (Psalm 56:8), "Your right hand holds me fast" (Psalm 62:9), "O God, you are my God" (Psalm 62:2), and so many, many more. Readers might like to make a collection for themselves so that, to use the words of St John Chrysostom, "we (shall be able to) season our actions with... the salt of the love of God".

Let me conclude this section as I started, with the reminder that as we pray the Prayer of the Church we have access to prayers which have been transformed and enriched by the coming of Christ. They are prayers which have been designated as the official prayer of the Church. After three thousand years they are 'still full of sap, still green' (Psalm 91:15) for all who use them thoughtfully and lovingly in praise of God.

# THE PROBLEM PSALMS

I have heard people say that the psalms are difficult; I would prefer to say that there are some difficulties in the psalms. Because of such difficulties, three whole psalms do not appear in the Prayer of the Church and others have been bowdlerised by the omission of certain verses.

Perhaps all the difficulties might be summed up most powerfully in the simple statement that the psalms are pre-Christian, not in the harmless sense that they obviously pre-date Christianity, but in the dangerous sense that they seem to be un-Christian, unsuitable therefore for Christian prayer. Of course, they are inevitably conditioned by the limitations which affect the whole of the Old Testament. Just as in becoming man Jesus accepted the limitations of our humanity, so in choosing to inspire the books of the Bible God accepted the limitations which the human authors brought to their task, at least to the extent that these limitations did not compromise his own holiness and truth. We cannot expect the psalms to contain the fullness of truth and moral sensitivity which we find in Christian revelation, but because they are prayers inspired by God, they cannot be completely contrary to what we have learned from Jesus. It's important to remember, however, that the Psalter, like any other part of Scripture does not stand on its own; it is part of a total collection – the Bible; and it is to be understood in the light of the whole. And so the 'shortcomings' of the psalms are 'remedied' by being read with a Christian understanding: even when we cannot share their sentiments to the full, there may still be much we can learn from them.

The four most common objections levelled against the psalms:

● *The psalmist often adopts a complaining – one commentator calls it a 'whining' – tone.* We have already noted that the majority of psalms are laments, and it is in them that this tone is at its best – or worst. The psalmist's enemies are lions lying in wait, they seek his life, they mock him and plot against him, lay snares for him and trample upon him, their lying tongues are swords and arrows. As for himself: "My life is spent with sorrow and my years with sighs" (Psalm 30:11). To some extent this may be explained by the fact that we are dealing with poetry; but also by the fact that orientals, ancient or modern, are less inhibited in the expression of emotion than are westerners.

● *The psalms sometimes show an extraordinary spirit of self-righteousness.* We who have been trained to go to God, saying "God, be merciful to me a sinner", even when we do not feel too sinful, sense unease when asked to say with the psalmist: "Give judgement for me, Lord; I am just and innocent of heart" (Psalm 7:9). However, what the psalmist is claiming is not an absolute holiness but a relative one, claiming that he is not to be classed with those who have completely rejected God. Moreover, it seems probable that some of these expressions of innocence belong to a situation where the psalmist has been wrongfully accused, and is simply making his 'not guilty' plea to the charge brought against him.

However, there is perhaps more to it than that. After all, do we not pray: "Forgive us our trespasses as we forgive those who trespass against us", the implication being that we always forgive those who have hurt us? Do we not proudly proclaim that we are children of God, though we often do not behave as though we were? Putting this another way, it seems that prayer, even undoubtedly Christian prayer, is sometimes more an expression of what we aspire to be than of what we are. So we need find no difficulty in praying: "O Lord, my heart is not proud, nor haughty my eyes..." (Psalm 130:1). That may not indicate what I really am, but it is certainly what I hope to be, and what I want to be.

● *There is no mention in the psalter of such basic beliefs as the after-life or the existence of only one God.* It is always dangerous to assert that others do not believe something because it is not mentioned in their writings. Nonetheless, the experts agree that it is not until the 2nd Century, in the Book of Daniel, that the first clear affirmation of individual resurrection to life beyond the tomb makes its appearance. If this is so, we cannot expect psalms which come from an earlier age to offer more than they do. It may surprise us that, according to the psalmist, no praise can go up to God and all human existence is diminished in Sheol – the dark, silent underworld to which all the dead descend. However, there are two points to be made. The first is that we cannot but be filled with admiration for our ancestors who, with no clear knowledge of an after-life, still strove to live according to God's law, still loved him and wanted him to be known, still clung to him with amazing faith as their sure Rock, as the everlasting One. And that leads to the second point: while there may be no explicit belief in an after-life, the seeds of that belief already seem to be present. It is as though these people are struggling towards the great truth: indeed, there are verses of the psalms which suggest that they have already reached it. Even if these texts are not as decisive as they appear, they are certainly milestones on the road to a clear belief in eternal life.

It is also rather disconcerting to find in some of the psalms what we might call a spirit of competition between the Lord and the gods of other nations: 'Among the gods there is none like you, O Lord' (Psalm 85:8). Did the psalmist, then, believe that there were many gods, and if so can we join him in his mistaken belief? The answer to the first part of the question is that in all probability he never stopped to think about it; but what he knew was that all other deities were as nothing compared with the God of Israel: they did not deserve to be called gods. Whatever about the theory, in practice he was certain that there was no god to be compared with the Lord. We can surely join with him in that. Indeed, when we recall how the Hebrews were crushed by massive nations like the Babylonians, the Assyrians, the Persians, the Greeks, the Romans – each attributing its success to its gods – then it's a triumph of faith that the psalmist should still have asserted that the gods of the nations were false and empty. As one writer has said, the hymns of praise which compare the Lord God with the gods of other nations were in fact for the Hebrews a magnificent profession of faith. We who live in a world which has its own false gods – power, sex, science, technology, to mention but a few – should not experience any reluctance in using these same psalms as our own act of allegiance to the Lord our God.

● *Finally, we come to the psalms which cause most difficulty, those which seem replete with hatred and vengeance.* What are we to make of them? We might begin by noting that even in the New Testament there are 'hard sayings'. What do we make of parts of the Book of Revelation, for example, or of some of the words of Paul? What did Jesus mean by hating our parents and brothers and sisters?

We tend to adopt delicate ways of putting things, whereas the Hebrews were uninhibited in expressing what was in their hearts. In their passionate concern, they sometimes use blood-thirsty language. Faced with appalling injustices, they realise that God is on their side, they are involved in his conflict. And of course that is how the Hebrews saw it. They had a black-and-white view of things. People were either good or bad, for God or against him, in the right or in the wrong – there was no middle ground – and those who were bad ought to be got rid of. Israel's cause was God's cause and God's cause must prevail. Moreover, since, as we have seen, there was scarcely any awareness of an after-life, if there was to be any justice, if the universe was to be sane and fair, then God must be vindicated and the wicked punished now.

In a 'just war' we pray for the success of our armies, carefully avoiding any mention of what this will entail: the wholesale destruction of cities, the death and maiming of countless innocent people. The psalmist is prepared to spell out in detail what defeat will cost the enemy. In a very real sense he was not able to express his legitimate hopes and desires in a way that would be approved by a Christian theologian; after all, he was totally ignorant of the principle of 'double effect'. As for 'hate the sin and love the sinner', he might have found that beyond his comprehension, because he could see only too clearly that the sin did not exist on its own but in a person. How therefore could he hate the one without hating the other? We must not blame him because he may have lacked our ethical sophistication.

As for the Christian use of these psalms, that becomes not merely possible but a joy if we apply to them the response that Abraham Lincoln is reputed to have made when he was accused of being too generous towards his enemies: "Do I not destroy my enemies by making them my friends?" That is certainly God's way of 'destroying' his enemies, and it can be the way of his followers too. We are able to adapt these psalms for our use, by praying, and praying passionately, for the complete destruction of all the sin – God's chief enemy – that still flourishes within the world and within us.

# The Four Week Psalter

# THE DAILY RECURRING CANTICLES AND PSALMS

Psalms and psalm-like hymns are to be found throughout the Old and New Testaments. Unlike the 'official' psalms, Canticles (a 'canticle' means literally a little song) are usually set in a particular historical context. For example, Mary prays: "My soul magnifies the Lord" in response to Elizabeth's greeting on the occasion of her visitation to her elderly cousin. More than 50 canticles appear in the *Prayer of the Church*. Three of them (known from the first word in their latin translation as the *Benedictus*, the *Magnificat* and the *Nunc Dimittis*), as well as Psalm 94(95), are recited every day.

## Psalm 94 (95) Hymn/Didactic *

What a fine hymn with which to begin the office day by day. In this Invitatory psalm, as it is called, we are invited to come rejoicing into the presence of our great God. Whatever the troubles or difficulties we may face this particular morning, there is always room in a Christian heart for deep-down joy and gratitude. The motives for them are spelt out almost immediately (st 2 & 3).

In the first place, he is *a mighty God*, so mighty that the so-called *gods* of the surrounding nations are simply his subjects. In the words of the Negro spiritual: 'He's got the whole world in his hands': the very *depths of the earth*, down to the underworld of Sheol, and the topmost peaks of the *mountains*, up to the heavens themselves; the firm and steady *land* and the volatile, unstable waters of the *sea*. All, including ourselves, are of his making.

In the second place, not only are we and all creation sustained in the hands of the Creator King, we are also led by the hands of the Shepherd, Redeemer King. He *is our God*; what could be more

* In place of Psalm 94, Psalm 99, Psalm 66 or Psalm 23 may be used

natural than that we should *bow and bend low* and *kneel* before him in worship.

At this point (st4), there is a noticeable change of mood: the hymn of praise gives way to a 'didaction', or instruction. The explanation may lie in the fact that this psalm is associated with the feast of Tabernacles, when for a whole week the people dwelt in tents so as to 'relive' the experience of the Israelites during their years in the desert. We can imagine the excited pilgrims arriving in Jerusalem ready to take part in the liturgy. But they are brought to a halt by a Temple spokesman (a prophet, perhaps) who reminds them that the desert days were a time of temptation and failure. At *Meribah* and at *Massah* (two places in the wilderness whose names mean, respectively, 'dispute' and 'testing') their ancestors had disputed with God (Exodus 17:1-7). They had put him to the test by their unwillingness to listen to him and their lack of faith; and so they spent forty years in the desert and failed to enter the Promised Land. The pilgrims, therefore, are urged to *listen to his voice* and to do so with a docile heart.

The letter to the *Hebrews* (3:7-4:13) underlines the continuing relevance of this psalm. We too must be responsive to God's word, for only then shall we enter into his rest, the promised land of heaven. It is fitting that the first psalm we recite each day should begin with a call to worship, but also with a reminder that our worship, our praying of the psalms, will be of no avail, unless it is accompanied throughout the day by a readiness to listen to his voice and put it into practice. It was Jesus who warned: "It is not those who say 'Lord, Lord,' who will enter the kingdom of heaven, but the person who does the will of my Father in heaven." (Matthew 7:21).

## The Benedictus (Luke 1: 68-79)

This New Testament canticle is set in the context of the circumcision of John the Baptist. After much discussion about the name to be given to the child, his father Zechariah indicates that it is to be John.

At that moment his speech is restored and, filled with the Holy Spirit, 'he spoke and praised God'. It is his prayer of praise that becomes ours each morning in the *Benedictus*.

It falls into four sections. In the first (st 1), we bless *the Lord, the God of Israel* because of the gracious way in which he *has visited his people* and brought them salvation. In the second (st 2-4), our thoughts go back to King David; God has kept the promise he made, through the prophet Nathan, that he would raise up a son to David and establish his throne for ever (II Sam 7:8-17). Then, our thoughts reach back further still – to Abraham, 'our father in faith'. Because of God's *love*, a traditional covenant virtue, the solemn covenant he made with Abraham (Gen 17:1-14) is now fulfilled. The third section (st 5-6a) brings us to John the Baptist. His father looks down at the little boy in his arms and proclaims that he is destined to be the *prophet of the Most High ... to prepare his ways before him.* And when the Saviour comes, the people will know because he will bring *forgiveness of all their sins.*

And so to the final section (st 6b-7): this tiny child is like a bridge between the promises and covenants in the Old Testament and Jesus in the New, through whom all the longing and yearning of the past are to be realised. For he is the embodiment of the *loving kindness of the heart of our God*; his coming is a *dawn from on high*, bringing *light to those in darkness...* and *the shadows of death*, and guiding us *into the way of peace.*

Again we have reason to rejoice that the Church places on our lips at Morning Prayer so appropriate a hymn of praise:

● We bless the Lord who will visit us this day and offer us his saving help;

● We thank him that we live in the time of the new and eternal covenant;

● We pray that we may be apostles who will prepare his way before him and *serve him in holiness and justice*, living this day and *all the days of our life in his presence.*


## The Magnificat (Luke 1:46-55)

As evening draws on we pray the canticle that Pope Paul VI described as "Mary's prayer par excellence, the song of the Messianic times in which there mingles the joy of the ancient and the new Israel" *(Marialis Cultus, 18)*. This beautiful canticle of praise is the outpouring of the heart of one who holds within her the Saviour of the world.

Mary's whole being thrills with joy as she *glorifies the Lord*, acknowledging him as her *Saviour*. The reasons for the praise and the joy immediately become apparent. Mary thinks of the present and what God has done for her, then of the future and what God will do for all who love and reverence him, and, finally, of the past and what God has done to fulfil his promises.

In st 1b-2a she praises God who *looks on* her. This is a biblical way of expressing the gentle tenderness with which he stooped down to her at the annunciation. The implication is that he was drawn by her *lowliness,* a word with deep roots in the Old Testament, where there is frequent allusion to the *anawim* or 'poor ones'. Originally used of the physically poor, with the passage of time the word took on a more spiritual sense to include all those who through sickness, oppression, widowhood or other misfortune, had discovered their own 'lowliness', their utter need of God. Just as, in Luke's gospel, Mary is presented as the ideal Christian, so she also "stands out among the 'humble' and 'poor' of the Lord who confidently hope in him for salvation and receive it from him" *(The Constitution on the Church 55)*. If she now *glorifies* him (literally, makes him great) that is because he has already *worked marvels* (literally, done great things) for her, in making her, *his servant*, the mother of the Lord. She gladly foretells that *all ages will call me blessed,* knowing that ultimately all the glory goes to him for he is *almighty* and it is *his name* (he himself) that is *holy* in the absolute sense of the term.

As Mary associates herself with the 'poor ones' of the past, she also links herself with her Christian brothers and sisters of the future (st 2b-4), for *his mercy,* a covenant word implying love and grace and faithfulness, is not confined to her but spreads out *from age to age* to all the 'poor ones', who *fear him* and look to him with trust and reverence. But a different fate awaits the *proud-hearted* for they are the opposite to the 'poor ones': they are so self-sufficient that they recognise no need for God or his help, and they will be scattered like a defeated army.

The next few lines help us to understand why some dictatorships have condemned the Magnificat as subversive, while those who suffer at their hands – the poor, the marginalised, the have-nots – have hailed it as a Magna Charta of liberation. The God who has done great things for Mary, *puts forth his arm in strength* to bring about a complete reversal of fortune as between the *mighty* and the *lowly,* the *rich* and the *starving.*

And so Mary's hymn moves to its conclusion (st 5) as she praises God for his faithfulness to *his servant*, an expression often used of Israel in the Old Testament. He *protects* his people, in the sense of stretching out his hand to support them. Again, all is attributed to his loving *mercy*, a key word in the Magnificat, which stretches back even to *Abraham* and the days before Israel had come into existence.

"Mary's hymn", as Pope Paul VI reminds us, "has spread far and wide and has become the prayer of the whole Church in all ages". Many of its expressions – God's 'almighty power', his 'holy' name, his 'outstretched arm', his 'mercy', his 'remembering' of his promises – call to mind the mighty deeds performed in the exodus and through the covenant. Now they all take on a new depth of meaning: through Mary we have received Jesus, whose death and resurrection are the true exodus. Now we see the fulfilment of all that went before, the sealing of the new covenant, the birth of the new Israel, the definitive raising up of the poor and the lowly, the final overwhelming proof of God's loving mercy. "The *Magnificat* is .. the voice of Mary, singing in the heart of the Church, 'for ever', the spiritual song of salvation" (Isidro G Civit), and it is our privilege to share it with her, joyously and gratefully, at each Evening Prayer.

## The Nunc Dimittis (Luke 2:29-32)

This is the last of the 'psalms, hymns and inspired songs' (Colossians 3:16) which we pray each day. The Nunc Dimittis is part of Night Prayer.

A missionary once described how in a remote corner of Africa she came across a very old woman, more than 90 years of age, who had never before met a white person. Despite her age and the extremely difficult circumstances in which she lived, her face shone with peace and serenity. In the course of a conversation which, because of language difficulties, was slow and painstaking, the old lady explained that she accepted everything because she trusted in her 'father' to whom she talked each day. Her human father was long since dead, and so the missionary asked her to say something more about this 'father' of hers: who was he? did he ever tell her anything? The response to the last question was stunning: "Yes, he tell me that I do not die until white missionary pour water over my head"! Within hours the old lady had been baptized and confirmed – and two days later she was dead.

That incident sheds light upon the event which took place when the aged Simeon met Mary and Joseph in the Temple courts, where they had come to 'present' Jesus 'in accordance with the law of the Lord'. Simeon had been assured by the Spirit that he would not die before he had set eyes on the Messiah. With face alight with joy, he takes the child from Mary's arms and announces his readiness to die, because now, in this little bundle of humanity, his eyes are gazing upon our *salvation*, salvation for the whole human race – a *light* to the Gentiles and *glory* for Israel.

"Each day dies with sleep" wrote Gerard Manley Hopkins. That is why from early Christian times this canticle has been used as a night prayer. As we prepare for the 'little death' of sleep, we thank the Lord for the signs of his saving work and the radiance of his light which we have experienced this day. But might we not also express through this canticle our readiness to accept our 'dismissal', our death, whenever and however it may come?

# WEEK 1 SUNDAY

## EVENING PRAYER I
### PSALM 140 (141) Lament

We begin the four-week cycle of prayer with a psalm which admirably sets the tone for the rest. We beg that our *prayer*, and here it can mean all the psalms we say in the coming month, may ascend like a column of sweet-smelling *incense* before the Lord and that the accompanying gesture, the *raising of my hands, may be like an evening oblation.* Mention of incense and sacrifice turns our thoughts to Jesus, who gave himself "as a fragrant offering and a sacrifice to God" (Ephesians 5:2).

It is clear from the start that the psalmist is in considerable distress. Whatever the cause, we can join him in asking God to *set a guard* over our *mouth*, which speaks to him, lest it be used for sinful purposes, and over our *heart*, which is raised to him, lest it turn to what is wrong. We pray to resist those who tempt us. As the psalmist suggests, it is better to receive a reprimand, or even a blow, from a good person, than to be feted and banquetted by a wicked. The next few lines (st 4) are notoriously difficult. It may be best not to delay over them but quietly leave them to one side – like the person who moves a piece of unappetizing gristle to the edge of the plate. (We can always give the 'gristle treatment' to parts of a psalm that are hard to digest – so long as we realise that one day we may discover that they have more to offer than we thought at first). And the psalm ends in a spirit of faith: our eyes turned towards God and our lips making a plea not unlike the 'deliver us from evil' of the Lord's Prayer.

### PSALM 141 (142) Lament

This is another of the Church's traditional evening prayers. The loud and repeated cry *with all my voice* has an urgency about it like that of blind Bartimaeus, at the side of the road, crying out to our Lord as he passes by and refusing to be silenced (Mark 10:46ff). The plight is described in conventional terms: a fainting spirit, hidden traps, no means of escape, powerful enemies. But part of st 2 – *look on my right* (where one's advocate or friend might be expected to stand) *and see: there is no one who takes my part* – takes on a dramatic reality when in the garden Jesus experiences the loneliness of desertion by all his friends.

In st 4 we move from *prison* to *praise*. There are many kinds of imprisonment – being house-bound, or handicapped, bed-ridden or fearful – but if we have the trust of the psalmist we know that God will come to our rescue. If he does not bring us out of our particular prison into freedom, he will help us to find freedom within it. St Francis of Assisi prayed this psalm on his death-bed. Ultimate freedom from all that imprisons us is to be found beyond this life, where all the just will be assembled and rejoice because of your goodness to me.

### CANTICLE – Philippians 2:6-11
*Philippians* is one of Paul's finest letters, written in the late 50's or early 60s to one of his best-loved communities, at Philippi in northern Greece. This canticle, composed in the first decade or so of Christianity, links us with the earliest Christians, as we use it this Saturday evening in preparation for the Paschal celebration tomorrow.

One commentator has described its opening stanzas as a transfiguration in reverse. At the transfiguration on mount Tabor, Jesus' inherent glory shone forth in his body; but at his incarnation, though he *was in the form of God*, he did not cling to the external glory that was his of right, but *emptied himself* and became like us in all things except sin. Indeed, he went further than that, *humbling himself* in pursuit of the Father's will unto death, *death on a cross*, the kind of death reserved for a slave.

But crucifixion is not the end of the story: if his birth and death were a transfiguration in reverse, what followed was a renewed bursting forth of the glory that had lain hidden. *God has highly exalted him*, through resurrection and ascension, and given him *the name which is above every other name*, the name "Lord", reserved in the Old Testament for God himself. Now the dazzling glory, once hidden, is revealed and *every knee* bows in adoration before him.

Paul uses this hymn, perhaps already known to his readers, in order to teach them that, following the self-sacrificing example of Christ, they must forgo everything that threatens peace and unity among themselves. That lesson has lost none of its relevance with the passing of the years.

## OFFICE OF READINGS
### PSALM 1 Didactic
When the psalter reached its present form, this psalm was added as a curtain-raiser to all that follows. It is didactic in form, encouraging the wisdom that leads a person to lay hold of true happiness. Its author, good teacher that he is, presents his lesson in three ways.

First of all (st 1a), negatively, by showing what the wise man does not do: he does not become involved with the wicked; the three verbs – *follows, lingers, sits* – may suggest growing degrees of intimacy with those who are evil. Similarly, *wicked, sinners* and *scorners*, may represent increasingly dangerous company, the scorners being those who scorn God and all that is good.

Secondly, the teacher presents his lesson positively (st 1b), by showing what the wise person does do. He or she find their *delight in the law of the Lord*, which means the whole of the Torah, the first five books of the Bible, and prayerfully *ponders* that revelation and its implications *day and night.*

Finally, he presents his lesson by contrast (st 2-3). From the tree of Life and the tree of Knowledge in the garden of Eden (Genesis 2:17) to the fate of the 'sheep' and 'goats' at the Last Judgement (Matthew 25), the Bible loves to draw comparisons between good and evil. This psalm is in that tradition. On the one hand there is the wise person, who is like a fine up-standing ever-green, planted close to life-giving *waters*, so that its *leaves* never succumb to drought and it produces its crop of *fruit in due season*. We recall our Lord's words: "By their fruits you shall know them" (Matthew 7:16) and St Paul's about the luxuriant "fruit of the Spirit" (Galatians 5:22f).

On the other hand there are *the wicked*, who are like light-weight *chaff*. At harvest time, when the farmer throws the threshed corn into the air, the heavy grains fall to the ground while the chaff is ignominiously whisked away *by the wind*. So it is when judgement comes, *they shall not stand* – they will not have a leg to stand on, as we might put it – nor is there any place for them among *those who are just*.

And then a one-sentence summary. For each person there is a choice to be made, a road to be taken either *the way of the just*, which is guarded by the Lord, and leads to security and happiness, or *the way of the wicked* which *leads to doom*. Life is rarely so black-and-white as this psalm might suggest. Nonetheless, day by day we are forging our fundamental option in life, directing ourselves along that path which leads to eternal blessedness or that which leads inexorably to doom.

### PSALM 2 Didactic

This is the first of the royal psalms in the psalter, composed for the coronation (or anniversary of the coronation) of a Davidic king. The period between the death of one king and the enthronement of another was often a chaotic time, and so the ideal moment for revolution. The opening words of the psalm (st 1) show the world's rulers in a state of rebellion *against the Lord and his Anointed* (king) and eager to *cast off their yoke.*

In response to the *tumult*, God, who sits calmly on his heavenly throne, *is laughing them to scorn.* Of course, God does not laugh, but the use of such language is a powerful way of pointing up the folly of those who would set themselves against him: they earn nothing but his scornful laughter. That is frightening enough, but it is followed by threatening words, announced perhaps by a prophet, which *strike them with terror*: here in the Temple on the *holy mountain*, it is God who has *set up*, or consecrated, the king. To oppose the king, therefore, is to oppose God himself, and that is to court disaster.

At this point the king intervenes (st 3), expressing his trust in God. The coronation day was the occasion when, it was believed, the king was *begotten* by God, so that he became his (adopted) son. It may be that a special document or *decree* was drawn up, based upon the promise made to David concerning his heir to the throne: "I (God) will be a father to him and he a son to me" (2 Samuel 7:14). It is as son that the king has right of access to God in prayer and also the power to subdue all his enemies. Possibly the latter point was reinforced by a visual aid, as the king took up a *rod of iron* and with it began to *shatter* a row of pots, symbolizing the fate awaiting those who threatened him.

The final stanza (4) is a warning which the king now issues to all the *kings* and *rulers of the earth*. There is only one hope for them and that is submission to the Lord. To refuse that is to face *his anger*. This is a human way of describing the result of ignoring God and his rights. And the psalm ends with a word of wisdom: *blessed* (blissfully happy) *are they who put their trust in God.*

# WEEK 1 SUNDAY

On the face of it, a triumphalistic song like this, composed for the enthronement of the new king of a tiny nation some three thousand years ago, has no prayer value for us today, but we have seen how the royal psalms are Messianic. Their apparently extravagant language makes superb sense and their true meaning is revealed when we remember that, rather like the final pieces of a jig-saw falling into place, they look forward to the Messiah. Jesus is that Messiah, the one who at his baptism, as on the mount of transfiguration was acknowledged by God: ' You are (in the fullest sense of the terms) my Son, today I have become your father' (see Hebrews 1:5). This was quickly appreciated by the first Christians. Looking for spiritual comfort in their time of persecution, they found it in this psalm. In st 1 they saw a foretelling of the conspiracy (between the people of Israel and the pagan nations) which led to Jesus' passion and death (Acts 4:25ff). And if his Sonship and sovereignty lay veiled in the darkness of Calvary, they were clearly revealed in the resurrection (see st 3 of the psalm) when God proclaimed in action that Jesus was indeed his Son (Acts 13:33; Romans 1:4). And his royal power (see st 4) will attain its climax when he comes in glory to shatter all the powers of evil (Revelation 12:5).

Here then we have a psalm which invites us to meditate upon our Lord: upon his divine Sonship, his Messiahship, his death and resurrrection, his paschal victory, and beyond all these his ultimate triumph at the end of time. It is such a meditation that will enable us, as it has enabled the Church throughout the ages, to find that blessedness which is promised to those *who put their trust in God*.

## PSALM 3 Confidence

A gentle trust permeates this psalm. It has often been associated with king David in the grim days that followed upon the rebellion of his son Absalom, but it is enough that we know that it was prayed by a psalmist when he was going through some kind of 'desert' experience.

# WEEK 1 SUNDAY

The sheer number of his *foes* (notice the repeated *How many*) is frightening, as also is their jeer that even God cannot help him now (st 1). But he is undaunted, for the Lord is like a huge *shield* behind which he can safely find a hiding place. Thus he is able, instead of being downcast with despair, to hold up his head, confident that God *answers from his holy mountain* where he has his special dwelling among his people (st 2). St 3 reveals the extent of his confidence. He is able to *lie down, sleep* and *wake* without fear, despite the encircling foes, though he is still careful to pray (in st 4) that God may demolish them and that the whole people may be blessed.

As we celebrate the paschal mystery this Sunday, we might recall that, through the words of this psalm, some of the Fathers of the Church caught a glimpse of Jesus in his Passion, with every hand turned against him and yet continuing to trust in his Father. He goes down to the sleep of death, lies buried in the tomb and finally awakes to the glory of Easter Day, thereby proving himself *Lord of salvation* and winning a blessing for his people. It is this Easter Jesus who greets us today in our anxieties and fears with the words: "Have confidence, I have overcome the world" (John 16;33).

## MORNING PRAYER
### PSALM 62 (63) Lament
This psalm has proved to be one of the most popular of all. It is indeed among the most beautiful poems in the psalter.

The psalmist lives in a country which is not only closed in on two sides by desert, but also has many desert areas within its boundaries; it is hardly surprising, then, that when he looks for images to express his deepest sentiments, he finds them in the 'howling wilderness waste'. His longing for God is a terrible thirsting of body and soul;

it makes him feel like a patch of *dry, weary land* crying out for water. And so his thoughts turn to the *sanctuary* of the Temple where he can *gaze on* him and catch a glimpse of his *strength and glory*. (st 1)

Life may be the sum of all blessings, but he is ready to affirm that *your love* is a greater blessing than life itself. And so he resolves to praise and bless God throughout his life, with *lips* and upraised *hands*. Perhaps it is the thought of the communion sacrifices in the Temple that leads him to compare his meeting with God in prayer to a luscious *banquet*, bringing joyous satiety to his hungry, thirsting *soul* (st 2). He will pray to him night and day because he alone provides the help he needs. And, thinking perhaps of the huge gold-plated cherubs whose outstretched wings were thought to provide a throne for God above the Ark of the Covenant, he rejoices in the realisation that at prayer he is nestling *in the shadow of your wings*. (st 3)

In our Sunday Morning Prayer, maybe we too become aware of what C S Lewis called the God-shaped emptiness in the midst of our hearts. We experience a deep-down hunger and thirst which he alone can satisfy. And so we join our brethren at the Eucharistic assembly, where each one of us, by our very presence, will be asserting that *you are my God*. In the holy sacrifice, we dwell in the shadow of his arms outstretched on the cross and are invited to a more vivid awareness of his power and the glory of his holiness. We are invited to a banquet that can satisfy our hearts and fill us with joy, that brings with it the assurance of the help we need and a pledge that we shall praise him not only throughout our lives but for eternity.

And as we leave church today, ready to enter into the whirl of another week's work and cares and worries, we can be uplifted by the beautiful image which comes at the end of this psalm (st 3). At times during the week ahead it may feel as though all depends upon us, as though we are holding on to God by our very finger-tips, but the reality is that *your right hand holds me fast* and that is our security. How much easier to "Go forth to love and serve the Lord" when we take that assurance with us.

### CANTICLE – Daniel 3:57-88,56

This remarkable litany of praise from the book of Daniel (written about 165 BC) is the third of three songs sung by *Ananias, Azarias and Mizael*, three young men who were miraculously saved from a fiery death. Having refused to worship a huge idol set up by the Babylonian king, they had been thrown into a blazing furnace.

The Church calls upon us today, this day of rest, to nurture a sense of gratitude to God for this wonderful world that is all of his making. Like the Creator himself, we are to look upon what he has made and see that "it is good". All his creatures – whether it be those of heaven (st 1-7), or those of earth (st 8-10) – give him praise simply by being what they are, and, in a child-like spirit, we beg them over and over again to *bless the Lord*. However, only human creatures can give voice to the mute worship of the rest of creation. This song of creation would be incomplete if it did not include the free, conscious worship of the *children of men*, especially those who are true *servants of the Lord,* just, *holy and humble of heart* (st 11-14).

It can be a fruitful experience to recite this canticle out of doors, especially in the countryside, actually addressing the elements of nature and *the works of his hand* that are to be seen on every side. It may also serve as a reminder that ecological concern should be in the heart of a Christian, for it is difficult to see how we can join in this symphony of praise from the universe if we fail to respect God's creation.

# WEEK 1 SUNDAY

**PSALM 149 Hymn**

There is an almost tangible exuberance in this psalm, which celebrates the solemn renewal of the Covenant. The *assembly of the faithful*, gathered in the temple, are asked to raise their voices *to the Lord* in *a new song*, befitting such an occasion. There is to be rejoicing and exulting, dancing and music, shouts of joy and resting in his presence, for he is their *Maker* and *king*. More than that: he actually *takes delight* in them (even more than they delight in him) and he bestows his *salvation* upon them like a crown.

At this point, however (the end of st 2), praise of God gives place to *a two edged-sword*, and talk of *vengeance* and *punishment* and *fetters of iron*. No doubt the sword, like the preceding song of praise, was taken literally by those who sang this psalm originally. But it can be understood in a different sense: we who are engaged in a spiritual warfare against powerful enemies must put on the armour of God (Ephesians 6:10ff) and carry the "two-edged sword" of the word of God (Hebrews 4:12-13). Did Jesus himself use the psalm in this way? True, in the Garden of Gethsemane, he told Peter that "all those who take the sword will perish by the sword" (Matthew 26:53), but at that very moment he was taking up the sword in the sense that he was embarking upon the most bitter battle of his life, the battle which took him to Calvary. Thus it was that he earned the Paschal joy we experience today in the sure knowledge that he has conquered all our enemies. So let us *sing a new song to the Lord!*

# PRAYER DURING THE DAY

**PSALM 117 (118) Thanksgiving**

This psalm is one of the most complete examples we have of a thanksgiving liturgy. Its chief character seems to be the king who, having been victorious in battle, comes to the Temple to offer thanks.

Among those present are priests, levites (who assist the priests) and the festal pilgrims, including proselytes (or God-fearers, Gentile converts who did not accept Jewish regulations in their entirety). Presented in dramatic form, the 'script' for this psalm might look like this:

**Scene One** A call to praise God for his covenant faithfulness

Levites: *Give thanks to the Lord for he is good, for his love endures for ever.*

(Then, summoning the people) *Let the sons of Israel say -*

People: *His love endures for ever*

Levites (summoning the priests): *Let the sons of Aaron say -*

Priests: *His love endures for ever*

Levites (summoning the proselytes): *Let those who fear the Lord say*

Proselytes: *His love endures for ever*

**Scene Two** The King appears.

The King (recalling his fearlessness because of his trust in God): *I called to the Lord in my distress; he answered and freed me./ The Lord is at my side; I do not fear./ What can man do against me?/ The Lord is at my side as my helper;/ I shall look down on my foes.*

Priests (reflecting on the king's words): *It is better to take refuge in the Lord/ than to trust in men;/ it is better to take refuge in the Lord/ than to trust in princes.*

The King (continues his story, telling how he was in a fearful situation, surrounded by foes on all sides as though by a swarm of bees; the rhythm of the language is suggestive of the see-sawing flow of the battle. But the crisis came to an end quickly, like fire in a thorn bush, thanks to the Lord, whom he humbly acknowledges as his strength, his song (of joy) and his saviour): *The nations all encompassed me;/ in the Lord's name I crushed them./ They compassed me, compassed me about; /in the Lord's name I crushed them./ They compassed me about like bees;/ they blazed like a fire among thorns./ In the Lord's name I crushed them./ I was hard-pressed and was falling / but the Lord came to help me./ The Lord is my strength and my song;/ he is my saviour.*

(A 'stage direction', indicating the response of the festival pilgrims, and suggesting by its mention of the 'tents of the just' that this event took place during the feast of Tabernacles). *There are shouts of joy and victory in the tents of the just.*

The people (visualising God as a mighty warrior with hand raised in victory): *The Lord's right hand has triumphed;*

The King agrees with them: *his right hand raised me./ The Lord's right hand    has triumphed;/ I shall not die, I shall live/ and recount his deeds.(*He ponders on the fact that though God has put him to the test, he has not handed him over to death but rather given his life new meaning). *I was punished, I was punished by the Lord,/ but not doomed to die.* (He is now before the gate of the Temple and addresses the priests).

*Open to me the gates of holiness:/ I will enter and give thanks.*

### Scene Three  Within the Sanctuary

Priests:*This is the Lord's own gate where the just may enter.*

King (enters inner court and humbly bows in prayer):*I will thank you for you have answered/ and you are my saviour.*

Priests (taking up a common saying for an unexpected turn of events):*The stone which the builders rejected/ has become the corner stone.*

People (amazed at the extraordinary reversal of fortunes): *This is the work of the Lord,/ a marvel in our eyes./ This day was made by the Lord;/ we rejoice and are glad.* (They are encouraged to make further requests for deliverance) *O Lord, grant us salvation;/ O Lord, grant success.*

Priests (responding with a blessing upon King and people): *Blessed in the name of the Lord/ is he who comes./ We bless you from the house of the Lord./ The Lord God is our light.*

Levites (summoning the people to a festal dance with branches round the altar): *Go forward in procession with branches/ even to the altar.*

*King: You are my God, I thank you./ My God, I praise you.*

Levites (addressing the assembly, as they did at the beginning): *Give thanks to the Lord for he is good.*

People: *for his love endures for ever.*

This impressive psalm, Martin Luther's favourite, was the last of the group known as the 'Egyptian Hallel' [Psalms 112-117 (113-118)], which were sung at Passover to celebrate the Exodus from Egypt, the first two before the meal and the other four after it. This, then, was the final psalm that Jesus sang with his friends on Holy Thursday night before entering upon the greatest Exodus of all, the one that redeems the world. Only a few days earlier, on Palm Sunday, the crowds had greeted him with words taken from this psalm: "Blessed in the name of the Lord is he who comes" (Matthew 21:9), and, shortly after, Jesus identified himself with "the stone which the builders rejected" and yet which becomes "the corner stone" (Matthew 21:42). St Peter takes up the thought when he declares that "He is the living stone, rejected by men (in his Passion) but chosen by God (through his Resurrection ) and precious to him"; and so he urges: "set yourselves close to him, so that you too...may be living stones making a spiritual house" (1 Peter 2:4ff). The Church in her liturgy sees this psalm as referring to Jesus and, in particular, applies the words "This day was made by the Lord..." to Easter Day itself. And so psalm 117 finds a place in the Prayer of the Church every Sunday, the day of the Lord's Easter triumph.

## EVENING PRAYER II
### PSALM 109 (110) Didactic

This royal psalm, which appears more frequently than any in the Prayer of Church, is also among the most difficult, though its general sense is clear: in the first section (st 1-4) a prophet speaks to the king on God's behalf, and in the second (st 5-6) he speaks to God on the king's behalf.

The occasion, as in Psalm 2, is the coronation of a king, or the anniversary of his coronation. The Temple prophet delivers an oracle, *the Lord's* (i.e. God's) *revelation to my Master* (i.e. the king). He invites him to ascend the throne and, since the royal palace is sited on the right side of the Temple, God's house, he is being made to *sit on my right*. With this honour goes the task of being associated with God, as the instrument of his victories, so that all his enemies will have to make their submission by the traditional gesture (recorded in ancient sculptures) of placing their neck under his feet. At this point he receives the *sceptre*, symbol of royal power, as the prophet calls upon him to: *rule in the midst of all your foes* – they may be all round you, but have confidence in the Lord (st 2).

What follows (st 3) has been described as the most difficult verse in the whole Bible. It has been translated in a variety of ways, but in the version used by the Prayer of the Church it means: the king's enthronement is a new birth: in this ceremony *I begot you* (see Psalm 2) *on the holy mountains* (a probable reference to mount Sion, with the plural being used to convey the utter majesty of the city of God). Indeed, he was God's son even before the dawn of creation, because that was always in the divine plan.

And now (st 4) the prophet presents the king with another message: by the irrevocable *oath* of God: *You are a priest for ever.* In pre-exilic times the king often fulfilled the role of chief priest also, the principal mediator between God and his people (see 2 Samuel 6:13). His is not the priesthood of Aaron (from whom the other priests of Israel were descended), but rather that of *Melchizedech of old.* This strange king-priest from Salem (i.e. Jerusalem) met Abraham returning from battle, offered him gifts of bread and wine, blessed him and received from him a tithe (one tenth) of the booty (Genesis 14:18-20). The fact that nothing is said about his earlier or later history is taken to mean that his priesthood is eternal. It is this mysterious priesthood that the king is to enjoy.

The king has received royal and priestly powers; now (st 5) the prophet turns to God, describing how *the Master* (the king) *standing at your right hand...* will fulfil his awesome role and defeat the mighty kings ranged against him. He will *drink from the stream by the wayside and therefore... lift up his head,* a reference either to the rite in which a new king drank from the spring of Gihon at the foot of Sion to symbolize reception of new life from God, or to a warrior pausing for a moment to slake his thirst, before continuing on his victorious way.

The royal psalms are Messianic, looking towards an ideal king who will come. In fact, Psalm 109 is expressly quoted by our Lord in a Messianic sense (Mark 12:35-37). Arguing from traditional belief in the Davidic authorship of the psalms, he reminds his hearers that David calls the Messiah, to whom God addresses his revelation (st 1), *my Lord*; clearly, therefore, though the Messiah is a son of David, he is also something more, i.e. his Lord. Jesus is also hinting that he himself is the Messiah "and the great majority of the people heard this with delight".

Once its messianic import is accepted, this psalm opens up its riches. Jesus used it when he was on trial before the Sanhedrin (Matthew 26:64), promising that they would see him seated at the right hand of God. Similarly, Peter uses it on Pentecost day to affirm that Jesus is ascended to God's right hand (Acts 2:34f), and the same idea appears elsewhere in the New Testament: in relation to Stephen (Acts 7:57), for example, and in Paul's hymn to God's love for us (Romans 8:34).

The final line of st 1 is re-echoed in Hebrews 10:11-12: "Christ has...taken his place at the right hand of God, where he is now waiting until his enemies are made into a footstool for him" (see also 1 Corinthians 15:24). Jesus, as the letter to the Hebrews is at pains to show (5-7), is the fulfilment of st 3-4: for he is the eternal, only-begotten (not adopted) Son of God; and if Melchisedech's priesthood was superior to that of Aaron – since he blessed Abraham, the ancestor of Aaron, and received tithes from him – Jesus, the High Priest, is superior to Melchisedech. His priesthood is truly for ever and under the form of bread and wine, he offers a sacrifice infinitely more wonderful than Melchisedech's (see the first Eucharistic Prayer).

The final stanzas (5 and 6), too, are a prophecy of what Jesus accomplished through the strife of his Passion, after which he lifted up his head, radiant with the glory of the Resurrection.

Despite difficulties in the text and language that may seem a little strange to us, this is a marvellous psalm to sing on Sunday when we hail Jesus our King and Great High Priest, risen from the dead, ascended into heaven and crowned in glory at the right hand of his Father.

# WEEK 1 SUNDAY

### PSALM 113A (114) Hymn

This psalm, with its flights of poetic fancy, its parallelisms and vivid imagery, proclaims the Exodus and its accompanying marvels, not simply as past history but as an event which is still effective. It was the Exodus (st 1) which dramatically transformed a group of slaves, living among al*ien people*, into God's own *temple* and *kingdom*, living proof of his holiness and his power. The whole of nature was convulsed by the wonder of it all (st 2). The *Sea* (of Reeds) *fled at the sight* so that God's people might pass (Ex 14:21f). *The Jordan turned back on its course* so that they might enter the Promised Land (Joshua 3:14f). Mount Sinai *leapt* like a lamb as it quaked at the divine presence (Exodus 19:16), and in response to Moses' rod, the flint-hard rock (st 4) turned into *a pool, a spring of water* to quench the thirst of the parched desert pilgrims (Exodus 17:5f).

Humourously, or perhaps ironically, the question is raised: why did all this happen? (st 3) And back comes the answer (st 4), already hinted at earlier in the psalm but not expressly mentioned, because the Creator God was at work on behalf of his people. And when he is present, how right that the whole *earth* should *tremble* before him.

Allowing for poetic licence, we may still find it strange that a small nation like Israel should see itself as singularly precious in the sight of God and the beneficiary of such wonders. But is not the Church made up of only a minority of the world's population? The Church is his 'little flock', and yet, as Vatican II's Constitution on the Church explains, it is also a 'sign of intimate union with God, and of the unity of all mankind'. As we recall each Sunday, it has been saved, re-created by wonders, including the defeat of death itself, even greater than those recalled in this psalm.

**CANTICLE – Revelation 19:1-2,5-7**

This canticle transfers us in spirit to heaven where the mighty voice of 'a great multitude' of angels and saints celebrates the final victory of *the Lamb*. Crucified and risen, he prepares for his *marriage* with his bride, the Church. He "loved the Church and gave himself up for her" (Ephesians 5:25), and, despite the sins and weaknesses of her members, she has at last *made herself ready for him*. We, who are still on this earth, join the heavenly throng in giving him the glory. And as we cry out our *Alleluia* (Praise the Lord), we realise that this scene represents the intimate union with God which is the end for which we were made, the end for which we prepare in our daily recitation of the psalms.

*During the season of Lent there is a special Canticle:*
**CANTICLE – 1 Peter 2:21-24**

In St Peter's day many Christians were slaves and these words are addressed specifically to them. They show that the mysterious Suffering Servant spoken of by Isaiah (see especially Isaiah 53) finds fulfilment in Jesus. He is sinless yet suffering, reviled yet refusing to respond with threats, oppressed yet trusting to his Father. In this he is an example not only to slaves but to us all, for through baptism we have the honour of being the slaves of Christ (Romans 6:22). We are committed to following in his footsteps, to bearing the sufferings and hardships involved in living out our lives as Christians.

However, our Lord did not only set us an example; he also *bore our sins in his body on the tree*, so that we in our turn might be ready to *die to sin and live to righteousness*. In the measure that our Lenten exercises enable us to die to all that is un-Christian within us – and the wonderful thought that *by his wounds you have been healed* encourages us when the going is hard – we shall be ready to renew our baptismal commitment and receive "life to the full" from the Risen Lord in our celebration of the Easter Vigil.

# WEEK 1 MONDAY

## OFFICE OF READINGS

### PSALM 6 Lament

This lament is concerned with a serious sickness (the mention of *foes* in st 3 and 4 may simply refer to evil agencies to which the sickness is attributed); both *body* and *soul* are affected. There is a plea for God to relent, to bring healing; and the poignant cry *But you, O Lord...how long?* expresses the anguish of one waiting for a response; reference to the *groaning* and the *weeping* underline the suffering that is being endured. While trusting in God's *merciful love* the psalmist, relying upon current belief about the after-life, is not beyond a little gentle blackmail. If the prayer goes unheard – well, *from the grave, who can give you praise?*, from the abode of the dead *no one remembers you*, in the sense of taking part any more in the worship of the Lord. But then, as is not unusual in the psalms, the sadness and appeals for help suddenly give way to relief: the plea has been heard, the prayer been accepted (st 4).

Words from this psalm were used by Jesus to describe the fate of those who cry "Lord" but fail to do the Father's will (Matthew 7:23) and may lie behind his anguished cry before the coming Passion ("now my soul is troubled" John 12: 27). The Church in turn has adopted the whole psalm as the first of the seven Penitential Psalms: the sickness of sin is more to be feared than any bodily ailment. It tortures the conscience, prevents sleep, can even be fatal; but Jesus has assured us that if we turn to him with contrite heart the prayer will always be heard, the sin will always be forgiven.

### PSALM 9A Thanksgiving

In the psalms, "I" often stands for the whole nation, and even where it does not, the language used is frequently borrowed from the great liturgical occasions which celebrated, for example, a national deliverance. Whatever may be the case here, we can happily add our voices to that of the psalmist as, with all his heart, he praises and thanks the *Most High* for all his *wonders*. (We need to remember not merely the great and mighty ones but the small and humble ones that take place day by day and so easily go unnoticed). He reflects, in the larger-than-life language of the poet, on all that God has done to defend his people, insisting that he is *a stronghold* for the oppressed. What that means is beautifully brought out in the last line of §I st 5: *you will never forsake those who seek you.* A further call to the assembly to *sing psalms to the Lord* and *proclaim* his mighty deeds (2 st 1) is followed by a request for his own personal needs: may he be saved *from the gates of death* so that he may recount God's praise *at the gates of Sion.* Again his thoughts turn to the way God has dealt, on the one hand, with those who are *forgetful* of him, i.e. choose to ignore him, and, on the other, with those who are *needy* and *poor.* *Arise*, he calls, remembering no doubt that that was the cry that used to greet the Ark when it (and with it, God's own powerful presence) was taken out to battle (Numbers 10:35). The final words of the psalm take us back to the beginning: human beings, however powerful, *are but men;* to God and him alone the glory and praise belong. The Prayer of the Church expresses an act of faith that the ultimate outcome of all our struggles, whether as individuals or as Church, is never in doubt, so long as we courageously seek the Lord, for he will come again to judge the living and the dead. We can have the confidence of Jesus who, even before calling Lazarus from his tomb, was already sure that his prayer was answered: "Father, I thank you for answering my prayer" (John 11:41).

## MORNING PRAYER
### PSALM 5 Lament
Some people suffer from the Monday blues: the week-end is over; it's back to work again. If that is how we feel, this psalm should prove an ideal Monday morning prayer. To our *King* and *God* (the very

words are comforting) we bring our *groaning* and, still more, that of our brothers and sisters who really do have something to groan about: those perpetually in pain or distress, those who seldom if ever get a break – even at week-ends. We ask him to be a Shepherd and *lead* us in the right paths, despite *all those who lie in wait* for us: colleagues at work, perhaps, or next-door neighbours who ignore God or live by standards different from those we strive to follow, and whose mischievous hearts and honeyed speech is often a source of temptation to us.

Our problems, whatever they may be, we set before him expectantly, *watching and waiting* for his help. There are good reasons for our confidence. First, *the greatness of your love* (st 5), secondly the fact that he brings joy (*those you protect ... ring out their joy* [st 8]), and finally the conviction that when the Lord blesses anyone (and that is what we are asking for in this psalm) it is like being surrounded by a sturdy *shield* (st 9).

The words of st 5, *I through the greatness of your love have access to your house*, are particularly moving when we think of the Mass which is celebrated each day. It is thanks to his love that such a thing is possible. But those who are unable to get to church for the Eucharist can still rejoice in the thought that each time we pray, each time, for example, we open the breviary to say the Divine Office, we are given immediate access to God's presence. "Through him (Jesus Christ) we all have access to the Father in the one Spirit" ( Ephesians 2:18). The realisation that we have a God who loves us like this is indeed wonderful – even on a rainy Monday morning.

### CANTICLE – 1 Chronicles 29:10-13
The canticle at Morning Prayer, which is taken from the Old Testament, is always sandwiched between the two psalms, while the canticle at Evening Prayer, because it comes from the New Testament, always follows them.

# WEEK 1 MONDAY

The two books of Chronicles, in which this morning's canticle is to be found, offer a view of Israel's history from the time of David to that of the Exile. Its author, a priest, is particularly interested in the Temple and he sees king David as its inspirer and the organiser of its liturgy. It is he who collects expensive offerings for the construction of the Temple, having first set the example of his own generosity. He then prays this splendid prayer acknowledging that the gifts offered have all come from God's own hands; his kingdom is for ever and to him alone are honour and glory to be given.

At the beginning of a new week it is good for us too to recognise that all we have comes from God and to ensure that our voices join the unending chorus of thanks and praise that ascends from earth and in heaven to his *glorious name*.

## PSALM 28 (29) Hymn

According to an ancient myth, thunder is a sign that someone has died and gone to heaven and the great noise is God dancing up and down with joy. We may smile at such unsophisticated ideas, but behind them lies a wealth of theology; life beyond death, heaven as a joyous homecoming, and – a notion worthy of a prophet (Zephaniah 3:17) – a God who dances with joy. Similarly, there is often profound theology in psalms which may at first hearing strike us as strangely primitive. This psalm is a case in point, a splendid poem, vigorous in its power, which sees the glory and majesty of God revealed in a storm. The reverberating claps of thunder are nothing less than *the Lord's voice*, in fact in Hebrew the word for thunder (qol) also means 'voice'. The expression is repeated seven times, as though mimicking the sound of the reverberating thunder and so the psalm is often called 'the psalm of seven thunders'. Some scholars believe that originally it was a hymn in honour of the Canaanite storm god, Baal-Hadad. Representations of him, discovered in the Syrian coast city of Ras Shamra, show him brandishing a thunderbolt in one hand and lightning in the other. But if the poem was taken over from the Canaanites, the psalmist has refashioned it in terms of his theology. One sign of this is that the *sons of God* in the first line, which may well have been 'gods' originally, are now simply servants of the one Lord God. Another is that 'Yahweh', Israel's special name for God, appears no less than eighteen times.

The poem unfolds in three scenes:

**Scene One** takes place in the *holy court* of heaven where the sons of God (or, as we might say, the angels) are called to worship God in all his towering majesty and render him the *glory of his name* (st 1).

**Scene Two** describes the path of a fierce thunderstorm: violently, it sweeps in from the Mediterranean sea, where it could be heard *resounding on the waters* (st 2), and crashes upon *Lebanon*, shattering the giant *cedars*, renowned for their strength. Even the huge mountains of Lebanon and *Sirion* (Mount Hermon) are shaken to their foundations, so that they jump like a gamboling *calf* or *young wild ox* (st 3). The thunder is accompanied by flashes of lightning. Finally, the storm, coming from the north and making its noisy way down the country, rumbles off into the wilderness of *Kadesh*, which lies to the south of Palestine; in the Old Testament it is associated with Sinai where God's voice 'spoke' with thunder, smoke, fire and earthquake (see Exodus 19). There the gyrating winds strip the *forest* of its foliage and split the mighty *oak tree* (st 4). It is all a magnificent display of God's power and majesty.

**Scene Three** introduces us to the Temple where the God who revealed himself in the storm is greeted by the worshippers with the mighty cry of *Glory*. Just as in the time of Noah (Genesis 6-11), *the Lord sat enthroned over the flood*, unperturbed by all that was happening below, so he *sits as king for ever* (st 5). However, he is not simply a Lord of naked power, as suggested by the storm, but also a Lord of love, bringing *strength* and peace to his *people*(st 6).

More than one commentator has noted that this psalm, beginning with 'Glory to God in the highest' (st 1) and ending with 'peace to men of good will' (st 6), is reminiscent of the hymn of the angels over Bethlehem on the first Christmas night. Similarly, the conjunction of wind and fire (lightning) and the 'voice of the Lord' is a reminder of the events in Jerusalem on Pentecost day. As we raise our voices in the *Glory be to the Father* at the end of this psalm, we are giving praise to the mighty God, revealed in the wonders of nature, to Jesus, born in the peaceful silence of the cave, and to the Holy Spirit, descending in a mighty wind and plumes of fire – the three-personed God, to whom be glory for ever and ever.

## PRAYER DURING THE DAY
### PSALM 18(19)B Didactic
The Commandments have frequently been viewed in one of two ways. Either they were imposed by a selfish, autocratic God who was annoyed at seeing his people enjoying themselves, or they were given as a gift by a loving, caring God who was in anguish at seeing his people bringing ruin upon themselves. There is no doubt which view was held by the author of this psalm and others like it. *They* (God's laws), he declares, *are more to be desired than purest of gold and sweeter are they than honey* (st 4). The *law of the Lord* is so vast a concept (it includes the whole of revelation) that it has many synonyms. In this psalm we meet five of them, and each of them is briefly described (st 1-3). *The law of the Lord revives the soul*, it literally brings back spiritual life and vigour; his *rule gives wisdom*; his *precepts* bring joy to the heart; his *command* enlightens the eyes; *fear of the Lord* endures for ever; and his *decrees* are all of them upright. The psalm also characterizes the many-facetted Law of God

as *perfect* (mirroring his goodness and holiness), trustworthy, *right*, radiantly *clear*, morally pure and *holy*; and, finally, as *truth* itself.

Small wonder that the psalmist is convinced that *great reward is in their keeping*, or that he begs for divine help to overcome sin and to be acquitted of *hidden faults*. As Christians, we share the same outlook for we have heard from Jesus' own lips: "You are my friends if you do what I command you" (John 15:14). We scarcely need reminding that the sins of which we are aware often represent only the symptoms of the deep-rooted evil in our hearts. And so we beg that we may be safeguarded from *presumption* and instead turn with confidence to the Lord who is our *rescuer* and *rock*.

### PSALM 7 Lament

Though faced by an enemy who is like a fearsome lion which drags its prey off into the bush and rips it to pieces, the psalmist begins his prayer with a fine act of faith: *Lord God, I take refuge in you.* Against the cruel *pursuer*, the psalmist insists on his innocence and flings down the challenge. *If* (as has been alleged) *my hands have done wrong, if* (as you say) *I have paid back evil for good*, then I accept the consequences: *let my foe.. trample my life to the ground* (§1st 2). It is time for the Lord to *awake*, to *rise up* in his anger (Arise! was a cry associated with the Ark when it was about to be taken into battle; [Numbers 10:35]), and to *give judgement* (§1st 3). Not only in this particular case but wherever wickedness flourishes, so that the *evil of the wicked* may be brought to an end and *the just* may *stand firm* (§1st 4).

God is not only a protective *shield* and a *just judge* who is able to *test mind and heart*, but also a warrior fully-armed, who will use his sharpened *sword* and fiery *arrows* against those *who will not repent* (§2 st 1-2). The evil person is storing up trouble for himself. He is *pregnant* with malicious desire and will give birth to *lies.* St James who uses a similar image (1:15), adds that the final outcome will be death. The psalmist makes the same point with a change of metaphor: evil is self-destructive, so that the evil person falls into the hole he has scooped out as a trap for others, and *his malice will recoil on himself* (§2 st 3).

As so frequently in the laments, the final words are of gratitude and praise. The trust expressed at the outset has been vindicated, so let us *sing to the Lord, the Most High.*

## EVENING PRAYER
**PSALM 10 (11) Confidence**

In daily life we sometimes meet with the jibe levelled at the psalmist: "it's no use depending upon God now; see, the troubles and trials that threaten, your only hope is to fly away like a bird". In our down moments we may fear that the very foundations of our world are in peril, not only from the nuclear threat but also from the wide-scale rejection of Gospel values. It is tempting to look for some escapist route; but we would be wiser to respond, like the psalmist, with a reaffirmation of trust. Despite everything, *In the Lord I have taken my refuge.* He *is in his holy temple,* the heavenly temple where he has his *throne* and from whence he *looks down upon the world,* so that no-one, *just* or *wicked,* can escape his discerning *gaze* (st 3). As at Sodom and Gommorrha, *fire and brimstone* will rain down like a *scorching wind* upon the wicked. They have cut themselves off from his love; what they now experience can best be described as his 'hatred' (st 4).

Because of what the Lord is (*just*) and because of what he does (*loves justice*), the *upright* can remain confident: he or she *shall see his face* (st 5). For the psalmist the possibility of a face to face vision of God was scarcely within the realm of hope; for us it is a certainty of faith.

### PSALM 14(15) Didactic

It is customary for worshippers, as they enter a church, to bless themselves with holy water – a symbol of their baptism and a reminder that they must be in the right dispositions if they are to worship God worthily. This psalm refers to a similar moment of reflection before worship. The psalmist ask the Lord through the Temple priest what is required of one who seeks admission to *your tent* (st 1). The reply is not couched in terms of ritual requirements but reaches down to the depths of conscience. It sets out the qualities of a person of integrity. Though the list is not exhaustive, it covers many important aspects of life. The person of integrity is recognisable by his/her:

*Actions*: on the negative side, walking without fault and, on the positive, acting with justice;

*Speech*: always truthful, steering clear of slander or slurs upon the neighbour;

*Attitudes*: displaying loyalty to God by disdaining the godless (perhaps in the sense of "follows not the counsels of the wicked" [Psalm 1:1]) and honouring those who fear the Lord;

*Dealings with others*: always faithful to a pledge that has been given, claiming no interest on a loan (where it involves taking advantage of the misfortunes of a brother or sister) and accepting no bribe against the innocent.

The psalm began with a request not only about *admission* to God's tent, but also about a permanent dwelling on his holy mountain. It ends with the wonderful assurance that the person who fits the description given by the psalmist will *stand firm for ever*.

A world in which individuals and nations followed the moral conduct outlined by the psalmist would be a world transformed. It would be a world in which justice would reign supreme, with all peoples having access to the riches of the earth. It would be a world in which politicians would always respect the truth, in which business would be honest in its dealings, and men and women would not deceive each other or indulge in tittle-tattle (st 2). It would be a world in which people would be faithful to their promises – their marriage vows, their priestly commitments, their baptismal promises (st 3). It would be a world in which there would be no threat of nuclear annihilation, where wealthy nations would not give loans in order to make fortunes at the expense of those of the Third World (st 4).Such a world would not be far from the Kingdom. But the arrival of such a world depends upon the conduct of individuals, including what you and I have done – and been – this day.

### CANTICLE – Ephesians 1:3-10

This splendid Christian hymn is based on a popular form of Jewish piety, the *berakah* or blessing, which is not a request for a blessing *from* God but a blessing *of* God for what he has done or what it is hoped he will do. In this case *God the Father of our Lord Jesus Christ* is blessed because of the way in which he *has blessed us in Christ with every spiritual blessing*. These blessings, given us by the Spirit and drawing us into closer union with the Lord, were won for us by Christ and so are most clearly operative where the Risen Jesus is – *in the heavenly places* (st 1).

Four of these blessings are spelt out in the succeeding stanzas:

# WEEK 1 MONDAY

*Election*: from all eternity, *before the foundation of the world*, God made his choice of us, so that we are now to live *holy and blameless* lives (st 2).

*Adoption*: It was *in love* that God chose us, and in that same love has adopted us as his sons and daughters. It is all *according to the purpose of his will* and it all leads to the *praise of his glorious grace* (st 3).

*Redemption*: Together with our adoption as God's children has come *redemption, the forgiveness of our trespasses*. Again this is due, not to any merits on our part, but to *the riches of his grace which he has lavished upon us* (st 4).

*Revelation: The mystery of his will* is by definition beyond our full understanding, but he has raised the veil so that we are now privileged to catch a glimpse of the divine plan. That plan, as presented in the letter to the Ephesians, is the reconciliation of the whole human race, whatever the barriers of colour, culture, sex or social status (see Gal 3:28), and even of the whole universe, *things in heaven and things on earth* (st 5).

Though the Father is the one whose plan has been unfurled and the one to whom praise is due, yet at every stage the centrality of our Lord is driven home. He is the means by which we return to God. It was *in him* that we were chosen, *through him* that we received our divine adoption; *in him* and *through his blood* that we are redeemed; and, finally, it is *in Christ* that God's revelation has been *set forth*.

At the end of a busy day, how wonderful to be able to ponder for a while on God's amazing grace. To think on these mighty events in which Father, Son and Holy Spirit have conspired to pour out their love upon us and to carry us forward, as on the crest of a mighty wave, with the hope of final glory.

# WEEK 1 TUESDAY

## OFFICE OF READINGS
### PSALM 9B (10) Lament

The first part of this psalm, which we used at Readings on Monday, is a song of thanksgiving, but this part is more in the nature of a lament. It speaks of a situation with which we are all too familiar. The wicked are taking advantage of the poor, while the Lord seems to *stand afar off,* nowhere to be found when he is most urgently needed. Meanwhile, the wicked person grows in confidence: God won't touch me, he thinks; and then, more arrogantly still: *There is no God.* Indeed, his ways seem to prosper; it looks as though *misfortune shall never be his lot.* And so he becomes like a man-eating lion, lurking *among the reeds,* eyes stealthily watching for the helpless passerby, powerful limbs coiled *preparing to spring,* and proud heart assuring him: *God forgets...he does not see.*

The colourful language is hardly too bold to illustrate events which are taking place in many parts of the world today, and perhaps even nearer home. Our television screens and newspapers constantly draw attention to areas where the poor are at the mercy of those who, for all intents and purposes, have no God. Even where the oppression does not amount to active persecution, the poor are made to feel helpless and hopeless.

But that is not the end of the story. As in this psalm, wherever there is injustice and oppression, individuals of irrepressible faith are always to be found. The psalmist raises the age-old battle-cry: *Arise then, Lord!* The enemy may think you do not see, *but you have seen* and, what is more, *you take it in hand.* Just as the wicked man grew more and more confident in himself, so the psalmist grows more and more confident in God, asking him *to break the power of the wicked* and show that he is *king for ever and ever.* The psalm ends with a profession of faith that God will indeed respond and rise in defence of the oppressed. That is our belief too, as we pray for all the ill-treated poor of the world, though we are well aware that their final vindication may not be till the Lord comes in his glory and all must answer for their conduct before his judgement seat.

### PSALM 11 (12) Confidence

John Dryden described truthfulness as the cement of a society. When, through lies and deceits, that cement crumbles the whole fabric of human relationships is put in jeopardy. And when lying is compounded with boastfulness: *our tongue is our strength*, we can hide our wrongdoing by lies, then the situation becomes frightening. It is out of such a situation that the psalmist and those with him made this prayer. They are living in a world where, it seems, *good men have vanished.* The misuse of the God-given and God-like gift of speech is not only an affront to fellow human beings, it is little short of blasphemy against God himself. And so they call upon the Lord for help and beg him to *destroy all lying lips* (st 1-2). A priest or prophet from the Temple responds in God's name, assuring them that divine action will be taken and reminding them that God's words, unlike ours, are as genuine as silver refined by fire till all trace of alloy is removed (st 3-4).

Renewed by this promise the assembly declare their complete confidence in God's word that he will *protect us for ever*, however much *the wicked prowl* and *the worthless are prized highly* (st 5).

St Thomas More used to say: "The things we pray for, Good Lord, give us grace to labour for". We, who are followers of the Word, who is also the Truth (John 14:16), dare not recite this psalm without recognising its challenge to live with an honesty and an integrity which bear witness to our Lord and Master.

# WEEK 1 TUESDAY

## MORNING PRAYER
### PSALM 23 (24) Didactic

Like Psalm 14(15) at Evening Prayer yesterday, this psalm is, at least in part, concerned with the conditions for true worship. We can picture the pilgrims wending their way towards the Temple, singing as they go of God the Creator. To him belongs *the earth and its fullness* and *the world and all its peoples* . The whole world owes its solidity to him, for, like a man who gives his house a firm foundation by driving piles into marshy ground, so he has made the world firm and secure on the shifting *waters* of the deep (st 1).

By now the procession reaches the gates of the sanctuary and the cry is raised *Who shall stand in the holy place* (worthily)? From inside the Temple, the priests respond. What is required of a true worshipper is *clean hands* and *pure heart* (integrity in deed and in intent) and honest dealings with his or her *neighbour*; such a person will receive *blessings from the Lord.* With surprising boldness (there is no mock humility here), back comes the response from outside the gates that those who *seek the face of the God of Jacob* fulfil these requirements (st 2-3).

The second part of this psalm, composed at a much earlier date and added to the present Psalm 23 (24), envisages the ark being borne in procession. Since it is the throne of God (or, according to Psalm 131:7, *his footstool*), the gates are called upon to *lift high their heads* and the *ancient doors to grow higher* so that the mighty king of glory may pass through without his having to bow his head (st 4). The priests, as though asking for a password, demand *Who is the king of glory?* The response of the pilgrims is that he is the great warrior king of Israel, but, more than that, the cosmic king who haall the stars of heaven at his command (cf. Psalm 146:4); therefore the gates must raise their heads and the doors grow higher. 'Not so quickly', the priests seem to say, 'no one can afford to make mistakes in such a momentous matter; once again, who is this king of glory?' The response, though phrased in slightly different words, is the same. And there the psalm ends, but the implication is that the doors are swung open and the ark, which began its pilgrim way in the desert, now completes its ascent to its home in the Temple (st 5-7).

The Church uses this splendid psalm in its celebration of the Ascension. But it also uses it during Advent, when we recall with gratitude how Jesus, with "the glory that is his as the only Son of God" (John 1:14), slipped unobtrusively from the Virgin's womb into this world and came to dwell among us. But Advent commemorates not only the past (the birth in Bethlehem) and the future (his coming again in glory) but also the present. Throughout this day the same Lord stands knocking at the door of our hearts; if we will open he will enter in and allow us, as dear guests at his table, to be 'side by side with him' (Revelation 3:20).

## CANTICLE – Tobit 13:1-5b,7-8

*Tobit* is one of the most delightful books in the Old Testament. Its devout hero, after whom the book is named, lives as an exile in Nineveh, the capital of Assyria. There he and his wife, Sarah, meet with misfortune: though reduced to poverty and though Tobit himself becomes blind, they remain faithful to God. However, the story has a happy ending: the Archangel Raphael guides their son, Tobias, on a dangerous journey and into a happy marriage and finally restores Tobit's sight. It is Tobit's song of thanksgiving which provides this lovely morning canticle.

It begins with an acknowledgement of God's eternal existence and reign, and of his power: *he brings down to Hades* (or Sheol, the underworld) *and brings up again*, probably referring to the way he saves even from the brink of death (st 1). Tobit calls upon his countrymen to raise their voices in praise of him *before the nations* and *make his greatness known there*. It was because of their unfaithfulness that God had allowed them to be overtaken by disaster and driven into exile; yet, he still remains *our Lord and God... our Father for ever*. More than that, he wants to use Israel, scattered among the pagan nations in the 'diaspora', to make him known (st 2). And so sinners must repent and *give thanks to him with full voice, praise the Lord, exalt the King of the ages* (st 3-4.)

It is particularly moving that even *in the land of my captivity*, Tobit is ready to thank God, and exalt him and *rejoice in his majesty*. His final words may even suggest that he looks forward to the day when exile will be over and Jews and Gentiles *give him thanks in Jerusalem* (st 5).

As Christians we may feel that we are in a 'diaspora' situation, scattered among people who do not share our understanding of Jesus Christ. Painful though this may be, it is also challenging. The challenge is to bear witness to him, to make his greatness known, to show by words and still more by deeds that God is our Father. If that is the way we try to live today, we shall find that, like the elderly Tobit, our hearts are filled with gratitude and praise – even in this land of exile.

## PSALM 32 (33) Hymn

This is a beautiful example of a hymn of praise, praise of God as loving Creator and Lord of history; its twenty-two verses, each beginning with successive letters of the Hebrew alphabet, are suggestive of the all-encompassing extent of his reign and influence. It begins with great enthusiasm; we are to *ring out* our *joy* and *give thanks* with *lyre* and *ten-stringed harp* and to sing and *play loudly* and *with all your skill* (st 1-2). There is to be nothing half-hearted about this act of worship. It is based on the fact that God *is faithful* and all his actions *to be trusted*. He *loves justice and right*, and, by implication, expects the same from loyal friends (st 3).

What follows might be compared to a diptych, one side representing us gazing up to heaven in worship (st 4-6), the other God gazing down on us in love (st 7-12). God's word is not only faithful, it is creative. By the mere *breath of his mouth* he has made the immeasurable heavens and their innumerable *stars*; as a farmer might fill a skin with water or gather his crops in a barn, he *collects* and *stores up* the boundless mass of water from the seas and oceans. Confronted with such marvels, what can one do but *fear the Lord* and *revere him*? The Hebrew, *dabar*, means both word and event. In God the two coincide, his word is instantly effective, it does what it says. *He spoke and it came to be. He commanded: it sprang into being* (st 4-5). Everything is of his making, but the secret which lies at the heart of it all, its motive force, is his love (see last line of st 3). And just as the glorious power of God is revealed in creation, so also is it in history. Though Israel may be surrounded by powerful nations and often suffers at their hands, yet it is God who is in charge, and *his designs, the plans of his heart* are what matter. They *shall stand for ever* (st 6).

What joy to have such a Lord and to have been *chosen* by him *as his own*. And what stupidity to depend upon one's own strength or upon any of his creatures. He *looks forth* from heaven; he *sees* us; he knows us to the centre of our being for it is *he who shapes the hearts* of us all; and he is *our help and our shield*. (We are close to that assurance given us by Jesus: "Can you not buy two sparrows for a penny? And yet not one falls to the ground without your Father knowing... there is no need to be afraid; you are worth more than a hundred sparrows" [Matthew 10:29-31]). Joyously trusting in him, then, we face the new day with a 'new song', knowing that he *fills the earth with his love*, and fortify ourselves with the prayer of the psalmist: *may your love be upon us, O Lord* in all we do.

## PRAYER DURING THE DAY
### PSALM 118 (119) I Didactic

Psalm 118, with its one hundred and seventy six verses, stands as a blockbuster among psalms, It is an alphabetical psalm with a difference: not only does it go through the 22 letters of the Hebrew alphabet in sequence, but it devotes a section of no less than 8 verses (16 lines in our translation), all beginning with the same letter, to each of them. The English equivalent would be a poem, each of its first eight verses beginning with the letter 'A', each of its next eight verses beginning with 'B', and so on. Within the constraints of that alphabetical framework, this huge poem is concerned with God's *law*, ringing the changes on no less that eight synonyms. However, this preoccupation with law is very different from legalism. For the psalmist, the law is the whole of God's revelation, including the Scriptures; more than that, it is in some way an expression of the personality of its author.

The Prayer of the Church feeds us this psalm in digestible portions, one section at a time. In the breviary each section is numbered and, following the number, the corresponding letter of the Hebrew alphabet is added. And so today we begin with the first of them, which sets before us, in words and ideas familiar to us from Psalm 1 and Psalm 18 (19), the way to achieve true happiness – by following his *law*, doing *his will*, *seeking him with all* our *hearts*. And so we pray that our *footsteps be firm* today – that they may be in our Master's own footprints – and that he will *not forsake me*.

### PSALM 12 (13) Lament

*How long, O Lord* is a cry that wells up from so many hearts, as individuals struggle with God's apparent forgetfulness of them, his readiness to play a cruel game of hide-and-seek at their expense (st 1). We might think of the hostage, or the prisoner in the hands of his or her torturers, or the bereaved, or the old-age pensioner living alone, or the young person struck down with an incapacitating disease, or many another who faces trouble or suffering which seems to be senseless. Like the psalmist, they want God to *look at me*, take notice of my plight, put the sparkle back into *my eyes* (st 2).

However, the very earnestness of their prayer is perhaps already a beginning of trust in God's *merciful love* and of conviction that they will in the end *rejoice in* his *saving help*. If that be the case, they are close to the mind of the psalmist who believes that a time will come when he or she will *sing to the Lord for his goodness* (st 3). On that day they will understand what St Paul meant when he promised that "in all things God works for the good of those who love him" (Romans 8: 28)

### PSALM 13 (14) Didactic

This psalm appears, in a slightly different version, as Psalm 52 (53). It also has similarities with Psakn 11 (12) in that it presupposes a situation in which *the fool* arrogantly denies God's existence and *not a good man is left*, so that as *the Lord looks down* he finds that *all have left the right path* (st 1-3).

And so, through his prophet, God pronounces judgement. Do not the *evil-doers*, those who *never pray* and who *eat up my people as though they were eating bread*, understand what they are doing? They may *mock the poor man's hope*, but *his refuge is the Lord* and it is they who will *tremble* in the end (st 4-5).

Responding to this message, the people yearn for the time when God will perform a mighty work *from Sion*, by delivering his people from the *bondage* of sinners, so that they, the sons of *Jacob* and *Israel* , will live in joy in his presence (st 6).

The picture painted by this psalm may seem unduly pessimistic, though there may be times when we feel it is uncomfortably close to the truth. St Paul quotes part of it in chapter 3 of Romans, at the end of his description of the hopelessness of fallen humanity. But, like the psalmist, his final thought is not a negative one. There is justification and redemption and reconciliation offered as a free gift of God's grace, for "everyone who believes in Jesus" (3:21).

## EVENING PRAYER

*Today's evening prayer might be described as an office in honour of Christ the King, for it consists of two royal psalms and a canticle that centres on One sitting on the throne.*

## PSALM 19 (20) Lament

This liturgical prayer was a petition for the king on the eve of battle (st 1-3). After the prayer and his own *offerings* and *sacrifice*, the king expresses confidence that victory awaits him. However, victory will be due not to *trust in chariots or horses*, but to trust *in the name of the Lord* and the power of *his hand* (st 4-5). And that only leaves the assembly to repeat their request for God's help (st 6).

This is a royal and therefore a Messianic psalm, and so our eyes are fixed on Jesus. He goes forth to do battle as our representative but he makes it clear that he 'does nothing of himself'; through his whole career *the name of the Lord* (three times mentioned in this psalm) is fully revealed; *in his time of trial*, he pleads with his Father that if it be possible the anguish may pass; he offers the *sacrifice* in which he himself is the victim, but in that 'defeat', to our everlasting *joy*, he gains the *victory*. He is King of Love on Calvary. I have heard st 2 and 3 (May he give you your heart's desire, etc.) used very effectively before the blessing at the end of Mass. They could be used equally well for anyone beginning a new task in life.

**PSALM 20 (21) Thanksgiving**

This psalm seems to make a pair with the preceding one; there the battle was awaited, here the victory is celebrated. A chorister, or possibly the king himself speaking in the third person, proclaims that it is God's *strength* and his *saving help* which have won the day. But he has gone further than that, investing him with *a crown of pure gold*, guaranteeing him long life and granting him *blessings for ever* (st 1-3). The people joyously respond, giving thanks to God to whom the king's victory belongs.

The very extravagance of the language makes this psalm inappropriate for any one but the King of kings. It is in the risen Jesus that we see it verified. In him is complete victory even over death; he is invested with *majesty and splendour*, his *days last from age to age* and, in his humanity, he rejoices *with the joy of* (the Father's) *presence*. With the people who sang of *the mercy* (the loving-faithfulness) *of the Most High*, we too can *sing and praise* his power, knowing that we, the members of his Mystical Body, are destined to share for ever in his glorious victory.

**CANTICLE – Revelation 4:11; 5:9,10,12.**

This canticle is a composite of three others which appear in the book of Revelations. The first (st 1) is a vision of God seated on his heavenly throne, surrounded by the twenty-four elders, twelve representing the twelve tribes of Israel, the other twelve representing the twelve apostles, and all twenty-four representing the whole People of God in the Old Testament and the New. They praise him as *worthy to receive glory and honour and power* because he is creator and sustainer of all that exists. The King hands over a mysterious scroll to the Lamb (Jesus, the one who went 'like a lamb to the slaughter'). And so we move to the second vision (st 2) where the same saints now address our Lord, acknowledging that he is worthy to *take the scroll and to open its seals* because *by your blood* – a reminder of how deeply he loves us – you have won for God people *from every tribe and tongue and people and nation.* All are made sharers in his kingly and priestly dignity (st 3).

Finally (st 4), a third vision opens up in which the hosts of angels raise their voices in praise of the Lamb, saluting him in words more generous, if anything, than those addressed to God himself in the first vision. I find it hard to recite this stanza without 'in my head' hearing it being sung by a massed choir in a performance of Handel's Messiah. But even those who have no mind for music must be impressed by this stirring hymn of praise rendered to Jesus our King who has been so close to us throughout our Evening Prayer today.

# WEEK 1 WEDNESDAY

## OFFICE OF READINGS
### PSALM 17 (18) Thanksgiving

It is with a flood of imagery that this psalm gets under way. It is as though no single image – *rock, fortress, shield* – can adequately describe the God who has shown such goodness, nor for that matter the terrible ordeals that the psalmist has been through – *waves of death, torrents of destruction, snares of the grave.* But the Lord, whom he loves, finally *heard my voice* crying out to him *in my anguish* and *saved me from my foes*(§I).

In §II the powerful imagery continues, as the psalmist tries to paint a picture of how God rescued him, in terms familiar from the exodus and Mount Sinai – storms and earthquakes, *flashes of fire* and hailstones. God appears on the scene, riding on the *wings of the wind* and *enthroned on the cherubim* (the heavenly winged creatures, part man and part beast, which were well known in the ancient near East). Then, a touching note, from the midst of this glorious 'theophany' (divine manifestation) God *reached down and seized me and brought me forth into freedom.* (Some scholars believe that this passage reflects a liturgical act in which the events of the Exodus and mount Sinai were ritually enacted and 'made present', with the king playing the leading role).

After the excitement of the preceding sections, §III may seem not only an anti-climax but also in rather poor taste. 'I've been saved', the king declares in effect, 'because God knows that I am without fault.' In addition to what has been noted about the disturbing self-righteousness which the psalmists sometimes seem to display (see p.26 ), two further points must be made. The first is that because it is Messianic, this psalm finds its fulfilment in Jesus. In snatching him from the tomb and in raising him from the abasement of Calvary, the Father was both responding to the perfect obedience of his Son who had *always been upright before him* and at the same time performing an action of cosmic significance. The second is that we dare not presume on the help of our Saviour King unless we are at least striving to keep *the way of the Lord* (see Luke 6: 36-38).

But the high point of this psalm is surely the last line of §II: *He saved me because he loved me*. Our creation and our redemption are due solely to the fact that he loves us. What more is there to say?

## MORNING PRAYER
### PSALM 35 (36) Lament

This is a psalm of darkness and light. The psalmist sketches the character of a person completely under the sway of sin (st 1-3). It *speaks* to him *in the depths of his heart*. The Hebrew word translated 'speaks' suggests that 'sin has for the wicked the same authority.. that God has for the prophet' to whom God mysteriously murmurs his word. The apparent freedom he has gained in rejecting God has made him sin's slave. His words (*mischief and deceit*), his thoughts (plotting evil even *as he lies on his bed*) and his actions (a clinging subservience *to what is evil*) show that *all* true *wisdom is gone*; he no longer behaves like a reasonable human being.

After the darkness comes the light: in contrast to the evil person, the psalmist glories in God. God's *love* and his *truth* (his covenant faithfulness), tower high beyond our comprehension, his *justice* (his goodness) is as solid as a *mountain* and his *judgements* as profound as the ocean *deep* (st 4). And if all this is too breath-taking, the psalmist, drawing from personal experience, speaks in more intimate terms of the precious nature of God's love for all his creation, but above all for the *sons of men* who, in contrast to the evil-doer, *find refuge in the shelter of his wings*. There they *feast* and *drink from the stream of your delight*, a probable reference to the Temple and its sacrifical meals. Just as without the warmth and light of the sun all life would cease, so without *your light* all human life would be dark and meaningless (st 6-7).

The final section of the psalm, apart from the ruthless language of the last two lines, is what we might expect, a plea that God will *keep on loving those who know you* and not allowing the wicked to prevail.

There are so many foreshadowings of the New Testament in this psalm that it could almost stand as a Christian profession of faith. But if there is one thought we might carry with us to lighten up our day, it is *O Lord, how precious is your love.*

## CANTICLE – Judith 16:2-3a,13-15

The book of Judith, like that of Tobit, was written about 200BC in the form of an historical novel. It tells of the Jewish heroine who, by her courage and prayerful trust in God, overcame, single-handed, the enemy of her people and set them free. The chapter from which this morning's Canticle is drawn makes no direct reference to the story. It is largely a mosaic of texts from the psalms. There is an invitation to praise (st 1), followed by a song to God who is great and glorious, *wonderful in strength* and *invincible* (st 2), then a plea that *all your creatures* may serve him (st 3), and finally a recognition that though all things be *shaken to their foundation,* there is the assurance of God's mercy for *those who serve him* (st 4). The whole adds up to a fitting prayer with which to begin another day.

## PSALM 46(47) Enthronement Psalm

This psalm of praise must have had a liturgical setting. According to some commentators, it belongs to a New Year feast, celebrated in conjunction with the festival of Tabernacles, during which there was an 'enthronement' of the Lord as King (see 2 Samuel 6:15f). The ark was carried in procession up towards the Temple in a 'reconstruction' of God's arrival in the Promised Land after the victory of the exodus.

In the meantime the people are commanded to *clap* their *hands*, perhaps rythmicly in time with the music, and to *cry to God with shouts of joy*. The reason for the jubilation is the fearful majesty of God, who is *great king over all the earth* (st 1). All that they have received from him, victory over enemies and their *inheritance* and *glory* as his people, have been *given out of love* (st 2).

By now the procession is approaching its highest point, the Holy of Holies, and with it *God* himself *goes up with shouts of joy*. The thunder of many voices is heard and the blaze of *trumpet blast*. Whatever the precise liturgical ceremony, God is enthroned and greeted with the cry *God is King*. Not merely king, but *king of all the earth* (st 3-4).

This psalm looks to the past (the Exodus victory), but it also looks to the future, to the glorious day when *the princes of the people* (the Gentiles) *are assembled with the people of Abraham's God* (the Jews). Already this was hinted at in the opening line where *all people*, not simply the Jews, were invited to praise God as king. But in the final stanza the universality of rule is expressed more clearly. The history of salvation has come full circle, for it began with Abraham and now the promise made to him – that all the nations would be blessed in him (Genesis 12:3) – is realized. The Gentiles do not merely join God's people, they become themselves the people of God.

For us there is a still more tremendous hope: a new heaven and a new earth, one flock and one shepherd, and the final arrival of the Kingdom of God.

# WEEK 1 WEDNESDAY

It is in the Risen Christ that the prophetic words of this psalm achieve their fulfilment: 'all power in heaven and earth belong to him' (Matthew 28:18) and by him those 'who were once far off' (the pagans) have been brought near thanks to [his] blood' (Ephesians 2:14)

## PRAYER DURING THE DAY
### PSALM 118 (119) II Didactic

The second section of ps 118 (119) begins with a question, posed by a young person: *how shall the young remain sinless?* The predictable answer is given: *by obeying your word.* The rest of the section is made up of what seem to be assertions, but perhaps it would be better to view them as reflections on that answer. In the Gospels another young person poses a vital question: "What must I do to possess eternal life?" The young man had kept the ten commandments from his youth, but what was still wanting to him? The sequel shows that he had not come to terms with the price that may have to be paid by those who wish to follow the Lord (Matthew 19:16-22). Few of us, young or old, would dare to claim that we have either. That is why we would do well to turn the reflections of this psalm into a prayer: Help me, Lord, to seek you with all my heart, to rejoice in your will, to delight in your commands whatever they may be, however costly they may be and wherever they may lead me.

### PSALM 16 (17) Lament

It is terrible to be accused unjustly. The psalmist has had the experience, and so begins his prayer with a declaration of innocence. Then comes a confident request for help; already he knows that God *will hear* and he begs for a demonstration of his *great love.* The plea is repeated with two moving images. First, may God guard him *as the apple of his eye*, with all that instinctive protection that one gives to a precious but extremely delicate organ. Second, may he hide him *in the shadow* of his *wings*, like a mother hen protecting her young (§I). After comparing his enemies' behaviour to that of wild beasts, he calls upon the Lord to rise against them. (§II st 1-4). However, he is sure that their *reward is in this present life* alone, whilst he looks forward when *I awake* – logic would seem to imply that the reference is to his awakening from death – *to see your face and be filled with the sight of your glory* (§II st 5).

In the Innocent One, unjustly done to death, we see a living out of this psalm. Jesus "offered up prayer and entreaty, aloud and in silent tears, and he submitted so humbly that his prayer was heard"(Heb 5:9); he was saved not *from* but *out of* death, and his innocence attested by his resurrection and return in glory to the Father. Christ, in our fellow men and women, continues to be unjustly crucified every day. His example can mean so much to us as we face the injustices in our world.

## EVENING PRAYER
### PSALM 26 (27) Confidence

Depression can make us feel that life has lost all meaning, we are trapped in a dark hole. This psalm, from its initial acknowledgement that God is *light* and *help* and *stronghold* to its final prayer of trust, breathes hope and comfort for one assailed by fears and depression. *Though an army encamp against me even then would I trust,* says the psalmist. Unlike the priest or levite, he cannot spend all his time literally in *the house of the Lord* (which is also *his temple, his tent, his rock*), but like them he wants to be aware of God's abiding presence and to *savour the sweetness of the Lord.* That is *the one thing* that matters, and, if it is granted, his downcast *head* will be *raised* again and he will offer a thanksgiving *sacrifice*, with song and music (§I)

His thoughts slip back to the problem in hand. In spite of everything, it was God who put into his heart the thought: *Seek his face*, so that is what he will do. With great psychological realism, he is sure and yet continues to beg, that God will not hide his face, or abandon him. He is confident that, even if his own parents were to forsake him, *the Lord will receive me*. So he asks that he may be guided in *your way* and along *an even* (morally correct) *path*. And the psalm reaches its end in a climax of trust: *I am sure I shall see the Lord's goodness in the land of the living* ; and then, *Hope in him, hold firm and take heart (§II).*

A whole cluster of thoughts comes to mind:

1. Jesus himself declared: "I am the light of the world. Anyone who follows me will not be walking in the dark" (John 8:12). He is our assurance in the midst of fears, the temple in which we can find refuge; in seeking him, we are pursuing the only one thing needed (Luke 10:41).

2. It is not always easy to discern the 'spiritual' value of what is to be done. But this psalm provides a simple prayer that can transform the most mundane work we may be called upon to perform, like ironing clothes or mending burst pipes or doing the shopping; in all these things it is *your face, O Lord*, that we seek.

3. How can we hear the psalmist speak of God's care for him even if his own parents should abandon him, without recalling the burning words which God spoke to Isaiah: "Does a woman forget her baby at the breast, or fail to cherish the son of her womb? Yet even if these forget I will never forget you" (Isaiah 49:15). With these words of our Father/Mother God echoing in our hearts, cannot we too *hold firm and take heart?*

## CANTICLE – Colossians 1:12-20

In the year 112, Pliny the Younger, governor of a Roman province in northern Asia Minor, wrote a famous letter to the Emperor Trajan in which he reported that Christians were accustomed to meet together and "chant a song to Christ as if to God". This raises the intriguing question: could the song have been the Canticle we recite this evening? Colossae is in Asia Minor and the canticle is a liturgical hymn, which the early Christians used in honour of Jesus.

There is a brief introduction (st 1-2) in which thanks are given to the Father who has taken the initiative by transferring us from the dominion of darkness to the kingdom of his beloved Son (the same expression – Beloved Son – was heard at Jesus' baptism and transfiguration), so that we now have *redemption,* here described in terms of *the forgiveness of sins.*

Then begins a hymn in honour of Christ 'as if to God', for he is in fact the *image* or icon *of the invisible God.* Its two sections describe his primacy in creation and redemption. He is *the first-born of all creation*, in the sense that all created things are brought into existence *in him, through him and for him*; in time and in importance, he exists *before all things* and it is to him that they owe their continued existence for it is *in him* that *all things hold together* (st 3-4).

Just as he is Lord and Head of creation so also is he *head of the body, the Church.* And so starts the second section of the hymn, in which Christ is saluted as the beginning, the starting point, of a redeemed humanity. Just as he is first-born of all creation, so he is also *first-born from the dead* because he already experiences the life of the resurrection. In every way, therefore, he is *pre-eminent* and *all the fullness of God was pleased to dwell* in him. The constant repetition of the word *all* prepares us for the cosmic repercussions of our Lord's redemptive work which brings about the reconciliation of a*ll things, whether on earth or in heaven.* However, this lofty vision of Jesus is not something up in the clouds; for in its final words the hymn comes firmly down to a particular spot on this earth and a precise event –

# WEEK 1 WEDNESDAY

Calvary and the shame and anguish of a crucified Man who, despite all appearances to the contrary, is *making peace by the blood of his cross*(st 4-5). What an honour to be continuing this evening the hymn of praise which, for almost 2000 years, Christians have chanted "to Christ as to God".

# WEEK 1 THURSDAY

## OFFICE OF READINGS
### PSALM 17 (18) Thanksgiving

This is the second part of the psalm which we began at Office of Readings yesterday, and it continues the outpouring of gratitude. The two parts which make up this hymn soaring to heaven have been compared to twin spires of a cathedral. There is praise for God whose *ways are perfect* and whose *word is purest gold*. He is a *shield, a rock*. He is a God that no other can match. He has graced the royal hero (remember that this is one of the Royal Psalms) with a swiftness of foot like *the deer's* and with strength to cope with *the heavy bow* (§IV).

He has protected him and trained him in the use of weapons. There follows a breathless account of the king's exploits as enemies are *crushed* like *dust before the wind* and *foreign nations* come cringing *out of their strongholds*, to face the consequences of defeat (§V).

If it is the king who is crowned with the laurel leaf of victory, it is God who has made it possible: it is he who has done the saving and the subduing and *set me above my assailants*. Therefore, *I will sing a psalm to your name*, a psalm which is also an act of trust in the Lord who proves faithful to his promises to king *David and his sons for ever* (§VI).

We may find it disconcerting to pray so warlike and merciless a psalm. But what was said about the first part of the psalm is equally applicable here. It is God "who has taken us out of the power of darkness and created a place for us in the kingdom of the Son that he loves" (Colossians 1:13). St Paul explicitly places on Jesus' lips the triumphant words of the king in §VI st2 (see Rom 15:9); he is the conquering king, but his kingdom is not of this world (John 18:37) and his victory is secured not by force of military might but of self-surrendering love. As we pray this psalm, then, we might keep in mind the powerful words of Samuel Wesley:

# WEEK 1 THURSDAY

*Alleluia, sing to Jesus, his the sceptre, his the throne.*
*Alleluia, his the triumph, his the victory alone.*
*Hark, the songs of holy Sion, thunder like a mighty flood:*
*Jesus, out of every nation hath redeemed us by his blood.*

## MORNING PRAYER
### PSALM 56 (57) Lament

A twice repeated plea for help – *Have mercy* – is followed by an expression of confidence which will re-echo throughout the rest of the psalm. The psalmist seeks refuge in *the shadow of your wings*, like a chick nestling under the protective wing of the mother bird, *till the storms of destruction*, whatever they may have been, *pass by*. The thought that God *has always been my help* encourages him to ask that God's loving kindness and his steadfast faithfulness may be sent like two messengers to his support. Just as he has personified God's covenant attributes of *truth and love*, so now he presents his enemies as though they were savage beasts, lions with fangs like *spears and arrows* and a tongue like *a sharpened sword* (st 1-3).

The refrain – *O God, rise up above the heavens...* – which will be repeated at the end of the psalm, marks the end of the lament and the beginning of praise and rejoicing, for the enemies have come to grief in the very *pit* they made for him. I wonder if there isn't a note of humour here: they have slipped on the banana skin they set for us (st 4-5).

Perhaps the psalmist had spent an all-night vigil in prayer, but now it is a new day and he declares that his *heart is ready* (for praise of God). With a poet's turn of phrase, he summons his soul and his musical instruments, *lyre and harp*, to wake up *the dawn*. Then they can join him in proclaiming to *the people* and *the nations* the act of faith which we saw in Psalm 35 yesterday morning: God's *love reaches to the heavens* and his *truth to the skies.* And so he takes up the refrain in loving gratitude, praying that God's glory may shine and be acknowledged on all the earth.

It is not surprising that this psalm should be offered to us for Morning Prayer. Each dawn is a new day, a time to turn once again to God with confidence. Whatever *storms of destruction* we may have to face, we can take heart in the steadfast love and faithfulness of our God.

### CANTICLE – Jeremiah 31:10-14

To a people whose greatest hopes were centred upon Jerusalem (see Psalm 47 [48] below), Jeremiah had the unenviable task of announcing that the city would be destroyed. Perhaps it is not surprising that his name has become synonymous with prophecies of doom. However, Jeremiah was not all gloom. Today's Canticle comes from a section of his work which is known as the Book of Consolation because it looks beyond the coming disaster to a time when God will gather his exiled people and, like a shepherd at the head of his flock, lead them back, *to shout for joy on Mount Sion* and receive *the blessings of the Lord. Young and old, priests* and *people* alike will rejoice; *mourning* will be turned to *joy* and *grief* to *gladness.*

Because of the sufferings and troubles he endured, Jeremiah has come to be seen as a 'type' of Jesus himself. After reporting how the authorities in Jerusalem plotted the death of our Lord, St John explains that "Jesus was to die..to gather together in unity the scattered children of God" (John 11:51). By his passion, death and resurrection, our Good Shepherd has gathered us out of the exile of sin and death and led us back towards reconciliation with God and with one another and the perfect happiness of the heavenly Jerusalem.

# WEEK 1 THURSDAY

**PSALM 47 (48) Hymn**

The capital of any country symbolizes its people, but Jerusalem was not simply the social and political capital of the people of Israel: it was their spiritual home. And so this small city and its buildings – in size the Temple was more like a parish church than a grand basilica – are invested with enormous significance, as this psalm clearly shows. It is the *Great King's* own *city*. His Temple, sited on a high ridge in the north east of the city (the original Sion), already had a majestic appearance, but through the eyes of faith it is enhanced still further, becoming *the joy* and *true pole of all the earth.* (In the medieval *Mappa Mundi*, preserved in Hereford Cathedral, Jerusalem appears as the centre point of the whole world). But its strength rests not in its own defences but in God himself who is i*n the midst of its citadels* (st 1-2).

That is why when powerful enemies have advanced against it – the reference is not to a precise historical event but rather to all those occasions when men have dared to march upon God's city – they have been thrown into panic and *fled in fear*. They have been destroyed, as surely as the east wind shatters the huge *ships of Tharsis* (Tharsis is a word connected with the smelting of iron; the ships which carried the cargo of metal were particularly large and powerful) (st 3-4). These events have been actually *heard* and *seen* by the worshippers, which suggests that as well as being recalled in word, they have also been liturgically re-enacted. It has helped the people to *ponder your* Covenant *love* and reflect that God's *judgments*, his mighty acts on behalf of Sion, affect the whole world so that praise of God *reaches the end of the earth* (st 7-9).

The good news is to be shared and so, before leaving for home, the pilgrims are invited to tour the outer walls of the city, counting *its towers*, reviewing *its ramparts* and *castles*, all of them tokens of the protective presence of God. Then, with that picture etched on their memory, they can go back and tell the youngsters who were not in the pilgrimage about the wonderful experience they have had in the Temple ceremonies (st 8-9).

Just as the royal psalms achieve their fulfilment in Jesus, so the 'Songs of Sion' are fulfilled in the Church, the new Jerusalem which he founded to continue his mission in the world. It has an inner strength which nothing can overcome, for he has given the guarantee "I am with you always; yes, to the end of time" (Matthew 28:20) and so "the gates of the underworld can never hold out against it" (Matthew 16:18). It is in the Church, through the Scriptures and above all the Sacraments, that we hear and see re-presented the saving work which he accomplished for us. If the ancient pilgrims felt compelled to share with others their experiences in Jerusalem, "it is inconceivable", as Pope Paul VI put it, '"that those who have received the word and surrendered themselves to the kingdom (in the Church) should not themselves become witnesses and proclaimers of the truth".

## PRAYER DURING THE DAY
### PSALM 118 (119) III Didactic

This long alphabetical psalm is so permeated with love of God, especially as he has manifested it through his revelation and in particular through his law, that it has been called 'the alphabet of Divine Love'. It may help us to turn it into a prayer, and will not be untrue to its meaning, if each time we find law (or one of its equivalents) we substitute 'love'. Thus, the present section might read as follows: *Bless you servant and I shall live/ And obey (the demands of) your love./ Open my eyes that I may see/ The wonders of your love./ I am a pilgrim on the earth;/ show me your love./ My soul is ever consumed/ as I long for your love.* And so on to the end.

# WEEK 1 THURSDAY

### PSALM 24 (25) Lament

The contemplative spirit of this psalm is revealed in its opening sentence: *To you, O Lord, I lift up my soul.* The Hebrews did not recognise any body/soul distinction; for them, and for us as we pray this psalm, to lift up one's soul is to lift up one's whole self. The expression suggests the complete trust of someone in deep trouble, and that is confirmed by what follows. Despite the number and *violent hatred* of the threatening foes (see especially §II), all the psalmist wants is to *know your ways* and be taught *your paths* because *you are God my saviour* (§I st 1-2).

The trust rests upon personal experience: God has proved his trustworthiness. The memory of his *goodness, mercy and the love shown from of old*, floods back into the mind, but so too does the memory of past *sins* (referred to in §I st5 and §II st3). Yet even the recognition of sinfulness does not undermine trust. The God of the covenant is a God who takes the initiative, a God whose *ways are faithfulness and love*, a God who is patient with *those who stray* and *teaches his way to the poor* (especially the spiritually poor?). Therefore the psalmist is confident that there will be forgiveness for guilt, even though, or perhaps especially when, *it is great*, when it is clearly beyond our remedying (§I st 3-5). These reflections deepen trust and lead to a proclamation of the wonders that await the person who enjoys *the Lord's friendship.* His soul, i.e. his whole being, *shall dwell in happiness* (§II st1). However, the foes of the psalmist have still to be dealt with, and so *my eyes are always on the Lord: Relieve the anguish of my heart, set me free, do not disappoint me* and, a final act of faith, *my hope is in you, O Lord.*

In beautiful terms this psalm expresses so many of the things that we want to pray about: trust in God, forgiveness of our sins, recognition of his dependability, determination to lift our whole being towards our Covenant Lord and fix our eyes on him.

# WEEK 1 THURSDAY

## EVENING PRAYER
### PSALM 29 (30) Thanksgiving

"We should spend as much time in thanking God for his benefits," said St Vincent de Paul, "as we do in asking for them." The author of this psalm would agree. It had been a close run thing, he had been near to death, but when all hope seemed lost *I cried to you for help* and the result was amazing: *God raised my soul from the dead* (like a bucket drawn up from a deep well) (st 2).

So now he calls upon those who love God, those who are faithful to the covenant, *to sing psalms to the Lord* and *give thanks to his holy name.* As he explains, in two marvellous word pictures, God's *anger* is momentary in comparison with his life-long goodness; and *tears* can be compared to an overnight guest, whose place is taken at *dawn,* the time associated with God's salvation, by *joy.* He admits that in his complacency he had thought *Nothing will ever disturb me*, but God had only to hide his face for a moment and – disaster (st 3-4).

Now he rehearses the prayer he had prayed: If anything happens to me, you won't gain anything from it; indeed, you'll be one worshipper less! And it worked: *The Lord listened and had pity*(st 5). The psalmist can hardly contain his excitement: *my mourning* was transformed *into dancing*, as you stripped off *my sackcloth and clothed me with joy.* And in face of all that, what is there to do but *sing psalms to you unceasingly* and *thank you for ever?* (st 5-6)

The hand of the poet is clearly discernible in this psalm. It was another poet who used the analogy of child-birth to assure his friends that their sorrows would quickly give place to joy, as surely as a mother's labour pains are transformed into rejoicing when her baby is safely delivered (John 16:20-22). And if we feel that the psalmist was over-optimistic in estimating the length (only a moment) of our sufferings, we might reflect on St Paul's confident assertion that our

# WEEK 1 THURSDAY

"troubles are soon over (and they) train us for the carrying of a weight of eternal glory which is out of all proportion to them" (2 Corinthians 4:17).

**PSALM 31 (32) Thanksgiving**
The first line explains why this psalm came to be numbered among the seven Penitential Psalms: it is the prayer of one who wrestled with sin, found forgiveness and wishes to share his happiness with others: O, the joy of the person *whose offence is forgiven.*

He admits that for some time he was unable to face up to the truth about himself, but he paid dearly for it: it affected his health of mind and/or body till he felt that he had become *dried up*, like a plant whose sap evaporates in the burning summer heat. But then came the moment when he turned to God and made his confession, *And you, Lord, have forgiven the guilt of my sin.* He urges all people of good will to follow his example; if only they will turn to God in prayer, then no matter what floods of trials beset them, they will, like himself, find a safe *hiding place* (st1-4).

It is difficult to know whether the next two stanzas are spoken by the poet or by God himself, but in either case the meaning is clear. Here is my advice, he says, don't be headstrong, needing to be forced back to God, like an untamed *horse* which can only be controlled by the use of *bridle and bit.* Remember, *the wicked* has many sorrows, but those who trust in the Lord are surrounded by his *loving mercy.* Such truths are an invitation to God's people to raise their voices and make their joy resound in the sanctuary (st 5-7).

This psalm might almost be a poetic version of the parable of the prodigal son (Luke 15:11-32): the lad turns his back on his father, deciding to live his own life. But in his heart there is an emptiness and a guilt, which surface when disaster strikes. It is the moment of truth:

# WEEK 1 THURSDAY

he must return and acknowledge his sin, even if it means being reduced to the status of a slave. But he is met with a tender embrace and a joyous celebration; he is arrayed in a splendid robe, with a ring for his finger and sandals for his feet. No slave was ever dressed like this. How easy to share in the joy of the psalmist, when we have a Lord who welcomes sinners in such a way.

**CANTICLE – Revelation 11:17-18; 12:10-12**
Like the Canticle of Tuesday's Evening Prayer, this one is made up from separate visions in the Book of Revelation. In the first (st 1-2), the last of seven trumpets has sounded in heaven to announce the final consummation. If earlier, e.g. 1:4, God was described as he "who is, who was and who is to come", here he is simply you *who are and who were:* his future coming is now accomplished, he has *begun to reign* and it is the *time for the dead to be judged* and *for rewarding your servants.* The second vision (st 3-4) is set against the victory of Jesus which reached its climax in his death and resurrection: as in Psalm 2 (see page 42), *God* and *his Christ,* his Anointed One, have triumphed over every enemy and in that triumph the whole Church shares, especially the glorious martyrs who *loved not their lives even unto death.*

After what may have been a very ordinary Thursday at home or in the office, in the classroom or the workplace, here are powerful thoughts on which to end our day. God and his Son are triumphant, the victory already won, Satan *the accuser of our brethren thrown down* and ourselves *servants* who share in the victory. In principle, the kingdom has come; with heaven itself *and you that dwell therein*, we too are ready to rejoice and give praise.

# WEEK 1 FRIDAY

## OFFICE OF READINGS
### PSALM 34 (35) Lament

The fact that Friday is traditionally associated with the Passion of Jesus is reflected in many of the psalms which the Prayer of the Church offers us on this day each week. Psalm 34 is a case in point, as we are reminded by the scripture text which heads it in the breviary: "They united in making plans to arrest Jesus by treachery and have him put to death" (Matthew 26:3-4).

The psalmist begs the Lord to arm himself with *buckler and shield* and come to the rescue. In his agony in the garden of Gethsemane, Jesus too pleaded for the Father's help, and "an angel appeared..to give him strength" for his ordeal (Luke 22:43). Like the psalmist, he experienced the horror of *lying witnesses* accusing him unjustly. §II reminds us that his sufferings were the more bitter because he was repaid evil for good. He had entered into the sorrows of his people, mourning with the afflicted and often healing the sick; but now that he is in *trouble* he is met by *mockery on mockery*; they *tear* him *to pieces* with a terrible flogging.

At the foot of the cross they gather about him like a pack of *raging beasts*, taunting him, winking eyes at each other. On the night before he died, Jesus quoted from this very psalm (§III st2). He told how, despite his miracles, his enemies "have hated both me and my Father. But this is to fulfil what was written...*They hated me without reason*" (John 15:24-25). Even the psalmist's cry *O Lord, you have seen, do not be silent* is less awesome than Jesus': "My God, my God, why have you deserted me?" (Matthew 27:46). And yet for Jesus, as for the psalmist, it is hope not despair that triumphs, so that his prayer "Father, into your hands I commit my spirit" (Luke 23:46) expresses the confidence – *Lord, who is like you?* – that constantly shines through this psalm.

# WEEK 1 FRIDAY

Friday is a day on which we are urged to undertake some form of penance. Perhaps we might find an appropriate penance today in following our Master's example and accepting, with real forgiveness in our hearts, anyone who has done us wrong, especially anyone who has repaid us evil for the good we have done them.

## MORNING PRAYER
### PSALM 50 (51) Lament
Jesus died for our sins and so, each week, Friday's Morning Prayer begins with a splendid act of sorrow; it is the fourth of the Pentitential Psalms and one of the best known psalms in the psalter.

It is a fervent prayer that in his loving kindness God will *have mercy*, will *blot out my offence*(like erasing an error in a book) and *wash me more and more* (like the laundering of a filthy garment), so that I may be cleansed. There is a humble confession of sin and a bold recognition that while it may wreak havoc for many people, including the sinner, its real malice lies in the fact that it is rebellion against God: *what is evil in your sight I have done*. God cannot be faulted in his judgements; indeed, the roots of sin lie so deep in human nature that each one of us can say: *a sinner was I conceived* (st 1-3).

There is no way out of this prison of sin, apart from God's grace. But God loves integrity of heart, and the psalmist begs to be taught that kind of *wisdom*. He pleads again to be purified and made clean, until he is *whiter than snow*. Then he will be able to return to society, his very bones dancing with joy (st 4-5).

After another appeal for the 'erasing' of his sins, the psalmist turns to the positive side of forgiveness: the creation of a new *pure heart*, the abiding presence of the Holy Spirit and *a spirit of fervour*. If these are granted, the sinner will become a joyful messenger of God's goodness and graciousness. *Sacrifice* and *burnt offering* were regarded as essential to the forgiveness of sin, but now he realises that the real sacifice, which God *will not spurn*, is a *contrite spirit* (st 6-9). (It seems likely that the final stanza was added after the exile to assure the people that, given true repentance, the *lawful sacrifice* which took place in the restored Temple was still pleasing to God).

In times gone by Psalm 50(51) was known in this country as 'the hanging psalm' because a condemned criminal was often saved the noose if he could recite it by heart. It might more appositely be called 'the salvation psalm' because those who pray it with a humble and contrite heart are sure of the loving mercy of God. It is no accident that the full extent and depth of human sinfulness was revealed only when it could also be affirmed that where sin increased, grace abounded all the more'(Romans 5:20-21).

## CANTICLE – Isaiah 45:15-26

'Where is your God now?' is the question sometimes asked, especially in time of disaster. The truth is that he is *a God who lies hidden*, a God whose existence cannot be demonstrated in a laboratory. This is a truth which men and women find it difficult to take. Is that why they so often become *makers of idols*, worshippers of things that can only too easily be seen and felt and fondled? And yet the believer need not *be ashamed*, for this hidden God is *the creator of heaven* and the one who *made earth and shaped it*. The evidence of his presence is above us and all about us. Furthermore, his voice has *not spoken in secret, in some dark place*, but openly – through his prophets and apostles and, finally (though the writer of this passage could not know it), through his Word, Jesus (st 1-4).

He is hidden and yet so intimately close, the Lover who, through the dark cloud of faith, draws all people, as he silently whispers to their

# WEEK 1 FRIDAY

hearts: *Turn to me and be saved, There is no God but me, none but me* (st 5-7). "Lord, I do believe, help thou my unbelief" (Mark 9:24).

## PSALM 99 (100) Hymn

William Kethe's hymn 'All people that on earth do dwell' has made this psalm into one of the best loved throughout the English-speaking world. This morning's Canticle, which we have just prayed, laid a foundation of faith. The psalm builds upon it, urging *all the earth* to come before the Lord *singing for joy* and serving him *with gladness.* Why? Because, the psalm proudly proclaims, he is our maker and *we are his people: he made us, we belong to him.*The command is repeated: join the procession, *Enter the Temple courts with songs of praise* and thanks (st 1-3). And the psalm is rounded off with a brief but beautiful word portrait of God: the vastness of his goodness and the never-ending nature of *his merciful love* and faithfulness.

This is one of the psalms which can be used at the Invitatory in place of Psalm 94 (see p.32). The two have much in common: the call to joyful worship, to gladness and gratitude; the recognition of God's greatness and his shepherd-like care of his people. One notable feature of Psalm 94, the plea to listen and respond to God's voice, is absent from Psalm 99, though it must surely be presumed: in the words of St Augustine: "Make sure that your life sings the same tune as your mouth."

## PRAYER DURING THE DAY
### PSALM 118 (119) IV Didactic

The only English scholar who has attempted to reproduce the effect of this alphabetical psalm, by starting every line of its twenty two sections with a letter of the English alphabet, is Mgr Ronald Knox. This is how he translated the present section, which begins with 'D'(corresponding to the Hebrew letter 'daleth'):

# WEEK 1 FRIDAY

Deep lies my soul in the dust, restore life to me, as thou hast promised./ Deign, now, to show me thy will, thou who hast listened when I opened my heart to thee./ Direct me in the path thou biddest me follow, and all my musings shall be of thy wonderful deeds./ Despair rings tears from me; let thy promises raise me up once more./ Deliver me from every false thought; let thy covenant be my comfort./ Duty's path my choice, I keep thy bidding ever in remembrance./ Disappoint me, Lord, never, one who holds fast by thy commandments./ Do but open my heart wide, and easy lies the path thou hast decreed.

This translation illustrates the skill that went into the construction of the original psalm (as well as the artificiality that sometimes resulted from it); but, like any alternative translation, it may also add freshness to a prayer with which we are long familiar.

## PSALM 25 (26) Lament

Like Ps 7, which we met at Prayer During the Day on Monday, this is the prayer of a man who has been unjustly accused and now vehemently protests his innocence. Conscious of the Lord's love and faithfulness, he begs him to *test my heart and my mind*. He denies that he has associated with *evil-doers* and in proof of that he is prepared to perform the ritual act of washing his hands, in the laver that was situated close to the altar. That action will be a sign both of his innocence and of his worthiness to *take my place around your altar* and give thanks for *all your wonders*. How he loves the *house where you dwell!* (st 1-5)

Having been vindicated, he now asks that he may never be swept away with *sinners*, those whose hands are stained by violence or the taking of bribes. While once again protesting his innocence, he does not hesitate to ask the Lord to *redeem me and show me your mercy*, a clear indication that he is well aware that he is still a sinner. It is because of his trust in God that *his foot stands on level ground* and he vows to *bless the Lord in the assembly* (st 6-7).

We often show great skill in finding excuses for ourselves – even before God and even when we are clearly guilty. In contrast, Jesus was, in the astonishing words of St Paul "made into sin so that in him we might become the goodness of God" (2 Corinthians 5:21).

### PSALM 27 (28) Lament

Here is a psalm with the swing of mood that is characteristic of many laments. In st 1-3 we hear the desperate cry for help, as the psalmist lifts up his hands in suplication *to your holy place*, the most sacred part of the Temple known as the Holy of Holies. Repeatedly he calls upon God to hear, almost as though unsure whether he will really do so, and pleads in particular that he may not be dragged away *with the wicked.*

But st 4-5 makes it clear that God has indeed heard. There is joy and song and acclamations of confidence: *in him my heart trusts.* But the psalmist belongs to a people; and so he prays that the God who has proved himself *my strength and my shield* may also be *the strength of his people,* and *a fortress* for *his anointed* (the king). He prays that God will *save* them and *bless* them and, a charming picture, will *carry them* in his arms or on his shoulders as a *shepherd* carries the weaklings of his flock – and will do so *for ever.*

In our suffering and in our rejoicing we are meant to support and in turn be supported by one another. The Church's great prayer of thanksgiving, the *Te Deum*, includes words form this psalm: "Lord, save your people and bless your inheritance. Rule them and uphold them for ever and ever".

# WEEK 1 FRIDAY

## EVENING PRAYER

### PSALM 40 (41) Lament

Because of other possible translations, especially of the final stanzas, many scholars regard this as a psalm of thanksgiving, but it seems better to see it as a lament, the prayer of one who suffers sickness and betrayal. After a reflection on the blessedness of the person who pays attention to *the poor* (the helpless) *and the weak*, in that he or she will in turn by helped by the Lord when faced with misfortune, the psalmist tells his own sorry story. He recalls how he cried out to God in his sickness (attributed, as was then the custom, to sinfulness: *for I have sinned against you*); how his enemies who visit him prove to be Job's comforters and worse, whispering that he hasn't got much longer for this world; and how even his close friend is little better (st 1-3).

But he turns to the Lord who can help him, begging him to do so and thereby prove *that you are my friend*. Then, he will be able to repay his enemies, a very 'human', though hardly a New Testament, attitude. More importantly, he will be able to go to the Temple and enjoy *your presence for evermore* (st 4).

On this Friday evening, the psalm takes on a solemn meaning as we recall how Jesus spent his whole life considering *the poor and the weak*. Our Lord, though able to silence his foes with the challenge: "Can one of you convict me of sin?" (John 8:46), still had to contend with enemies who spoke evil against him and, worse still, with a friend, a table companion in whom he trusted, but who turned against him (Mark 14:18). We also recall how his cries for help seemed to go unheard, so that his enemies did shout in triumph over him; but how he triumphed and was set in God's presence for ever. And so we are ready to join in a doxology of praise to the Father, to the Crucified and Risen One and to the Holy Spirit, joint gift of both.

# WEEK 1 FRIDAY

**PSALM 45 (46) Confidence**

As the heading in the breviary suggests, this psalm might be called the psalm of Emmanuel, God-with-us. Written it would seem at a time of crisis, it is a song of amazing confidence: not in the strength of Jerusalem but in the mighty power of God who dwells there. *The Lord of hosts is with us; the God of Jacob is our stronghold*: that is the defiant rallying chorus, repeated three times, to draw attention to three areas of his sovereignty.

1. In Nature: In st 1 the psalmist probably has in mind the power God displayed in mastering untamed nature and bringing the world into being, a power which remains sure even though the created world should collapse. At a time when there are enough nuclear arsenals to 'dissolve' our planet several times over, the words are no longer poetic imagery. But whatever the *distress*, even though *the earth should rock* and *the mountains be shaken*, God is *a helper close at hand*.

2. In History: After the chorus, sung by the assembly, the poet turns to the city itself. Sited high on its rocky eminence, it would be vulnerable to siege, because no stream of water could reach it. But just outside the eastern wall there was a natural spring, and King Hezechiah ordered the cutting of a long tunnel to bring the precious spring water into the city. (Archeologists found, mid-way along the tunnel, a Hebrew inscription telling how the work had begun at either end of the tunnel and at this very spot the two gangs of workmen had heard the sound of each other's picks and knew the breakthrough was at hand). However, the eyes of faith saw the modest stream as *a river*, gushing up from under the earth or even from one of the mighty rivers of the Garden of Eden (Genesis 2:10). It was a gift from God, *bringing joy to God's city* and serving as a sign that *God is within* and therefore *it cannot be shaken*. It can overcome any enemy.

# WEEK 1 FRIDAY

3 At the End: Again the chorus is sung, and then the psalmist tells how God, who has proved himself by *the redoutable deeds he has done*, will finally put an end to wars, destroy all the accoutrements of battle and will *reign supreme over all the earth*.

Like other 'Songs of Sion', this psalm lends itself to confident prayer for the Church. On the night before he went into the darkness of the night and of his Passion, our Lord told his friends, the Church in embryo, "Do not be afraid". Like its Master, it can never be defeated, though the world should collapse or, as history has so often shown, terrible persecution be launched against it. He is always God-with-us. And the end of this world will mark the coming of his Kingdom of peace, the heavenly Jerusalem in which every one is a first-born son or daughter (Hebrews 12:23). We can find confidence in the words, spoken by a prophet in this psalm: *Be still and know that I am God.* We are safe.

## CANTICLE – Revelation 15:3-4

This Canticle takes over where the last psalm ended. It transports us to heaven where those who have successfully fought against 'the beast' (i.e. every enemy of Christ and his Church) gather to sing 'the hymn of Moses and the Lamb'. That hymn, this evening's Canticle, is the celebration of the Lamb of God, who on Good Friday achieved a greater deliverance than that accomplished by Moses at the Exodus, for through it the salvation of the world is secured and he is revealed as *King of the ages*.

The book of Revelation, written about the turn of the first century, brought comfort to hard-pressed Christians. Nineteen centuries later, it still brings comfort to us in all our troubles and givers us hymns of praise for our Saviour God.

# WEEK 1 SATURDAY

## OFFICE OF READINGS

### PSALM 130 (131) Confidence

Psalms 119(120) to 133(134) make up a group known as the 'Psalms of Ascent', in all probability because they were sung by pilgrims on their way up to Jerusalem. Since the city stands over 2000 feet above sea-level, it was a real ascent for the worshippers. Psalm 130, which belongs to this group, is a gem, one of the most tender and intimate psalms in the psalter. Its style is simple, its imagery evocative and its spirit close to that of the gospels ("Unless you become as little children" Matthew 18:3).

In st 1 the poet describes how he has learned, no doubt after many struggles, to steer clear of pride (*my heart is not proud*) and presumption (*I have not gone after marvels beyond me*). Instead, and this is the heart of the psalm, he has abandoned himself totally to God, *in silence and peace*, like a tiny child on its mother's breast; indeed, a more accurate translation would give the sense of a weaned child, a little one that seeks nothing, except to be close to its mother's heart (st 2). All God's people are urged to follow his example, *to hope in the Lord both now and forever.*

Could it be that the poet was in fact a woman, speaking from her own experience as a mother? In any event, if one of the Church's greatest needs is to discover the maternal face of God, this is surely a psalm for our times.

### PSALM 131 (132) Confidence

Before leaving Jerusalem, the pilgrims call upon God *to remember* their great hero king, David and by implication his successor. They recall David's *many hardships* on behalf of the city, including the vow not to sleep until he had rescued the Ark from obscurity and brought it to a worthy dwelling place in the sanctuary. The search had begun at *Ephrata* (probably Bethlehem, David's native town) and ended with the discovery of the Ark *in the plains of Yearim* (not far from Jerusalem). From there it was borne in triumph to the city. And now the worshippers are summoned to *go to the place of his dwelling* and to kneel beside the Ark, which serves as *his footstool.* The next stanza, especially the formula *Go up, Lord* suggests that this psalm was part of a ritual re-enactment of David's exploit. The Ark itself may have been carried in procession, while intercessions were made for the priests that they might be *clothed with holiness* befitting the splendour of their festive robes, and for the king, *your anointed*, that he might never be rejected by the Lord (§I).

What follows (§II) is God's response, delivered to the assembly by a Temple prophet. Like David (see §I st 1), God too has sworn an oath and he will *not go back on his word*, provided only that his people are true to the covenant. God's promises reflect the petitions that have been made: blessings for his *chosen Sion*, for the *poor*, for his *priests* and people, but above all for *David*: he will have descendants (his *stock will flower*), divine presence and protection (*a lamp for my anointed*) and a glorious reign (*my crown shall shine*).

This may seem an outmoded, even un-prayable, psalm until we remember that it is one of those Royal Psalms which the Jews continued to pray even when they had lost their king and the Ark itself (at the fall of Jerusalem in 587), and the new Temple was only a shadow of its glorious predecessor. They continued to use it because of their hopes for the future. We have seen those hopes fulfilled: in Jesus, David's stock has flowered (see the *Benedictus*); he is the King whose reign will have no end (Luke 1:33) and who is a light to the world (Luke 2:31); he is the Word made flesh who sought no special Ark as his home, but was happy to be made flesh and dwell among us, his creatures. We know of *the many hardships he endured* and that he has left his Church as a new Sion to replace the old. Come, then, let us praise and thank him.

*During Advent, Christmastide, Lent and Eastertide the above two psalms are replaced by the following:*

## PSALM 104 (105) Didactic

The historian Christopher Dawson once remarked that a people unaware of its own past is like a man who has lost his memory. The Israelites made sure that they could never be accused of amnesia. On great festivals, such as the one that lies behind this psalm, they loved to recall the events of their history, not out of nostaligia but in order to praise and glorify the Lord for *the wonders he has done* (§I st 1-3).

The remainder of §I centres upon the history of Abraham and the Patriarchs, and more especially upon *his Covenant* with them, which *he remembers for ever*. Though they were no more than a handful of people, he guaranteed that *Canaan* would be their *appointed heritage*. §II takes in the history of *Joseph*, who, having become a slave, then rose to a place of high honour. Thus God prepared for the greatest event in their history, the Exodus.

§III tells how Israel *lived in the country of Ham* (Egypt), how they increased in number until they seemed to pose a threat to the host community and were bitterly oppressed. But then God, the chief actor in their history, raised up *Moses his servant* and Aaron, and through them *showed his marvels*, the plagues of Exodus 4-11. The result was that *Egypt rejoiced to see them go* and God continued to care for them, providing them on the way to Canaan with *bread from heaven* and *water* that *gushed forth in the desert like a river*. And so they must be a people who *observe his laws*.

This story is our story, too, but we know its final chapter: the liberation accomplished by the death and resurrection of Jesus and the 'bread from heaven', given to nourish us on our pilgrim journey to the Promised Land.

# WEEK 1 SATURDAY

## MORNING PRAYER

### PSALM 118(119) XIX Didactic

This section of the long Psalm 118 (119) is a suitable prayer for any morning; it tells how the psalmist rose *before dawn* and cried for help. The reason for his plea is clear, he wants God to strengthen him so that he may be able to keep his law. And he is confident that he will receive help because of God's faithful love. However, his prayer is the more urgent because enemies are at hand. Perhaps they will tempt him into sin. But if they *draw near*, experience has taught him that already *you, O Lord, are close.*

As we begin this new day, we have the consolation of knowing that whatever the difficulties, the Lord is close, closer than any enemy could ever be.

### CANTICLE – Exodus 15: 1-4,8-13,17-18

This is the first and one of the most celebrated canticles in the Bible, parts of it dating back to perhaps within a hundred years or so of the key event of Israel's history, the Exodus, when *horse and rider* were *thrown into the sea*. It is a hymn attributed to Moses; aided by his followers, and his sister, Miriam, who together with the other women dances and sings, he recalls God's mighty victory over the Egyptians. With poetic licence he visualises the waters of the Red (or Reed) Sea being torn apart by *the breath* of God and being piled up *like a dam* so that his people can cross in safety. Then, when their enemies pursue them, *you blew with your breath* again, and the Egyptians sink beneath the waves *like lead* (st 1-5). Indeed, *the Lord is a warrior!* Having rescued his people, his *love guided* them and his *power led them* to the Promised Land, where he is installed in *the sanctuary* as *Lord, for ever and ever* (st 6-7).

At times of national disaster, for example during the Babylonian exile, the people of Israel looked forward to a new and even greater

# WEEK 1 SATURDAY

Exodus to come (see Isaiah 40-55). It was with Christ's victory over sin and death that their hopes were finally realised. As the breviary heading reminds us, the full fruits of his victory will be revealed in heaven to all "those who overcame the beast" and who now sing "the hymn of Moses, the Servant of the Lord". Until that glorious day arrives, *The Lord* (Jesus) *is my strength, my song* (of joy), *my salvation.*

### PSALM 116 (117) Hymn

This morning's prayer began with an excerpt from the longest psalm in the psalter and now ends with the shortest. It is a call for *all you nations* to praise and acclaim the Lord, because *of his love* and his covenant faithfulness. In his letter to the Romans Paul quotes this psalm to buttress his argument that Christ's purpose is "to get the pagans to give glory to God" (Rom 15:9). But, as the context of Paul's words indicates, Christ's purpose will not be achieved unless his followers are united, and, it might be added, unless there are missionaries to take his message to the ends of the earth. And so this little psalm might serve as a prayer for the cause of Christian unity and for the Church's missionary activity throughout the world.


## PRAYER DURING THE DAY
### PSALM 118 (119) V Didactic

Once again today a section of Psalm 118(119) provides us with our prayer. There is a note of urgency in the repeated requests: *Teach me, train me, guide me, keep my eyes, keep the promise you have made.* But behind the requests is the recognition, essential to all prayer, of personal weakness and of the absolute need of God's help.

Two of the requests are particularly attractive: first, the prayer that God will guide us in the path of his commands, will lead us in his way; and we remember that Jesus said "I am the Way". It is in that living Way that we wish to walk this day, and every day. Secondly, there is the prayer *Bend my heart to your will.* It is as though the psalmist was saying: take this hard heart of mine, but be gentle with it. Don't break it by your almighty power, but soften it, make it pliable, biddable, responsive and then bring it into harmony with your will. "Spirit of the living God, fall afresh on me. Melt me, mould me, fill me, use me. Spirit of the living God, fall afresh on me."

### PSALM 33 (34) Thanksgiving

Jean Vanier, from his experience with the mentally handicapped and the imprisoned, argues that: "The poor are the best teachers of theology, if we can learn to listen to them." This moving psalm is composed by a poor man and is directed especially to *the humble, those who revere* the Lord, those *who seek the Lord, his saints, his servants*, those who are *crushed*.

He begins with the announcement that he intends to *bless the Lord*, and not only now but at *all times*, and he calls upon the worshippers who surround him to *glorify the Lord with me*. He recalls his own experience of answered prayer: how he had *sought the Lord* and had been *set free, rescued from all his distress*. He stands, therefore, as living proof that angelic power surrounds the Lord's people like a mighty host, just as it did in the 'old days' when they camped in the desert. So he bids them to *look towards* the Lord *and be radiant*, like a mother whose face lights up with joy at the sight of her returning children (see Isaiah 60:5). *Taste,* he urges them, *and see that the Lord is good;* discover him from your own experience. Seek refuge in him and you will find happiness. (The intrepid missionary St Columba of Iona died as he was transcribing these words: he had so often sought refuge in the Lord, now he was to taste him and see him and find pefect happiness in him). The king of beasts may go hungry, but the

# WEEK 1 SATURDAY

Lord will not fail his frail human creatures when they seek him(§I).

In §II the psalmist acts as a 'master of spirituality', bidding his *children to come and hear me*. What he wants to share with them is the secret of how to live a long and happy life. It is to *turn aside from evil and do good*, because God's *eyes* (which see all) *and his ears* (which hear every prayer) are turned towards *the just*, while – a horrifying thought – he *turns his face* away from *the wicked*. So, though the just man may encounter *many trials* in life, God will always be near and provide a favourable outcome. Put simply, and beautifully, *those who hide in him shall not be condemned*.

This psalm is several times alluded to in the New Testament (e.g. 1 Peter 2:3), and it provides many points for reflection. One is that the nearness of God which the psalmist promises to the just, even in the midst of troubles, has been realised for the Church above all in the Holy Eucharist, where he is present among us and where we are invited to 'taste and see that the Lord is good'. A second we discover in St John when he quotes this psalm – "He will keep guard over all his bones" – to show that, in the horror of Calvary, Jesus' very bones are in the safe-keeping of his Father and also to indicate that Jesus is the true Passover Lamb (Exodus 12:46: "nor must you break any bone of it"). In both these points there is encouragement for us, as well as fruit for meditation.

# WEEK 2 SUNDAY

## EVENING PRAYER I
### PSALM 118(119) XIV Didactic

In Old Testament times a *lamp* was usually a shallow clay dish, serving as a reservoir for oil, with the rim pinched at one point to receive the wick; its flickering *light* could do little more than reveal the step immediately ahead. And so when the psalmist calls God's *word* (his law, his revelation) *a lamp for my steps*, he is acknowledging the brightness that God has brought into his life but also recognising that outside that pool of light there is much still shrouded in darkness – the reason for evil and suffering in the world, the uncertain future, death itself. *I carry my life in my hands*, he says, as though indicating his precarious hold on existence. Yet, in spite of the uncertainties and the fact that *the wicked try to ensnare me*, he pledges himself to continue to *carry out your will for ever*, for God's will is *the joy of my heart*. Though Christ has brought us the 'fullness of revelation', and though the area of light he gives us is so much vaster than it was in Old Testament times, we still find ourselves surrounded with darkness, so much that we cannot understand, so much uncertainty about where the future may lead us. But, like the psalmist, we learn that God will always provide light enough for the next step of our pilgrim journey. After that we leave ourselves in his hands.

### PSALM 15(16) Confidence

This is a thrilling song and, in the light of the New Testament, an excellent 'vocation prayer', a way of reflecting on our vocation as baptised Christians, sons and daughters of God.

We seek refuge in God and ask him to keep us faithful. With great daring, we claim: *My happiness lies in you alone*. We have a special affection for those who share the faith with us; but those who make 'gods' of other things or people, bring trouble upon themselves. We want no part in such deities (st 1-2). The Promised Land had been shared out by the drawing of lots, each of the twelve tribes receiving its own God-given *portion*; but God allotted the priests no territory because he had given them the wonderful assurance: "It is *I* who will be your portion and your inheritance" (Numbers 18:20). As Christians we are a priestly people; our portion and *cup* is nothing less than God himself. He is our *prize, the lot marked out* for us, *the heritage* that falls to us. How we should delight in our good fortune. (st 3)

As we reflect on our portion, we find ourselves blessing God, our constant counsellor and guide. However inadequately, we try to keep him *ever in sight*, and in quiet prayer or as our last thought before sleep we allow him to direct our hearts. The certainty that he is ever beside us is a source of great consolation and enables each one of us to declare: *I shall stand firm* (st 4).

Now the psalm moves towards its superb climax. The final two stanzas were applied to Jesus by both St Peter and St Paul (Acts 2:29 & 13:34-37). In him they are literally fulfilled, but because we have been 'caught up' in him through baptism, they apply to us too. *Heart and soul* we rejoice and are glad. The Lord will not allow us to come to any lasting harm. And though we must die and even decay, he *will not leave my soul among the dead*. It is through communion with him that we are introduced to *the path of life* – to walk this way is already *life* – which will one day open up *to the fulness of joy in his presence* (literally, 'at the sight of his face') and with him *happiness for ever*.

I called this a thrilling psalm: it began with our seeking refuge in God as his children; it ends with perfect and unending joy in our Father's house.

**CANTICLE – Philippians 2:6-11** (see Week 1 Sunday, page 40)
The aim of this canticle may be to contrast the first, 'earthly' man,

Adam, with the perfect, 'heavenly' man, Jesus Christ. Both were 'in the image and likeness of God' (Genesis 1:26), but whereas the first tried to seize equality with God (Genesis 2 & 3), the latter, though the very Son of God, "did not count equality with God a thing to be grasped" and as a result of his obedient self-emptying is now clearly seen to enjoy that equality.

## OFFICE OF READINGS
### PSALM 103(104) Hymn

Inscribed on the wall of a tomb, dating from the early 14th century B.C., is to be found one of the most astonishing Egyptian hymns, composed by the Pharaoh Akhenhaton in honour of the Sun. It may have inspired Psalm 103(104), as some scholars believe, but if so the alchemy of faith has transmuted it into a magnificent hymn in honour of the Creator God.

After a brief summons to *bless the Lord,* the psalmist cries out in wonder at the greatness of God. A commentator on this psalm refers to the "Lord of seven wonders" because as the psalm unfolds it mirrors the 7- day drama of creation (Genesis 1). He is a God *clothed in majesty* and surrounded by light as though *wrapped in a robe.* He has set up *the heavens* as a desert-dweller sets up his *tent;* above this canopy is the sea of heaven and in its swirling waters, on sturdy pillars, he has built his palace *dwelling.* All the elements are at his disposal: *the clouds* as his chariot, *the winds* as his messengers and the plumes of *flashing fire* as his servants (§I st 1-2). Like the author of the creation story, the psalmist now recounts, in a series of brilliant poetic pictures, the origin of the earth, which he visualizes as a circular disc, firmly fixed so that it will *stand firm from age to age.* Once, it had been covered with water, which reached *higher than the mountains,* but at *the thunder* of his word he tamed the waters, which fled to their appointed place and were prevented from ever again covering the earth by the boundaries he set. Having brought cosmos from watery chaos, God now uses the waters in the service of his creatures: from the subterranean ocean, *springs gush forth* so that the animals can *quench their thirst* and the wilderness can sprout foliage in which *the birds* of the sky nest and sing (§I st 3-5). From the heavenly ocean, comes *your gift* of rain which transforms parched land into green vegetation, meeting the needs of cattle and of human beings. *The cedars*, so mighty that God himself must have *planted* them *on Lebanon*, also *drink their fill* and so a home is provided for small *birds* and the more substantial *storks*. Even the apparently inhospitable rocks provide a refuge for some of the animals. The whole of nature exists in wonderful mutual harmony (§II 1-3).

In a world without clock or calendar, God in his munificence has created two mighty timepieces, *the moon to mark the months* and *the sun* to mark the days; and in his wisdom has so arranged night and day that the first belongs to the fierce *beasts* and the second to human beings, each group being able to go about its business without threat from the other; and, a delightful poetic touch, the powerful *lions* roaring for *their prey* in the night are praying to God for *their food*. (§II st 4-5).

After another outburst of praise at the wonders of creation, the poet shows that God's concern is not only with the earth but also with the ocean, so *vast and wide* that *the ships are moving there* and a home is provided for creatures *great and small*, even *the monsters* of the deep which he *made to play with* as pets. Having created them, he must preserve them: for if *you hide your face* they are in dire straits; and if *you take back your spirit* they are finished. But he who breathes the spirit of life into his creatures, continues to do so and the whole earth is renewed (§III st 1-4).

And so the hymn draws to its finale as the poet prays, in childlike fashion, that *the glory of the Lord*, whose might is revealed in the earthquakes and the lightning, may *last for ever* and that his creation may always bring joy to his heart. And if he prays for the disappearence of the wicked, that is because he wants all human beings to share in their Maker's joy, just as he finds his joy in the Lord and promises to *sing to the Lord all my life, make music to my God while I live.*

## MORNING PRAYER I
### PSALM 117(118) Thanksgiving (see Week 1 Sunday, page 48)

### CANTICLE – Daniel 3:52-57
Last Sunday at Morning Prayer we met the three young men who sang praises to God as they walked unscorched in the midst of a fiery furnace. Today's Canticle is the second of the songs they sang. Again it is in the form of a litany, with the constant refrain *To you glory and praise for ever.* The *Lord* and his *glorious holy name* are to be blest in *the temple of your glory*, whence he is able to *gaze into the depths*; *in the firmament of heaven*, where he walks *on the wings of the wind.* *Saints and angels* are called upon to bless him; praise is to go up to him from every part of creation, *from the heavens, the earth and the sea.* He is to be blest as *God of our fathers.*

In our Mass today we shall be taking up the song of the three youths, as we add our voices to all those through the ages who have praised God. But ours will be the privilege of being united with Jesus as he offers his perfect act of praise to his Father.

### PSALM 150 Hymn
"Praise I call the product of the singing heart", wrote Cardinal Hume. The author of this psalm must surely have had such a heart. It is a

psalm free of all self-seeking, it is simply praise, pure praise from beginning to end; indeed, the invitation to praise appears in every single line except one. God is to be praised in *his holy place*, the Temple, and in his home, *his mighty heavens*; he is to be praised for what he has done, *his powerful deeds*, and for what he is, *his surpassing greatness* (st 1).

Each section of the Temple orchestra is called to lend its voice to the symphony of praise: brass and strings, woodwinds and percussion. Above all the worshippers themselves must praise God, and not only with voices and musical instruments but also with their own bodies as they join the sacred *dance*. And then, as though to sum it all up, the psalmist begs that every single living creature should join in the hymn of praise (st 2-3).

It is a breath-taking psalm, which has been described as the keystone of the whole psalter, and, as a doxology of praise, it provides a perfect ending to this wonderful book of prayer. *Let everything that lives and that breathes give praise to the Lord* – at our Eucharist today let us praise him in our hearts, let us praise him for those who are dear to us, for those who are in our care, for those who never raise their voices in praise.

## PRAYER DURING THE DAY
### PSALM 22(23) Confidence

In 1971 the late Sir Geoffrey Jackson, British Ambassador in Uruguay, was kidnapped by guerillas and held for several months in a secret underground prison. He recalls how, after his first night in captivity, he awoke to see a rough concrete wall beside him. He blinked in unbelief, listened for the quiet breathing of his wife and then realised to his horror that he really was a prisoner. "Slowly and consciously, I unknotted my stomach, blessed myself and...found myself saying the one line of the 23rd Psalm (Psalm 22) which, by some odd block, was all that would come through to me for many days – *Yea, though I walk through the valley of the shadow of death I will fear no evil.*"

This psalm is held in affection by people the whole world over. Its imagery and serene confidence have brought consolation to many men and women who would claim that they are 'not at all religious'. The psalmist recognises the great Lord of the exodus as *my shepherd*, Someone with a personal interest in him. And so he is confident that *nothing shall I want*. As a sheep is led by its shepherd to luscious *pastures* and cool refreshing *waters* where it can find rest and renewal, so he too is cared and provided for by God (st 1). But he is no romantic; he lives in the real world, where terrible things happen, where there is no escape from the lonely walk *in the valley of darkness*. But the good Shepherd is with him in the midst of the darkness, bearing his *crook* (to direct) and his *staff* (to ward off enemies), and he can be relied upon for he is always *true to his name*. It is a thought which eases *fear* and brings *comfort*. Notice how at this point God is addressed familiarly and directly as "You" (st 2).

Then the picture changes to one of even greater intimacy: God has become host to the psalmist, has *anointed his head with oil,* prepared *a banquet* and *a cup* full to overflowing. Such generous hospitality forms an unbreakable bond between them, which even the presence of *foes* cannot destroy (st 3). And it fills the psalmist with overwhelming happiness and an assurance that the divine *goodness and kindness* will never desert him, and that he will have a place in *the Lord's own house* for ever (st 4).

This song takes on even greater beauty as a Christian prayer, reminding us, as it does, of Jesus our 'Good Shepherd' (John 10:11-18), of the glorious banquet and eucharistic cup which he makes ready for us at Mass to today, of the anointing with the Spirit which we received at Confirmation sealing us as God's for ever, of St Paul's affirmation that nothing can separate us from the love of God (see Rom 8), and of the fact that Jesus has gone ahead "to prepare a place" for us so that "where I am you may be too" (John 14:2-4).

Geoffrey Jackson describes as 'a nugget' (of gold) the day "when suddenly I awoke with the words of the whole 23rd Psalm entire in my mind". If we were to commit this psalm to memory, I suspect we too would find it as precious as gold, a source of strength and joy in all the eventualties of life.

### PSALM 75(76) Thanksgiving

The occasion for this psalm may have been a particular historical victory, but more probably it is a thanksgiving for all that God has done – and will do. He *is made known* (has made his glorious presence felt) and *his name is great* in both parts of the country – *Judah* (in the south) and *Israel* (in the north), but above all in his own *dwelling place in Jerusalem*: the gear of battle that was turned against it now lies in the dust. What a magnificent Lord we have! He is *more majestic than the everlasting mountains.* Pitted against him, *warriors* are of no avail and *soldiers* are powerless; at his word they are paralyzed with fear. (§I)

The first section of this psalm leads naturally into the second. The God who has proved himself powerful against every enemy is the God who is to judge the human race. And when he has risen to pass sentence the whole earth is *still* in expectation and in trembling of what is to come: disaster for the wicked and justice for the *humble* (the weak and the oppressed).

# WEEK 2 SUNDAY

The very *anger* of the first group will *serve to praise you*, because it will be a vindication of your justice, while the latter will be filled with gratitude towards you. And so the psalm ends with a call to all people to come and *pay tribute to him* by their worship (§II).

Amidst the warlike language of this psalm is the vital truth, proclaimed throughout the New Testament, that our God is a God of limitless power who will judge all people so that they will receive their just deserts. So often in history powers have risen against him and all he stands for, but as we look back we see the ruins of mighty empires, the destruction of apparently invincible armies, the end of persecutions which seemed destined to last for ever. Time and again, we join our forefathers who sang this psalm in proclaiming: 'Our God reigns' – and ever shall.

## EVENING PRAYER II
**PSALM 109(110) Didactic** (see Week 1 Sunday, page 52)

### PSALM 113b(115) Confidence
A priest working in West Africa reported how his little Christian community were filled with fear because the local witchdoctors had set up ju-jus (charms which were believed to bring harm). And so he organised a service to show his people that they were safe under God's protection. What impressed them most, he explained, were "these lines from the psalms: 'They have mouths but they cannot speak;...eyes but they cannot see;... ears but they cannot hear;...nostrils but they cannot smell'".

More than 2000 years earlier, in another service, the same Psalm 113b (115) had been sung by the people of Israel. Gathered in the Temple they plead with the Lord for the manifestation of his glory.

# WEEK 2 SUNDAY

It is not their honour but his that is at stake. The heathen may be tempted to ask: *'Where is their God?'* The answer to such a question is not only that he *is in the heavens*, but also, and more importantly, that he is infinitely greater (able to do *whatever he wills*) than the idols of his adversaries who foolishly worship *the work of their own human hands*. The graven images may have *mouths, eyes, ears, nostrils, hands and feet*, but they are utterly powerless. To take them as one's gods is *to become like them* – helpless and impotent (st 1-4).

A priest exhorts the whole community – *sons of Israel* (the laity), the *sons of Aaron* (the priests) and all who *fear the Lord* (perhaps other, non-Israelite, worshippers) – to trust in the Lord, and each group responds, acknowledging him as *their help and their shield*. In answer to their expressions of trust, the priest calls down upon them God's blessings, including that of a numerous posterity (st 5-8a).

The service ends with the assembly proclaiming once more the greatness of their God, *maker of heaven and earth*, who has given the earth to his creatures as their sphere of existence and activity. As this Sunday draws to its close, we are given both a warning and an assurance. The warning is that in every age and in every situation idol-worship is an ever-present reality. Human beings so easily begin to make 'gods' of the things of this world (money, power, sex, fame) and to worship "what their own hands have made". We need constantly to be on guard to ensure that our great God holds his rightful place in our lives. And the assurance is that, through the Paschal Mystery, heaven, as well as earth, has been given us and that the praise we offer God this evening is destined to last for ever.

**CANTICLE – Revelation 19:1-2, 5-7 or (in Lent) 1 Peter 2:21-24** (see Week 1 Sunday, page 56)

## OFFICE OF READINGS

### PSALM 30 (31) Lament

For a Christian, one sentence of this psalm stands out above all others: *Into your hands I commend my spirit* (§I st 3). These are among the last recorded words of Jesus (Luke 23:46), though with the significant addition of the word: "Father". Even as he writhes in his death agony, Jesus still calls trustingly upon his "Abba" (dear Father). Following his example, many other Christians – including St Stephen (Acts 7:59) – have made these words their dying prayer. Brother Charles de Foucauld found in them the inspiration for his widely-used Prayer of Abondonment. Indeed, they serve as a source of comfort to all who unite their sufferings with those of the Master.

Like him they turn to God in confidence, begging urgently that the Lord may be a granite *rock* or *a mighty stronghold* where they may find safety from all that oppresses them. Knowing that he is a *God of truth*, of utter faithfulness, they entrust themselves to his hands and to his redeeming power. Because their trust is not in *empty gods* but in *the Lord* himself, fear gives way to gladness and rejoicing, and already they anticipate an end to their *affliction* and *soul's distress* (§I st 1-5).

Surprisingly, however, the psalm does not end here: instead there is a recapitulation of the cries for help and the acts of confidence, together with a moving description of the sorrows that have been (or are being?) endured. Perhaps the sorrows have returned; perhaps, because of his trust in God, the psalmist now feels able to unburden himself of his story in a more detached way; his suffering was real – maybe it still is – but now he can accept it trustfully as part of God's plan.

It is helpful when reading §II to think of what our Lord had been through before uttering his cry from the Cross. He had been deserted by his friends, treated as *a reproach, an object of scorn*; he had become *like a thing thrown away*; he had been the victim of *slander* and enveloped with *fear* as men plotted and schemed *to take my life*. But it was in the depths of his distress that he called upon God and sought his help.

St Luke recalls that "With these words (i.e. *Into your hands..*) he breathed his last" (23:46). But God did indeed let his *face shine on his servant*; and so §III may be regarded as the prayer of thanksgiving of the risen Jesus for *the wonders of* his Father's *love*. And it is an encouragement to us his brothers and sisters who take up our cross and continue on our pilgrim way: *Be strong, let your heart take courage, all who hope in the Lord.*

## MORNING PRAYER

### PSALM 41 (42) Lament

The psalm opens with an unforgettable image: the psalmist, probably in exile, catches sight of a *deer* which in the harsh summer heat searches anxiously *for running streams* to quench its burning thirst. He too is aware of an almost animal-like craving, a dreadful *thirsting*, for the One who is so important to him that he describes him as *the God of my life*. His one desire is to *see the face of God*, to meet him in his Temple. But there is litle hope of that desire being fulfilled. Life has been reduced to a diet of *tears*, the more so as he hears the unnerving jeers of his pagan enemies: *Where is your God?* (st 1-3)

In his distress, he finds comfort in recalling days gone by when he used to go up to Jerusalem at the head of a *rejoicing crowd;* there was *gladness* and *thanksgiving* and unbelievable *joy* as they approached God's dwelling place. With these happy memories in mind, he enters into a dialogue with *my soul,* questioning the reason for his grief, urging himself to continue to *hope in God* and defiantly declaring that he *will praise him still,* his Saviour God (st 5).

Alas, the respite is short-lived: his very thinking about God has served only to intensify his home-sickness for the Temple. Gazing up at the towering heights of *Mount Hermon* and the waters, which feed the *Jordan* river, rushing down with such ferocity, he is reminded of his own unhappy situation. It is as though God's own *torrents and waves* had thundered down upon him; and at the foot of the waterfalls, where *deep is calling on deep*, the dark, swirling currents seem to reflect his own inner turmoil, pain and loneliness (st 6-7).

The psalmist tries to pull himself together, asserting that God will *send his loving kindness* to the rescue, and promising that he himself *will sing to him* in praise. During the watches of the night he will call upon *my rock* – a description brought to mind perhaps by the sight of the rock face, down which the waters cascade – and will reproach God for apparently *forgetting* him and allowing enemies to *revile* him *all the day long* with their soul-chilling taunts. Once more he tries bravely to find comfort in that dialogue with self which we saw in §I st 5 (st 8-11).

In his agony in the Garden Jesus echoes the thought of this psalm (Mark 14:34). 'Yearning' for God was the secret strength of the martyrs, like Blessed George Beesley who, when he was languishing in the Tower of London, carved into his cell walls the opening words of this psalm. There are many people in our world – ourselves included at times – who face Gethsemane experiences when God seems far away and everything is painful 'emptiness'. For them, and for ourselves, we can pray this psalm with conviction.


### CANTICLE – Sirach 36:1-7,13-16
The book from which this canticle comes takes its name from its author, Sirach. He wrote early in the second century BC, at a time when the Jews still felt the effects of being under Greek rule and in

# WEEK 2 MONDAY

fact would, before long, engage in a national uprising, spearheaded by the Maccabees.

He prays that Jerusalem may be delivered from *foreign nations*: by punishing his own people for their sins, God had *proved his holiness* to the unbelievers; now he should punish them and thereby *prove* his *glory to us* (st 1-2). He begs God to renew the *wonders* of former times, to draw all his people, *all the tribes of Jacob*, together in unity and make *Sion ring with your praises* (st 3-5).

This beautiful canticle serves as an invitation to us to pray for the Church today. Because of the sinfulness and shortcomings of its members, the Church stands in need of renewal. If the Church is to fulfil her task in the world, renewal must be an on-going concern. Let us pray this morning that we and all our Christian brothers and sisters may be so renewed that from the Church (the new Jerusalem) "there may radiate before all people the loveable features of Jesus Christ" (Pope John XXIII).

### PSALM 18(19)A  Hymn
The Christian apologist and English scholar, C.S. Lewis wrote of this psalm: "I take this to be the greatest poem in the psalter and one of the greatest lyrics in the world". Already we have considered its second part in Prayer during the Day of Week I Monday. There we saw how God is revealed through his Law; now we see how he is also revealed through his creation.

Even inanimate things – *the heavens*, the *day* and the *night*, – seem to possess the gift of speech for they bear witness to their Maker, they *proclaim the glory of God*. Paradoxically, the fact that their 'speech' is wordless makes it a language capable of being understood by all people *through all the earth*, and *to the utmost bounds of the world* (st 1-2).

The same is true of *the sun*, the part of creation which dominates the poem from this point on. It emerges each day with festive joy and splendid apparel, like *a bridegroom* leaving the tent where he has slept with his bride, and it runs its course with power and swiftness, like *a champion* athlete running his race. There may be an allusion in the first image to an ancient myth which tells how the sun-god sinks down each night into the ocean and, having spent the night with his bride, sets out once more in the morning. But if the poet uses that myth, how magnificently he has turned it to his purpose. Even the mighty sun – which others may regard as a god – is in fact just another part of God's handiwork. It is he who provides it with *a tent* in which it can live, and if *there is nothing concealed* from it, then that is but an image of the ubiquitous presence of our God (st 3-4).

Centuries later St Paul said that the pagans had no excuse for their unbelief, because: "Ever since God created the world his everlasting power and deity – however invisible – have been there for the mind to see in the things he has made" (Romans 1:19). However, we Christians are doubly fortunate, for we have not only the speechless voice of creation pointing to a Creator, but also Jesus himself who is both "the Bridegroom" (Mark 2:19-20) and "the Rising Sun" come to visit us (Luke 1:78) and show us the Father. Doubly fortunate, but also doubly obligated to live lives that will *proclaim the glory of God* and pass on the message which all creation *makes known*.

## PRAYER DURING THE DAY
### PSALM 118(119) VI Didactic

We beg that God's *love* may *come upon* us during the course of this day. What that means is brought out by the words which follow: *the saving help of your promise*. So long as we are assured of that saving help – and we can always *trust in your word* – we are able to face with equanimity those who *taunt* us, and testify to *the word of truth,* your steadfast faithfulness. And just as God is trustworthy, so we too promise to be faithful to the keeping of his law. We recognise that to obey him and follow his *precepts* is to find *the path of freedom* and the courage to speak up for him and his law before all whom we meet today, even *before kings,* if need be. And so, with the psalmist, we raise our hands in praise of his *commands* and of the whole of his revelation.

### PSALM 39(40) Thanksgiving

The psalmist *waited* and *waited* for the Lord to act, and now he has done so. There's something moving in the idea that God *stooped down to me,* like a father bending down to his troubled child. Whatever the trouble, when God intervened it was like Jeremiah's experience of being hauled out of *miry clay* at the bottom of a *deadly pit* (Jeremiah 38:6f): a rock-like security awaited him. God's goodness has *put a new song* of praise into the mouth of the psalmist, who cannot resist drawing a comparison between the *happy man* who trusts in God, and the unhappy one who follows idols. *The wonders* that God works mean that he has *no equal,* and their number means that we can never praise him enough (§I st 1-5).

God does not want even the Temple *offerings* of food or the blood-*sacrifice* of animals. One thing only suffices: the total giving of self – *here am I* – and the doing of *your will,* according to *the scroll of the book* – probably a reference to the book of the Law, which is *his delight* (§I st 6-7).

In §II the psalmist records how he has borne witness to God's goodness *in the great assembly* (st 1-2). But soon the hint of a change of tone creeps in: his reaffirmation of trust suggests that he is facing new perils. And in st 4 he confesses that he is *beset with evils too many to be counted.* As we have seen on other occasions, it may indicate that trouble has returned or that the psalmist is 'back-tracking' to tell of the sufferings for which he is now giving thanks. In any event, the psalm ends with a prayer for himself and for *all who seek you*, and, confident that *the Lord thinks of me*, he gently bids him *do not delay* (st 6-8).

The Letter to the Hebrews applies words from this psalm to Jesus, showing how he has come to replace all the sacrifices of old and to offer himself in an act of perfect worship to the Father (Hebrews 10). Our best response for what he has done will be the resolve to render God true worship 'in spirit and in truth' and that total submission to him which will enable us, even in dark times, to wait patiently upon him who is *my rescuer, my help.*

## EVENING PRAYER
### PSALM 44(45) Hymn

Just as a secular love song, the Song of Songs, has its place in the Bible, so a secular royal wedding song, Psalm 44(45), has its place in the Prayer of the Church. The court poet speaks of the inspiration which fills his *heart* and gives to his *tongue* the deftness of the *pen of a scribe* (an expert writer). His is a noble theme, the marriage of the *king* (§I st 1). A king who is outstandingly handsome, gracious in speech and *blessed* by God *for evermore*. One sign of that blessing is his skill in war, and so the poet urges him to take up arms and *ride on in triumph*. He fights in the *cause of truth and goodness and right* (§I st 2-4). The splendour of his rule is beyond doubt: his *throne will endure for ever*, his *sceptre* is one of *justice,* he has been *anointed* king by God himself, he is adorned in sumptuous perfumed robes and dwells in a *palace* inlaid with *ivory* and re-echoing to the sound of *music*. The psalm moves forward to its stunning climax: today the king's most precious 'possession' is revealed – the bride who stands beside him, arrayed in glistening jewellery of *gold of Ophir* (the finest gold then known, coming from south west Arabia) (§I st 5-7)

Now it is to her that the poet turns his attention, offering a few words of fatherly advice: she must *forget her own people and her father's house*, so that henceforth she may belong completely to her husband, who as king is also her *lord*. But her loss will also be her gain, for, having broken with her former home, she will find that the king's subjects are hers, just as his friends are hers; *the people of Tyre*, proverbial for their wealth, will bring her costly *gifts* to win her favour; and as she enters the palace, resplendent in dazzling *robes* encrusted with *pearls set in gold*, she is accompanied by the *rejoicing maiden companions* of her youth (§II st 1-3).

Once more the poet addresses the king, promising that he will be blessed with *sons* who will rule *over all the earth*. And he prays that through his own song the king's *name* will be immortalized and the *peoples* of all nations will be united in praise of him for ever (§II st 4).

His prayer has in fact been answered, but only because this royal psalm has a deeper Messianic significance. Behind the figure of the king are to be discerned the features of Jesus. He is *the fairest of the children of men*, such graciousness poured upon his lips that "There has never been anybody who has spoken like him"(John 7:46). Jesus is rightly addressed as God (see §I st 5); at the same time, as the Letter to the Hebrews points out, quoting from this psalm, he has been anointed by *God, your God* (§I st6), and thereby been given a superiority over the angels (Hebrews I:8-9). Furthermore, the Church (and each member of the Church) is his bride (Ephesians 5:32f); on Calvary he fought the battle for *truth and goodness and right*, bringing "many sons to glory" (Hebrews 2:10) by his paschal victory and making possible the wedding feast of heaven (Revelation 19). As we pray this psalm tonight, we make a lovely secular wedding song into a sacred hymn in honour of him who "first loved us". We also help to ensure that his name is *forever remembered*; and our thoughts turn, at the end of the day, to the last scene depicted in the Bible where the Spirit and the Bride (the Church), cry out "Come, Lord Jesus" as they await his final coming in glory when the Church is presented "as a chaste virgin to this one husband" 2 Corinthians 11:20 .

**CANTICLE – Ephesians 1:3-10** (see Week 1 Monday, page 66)

# WEEK 2 TUESDAY

## OFFICE OF READINGS
### PSALM 36 (37) Didactic

In every age the believer faces a burning problem: how to cope with the apparent triumph of evil in the world. It is a problem bravely tackled by the author of this psalm. As one *now...old* (see §II, st 8), he speaks from long experience; his aim is not to provide answers but to encourage trust.

§I sets the tone: Do not get worked up over *the wicked*, it seems to say, they will receive their reward. Armed with that assurance, your task is to *trust in the Lord and do good* and then you will find security *in the land*, and God himself, who is *your delight*, will bring forward *your cause like the noon-day sun*. Thus, your task is to *Be still before the Lord and wait in patience*, beware of allowing *anger* to take control of you and remember that it is only for *a little longer* that things shall be as they are. And then it is *the humble who shall own the land*.

§II st 1-5 points to the hostility of the wicked man, whose gnashing teeth are evidence of murderous intent, and to his *wealth*, as contrasted with *the just man's few possessions*. Yet, despite appearances, God *laughs at the wicked* ones – for he knows what the outcome will be: their weapons will be *broken to pieces* or even turned against them: they are no more permanent than *the beauty of the meadows* or a whisp of *smoke*.

Many contrasts can be drawn between *the just man* and *the wicked* man (§II st 6-10). The just one is *generous,* the other niggardly; the one is *blessed by the Lord*, the other *cursed* by him; the children of the one will *become a blessing* (a matter of crucial importance to people who had no clear notion of life beyond the grave), while those of the other will be *destroyed*.

# WEEK 2 TUESDAY

§III begins with the assurance that because the godly man has God's law *in his heart,* what he speaks will be true *wisdom,* and he will be *saved from stumbling.* It then repeats ideas from the earlier sections. There is the need to wait patiently upon God and *keep to his way,* the promise that the wicked will ultimately be destroyed, and, most significantly, the guarantee that while the *peaceful* can look forward to the future with hope, the wicked simply have *no future* – and therefore no hope. The elderly psalmist illustrates the last point from his own experience: he recalls an evil man who towered triumphant like a huge *Lebanon cedar,* but in a short time was *nowhere to be found.* And so he ends his poem with a serene act of faith that the Lord brings help, deliverance and salvation to all who place *their refuge in him.*

He might be accused of over-simplification in his portrayal of good and evil and of naivety in his perception of what happens to good people in this world. Yet his basic intuition is correct: the wicked will not prevail for ever, the good must be patient and trust, for it is God who will have the last word and he will not desert the *one he loves* or ever *forsake his friends.* And that message retains all its validity when we look out upon a world in which there are such gross inequalities. We see around us the haves and the have-nots, the over-fed and the dying of hunger, the desperately poor and the exorbitantly rich dwelling side by side. It has been said that there is no finer exposition of the third beatitude ('Blessed are the meek for they shall possess the land') than this psalm. If we who pray this psalm neglect our duty of working for the coming of the Kingdom of justice and peace, we have scarcely prayed at all.

# WEEK 2 TUESDAY

## MORNING PRAYER
### PSALM 42(43) Lament

There can be little doubt that this psalm together with Psalm 41 (42) (see yesterday's Morning Prayer, p 124) originally formed a single poem, divided into three sections. Each of the first two ends with the same refrain, and at the end of this, the third section, the refrain is picked up once more (st 5). Nonetheless, this part of the poem has its own peculiar tone. While earlier the psalmist had tended to speak *about* God; now he speaks *to* him: and the very repetition of the word *God* (no less than nine times in these few lines) seems to add to the earnestness of his prayer. It is a petition that the Lord will be his advocate, ready to *defend me, plead my cause* and finally to *rescue me*; that he will give orders for *light* and *truth,* like angelic escorts, to bring him safely back to God's house on the *holy mountain,* so that there he may rejoice in his *Redeemer* and make a sacrifice of thanksgiving. Again, we hear the refrain, which has occurred twice before, but though the words are the same the spirit is different: it is the spirit of faith and hope and even of victory.

Quite apart from Gethsemane experiences, there is in the life of each of us an emptiness, a yearning, a loneliness that nothing and no-one can satisfy. The human mind has been made for truth without limit, just as the human heart is made for limitless love. We can use this splendid psalm to express our homesickness for heaven, to reinforce our hope, to beg God that 'after this our exile' we may safely reach the *holy mountain* and the *God of our joy*, the God who alone can meet the hungriest longings of a human being.

### CANTICLE – Isaiah 38: 10-14,17-20

King Hezechiah enjoyed a long reign in Judah. He was a good king and this canticle is placed on his lips by the prophet Isaiah. It is a psalm of thanksgiving for recovery from grave illness. The early part (st 1-5) tells of the sickness which afflicted him when he was still a comparatively young man. It was so serious that he expected to die and thus be reduced to the shadowy life of *Sheol*. He saw his real life being *plucked* away from him as though it were *a shepherd's tent* being dismantled or a piece of woven cloth being cut off *from the loom*; morning and night he pleaded for mercy.

Like his contemporaries, he believed that illness was linked with sinfulness; and so when he recovered, it must have been because God had *cast all [his] sins behind [his] back*. Now he must give himself to thanksgiving, and tell his children of *your faithfulness* and give continual praise in the *house of the Lord* (st 6-9).

The scripture text which stands at the head of this canticle in the Prayer of the Church reminds us of One who did not merely draw close to death but who was dead and who is now alive. How deeply indebted we are to our Saviour God not only for the many favours he grants us, such as recovery from sickness, but for the mighty promise he holds out to us: that even death itself will not have the final victory, for he himself holds *the keys of death* and he will use them on our behalf.

### PSALM 64(65) Thanksgiving

This psalm, like so many others, bears testimony to the ingrained sense of gratitude of the people who wrote and sang the psalms: *to you*, it declares, *our praise* (thanksgiving) *is due*. It is a psalm which focuses upon God under three aspects:

i. The Lord of Grace: in Sion all can find intimacy with him, especially if labouring under the *burden of sin*; there too Israel celebrates with joy its own election, which enables it to *dwell in your courts* (st 2-3).

ii. The Lord of Nature and History: from Sion the psalmist's vision widens to take in the whole of creation, for it is God who is at work giving the *mountains* their massive security and holding in check the menancing roar of *the seas*. From east to west *the ends of the earth* stand awe-striken before his mighty *wonders*. The same Creator God is also *Saviour*, and throughout Israel's history has shown that his power over *the tumult of the people* is no less potent than his power over nature (st 4-6).

iii. The Lord of Plenty: the psalmist describes in lyrical fashion the magnificence of God's provision for his people. Like a farmer, he has taken care of *the earth*; his *river in heaven* has overflowed providing a plentiful outpouring of rain so that hard soil has become level and soft and *filled with riches*. His continuing goodness is like a *crown* placed upon the brow of the yearly cycle; *abundance* follows, wherever he goes. The psalmist seems to have in mind the delightful picture of a divine cart making its way across the earth and dripping its rich contents behind. At the Lord's passing the Palestinian landscape is transformed: the barren *hills* have *girded* themselves with *joy*, while *the meadows* with their *flocks* of sheep seem to be clad in festive garb and *the valleys* are decked out in ears of golden *wheat*. The whole of nature has put on its finest apparel, ready to *sing and shout for joy* at the festival (st 7-10).

This is a psalm which comes into its own at Harvest Festival. But it would be a pity if we did not see it as an invitation to thank God for all his blessings. We can thank him for forgiveness of our sins, election as his children, his creative and redeeming work, and the myriad of favours – like abundant crops and flowing water – which we so easily take for granted.

# WEEK 2 TUESDAY

## PRAYER DURING THE DAY
### PSALM 118(119) VII Didactic
It is not easy to be true to God's law when you have to face derision for your loyalty. The psalmist finds his *comfort* and his *hope* in God's word; it is *old* and trustworthy and brings with it the promise of life in the fullest sense of the word. And this fires him with fresh zeal for *the keeping of your precepts*, which have become to him like a song *in the land of exile*. We may be less than happy about his *indignation at the wicked*, but who would not admire and wish to imitate his resolute determination to serve God faithfully?

### PSALM 52(53) Didactic
This psalm is almost word for word identical with Psalm 13(14) (see Week 1 Tuesday, page 75)

### PSALM 53(54) Lament
This is a typical lament, beginning with a cry for help (st 1), followed by a brief account of the trial endured (st 2) and ending with the promise of a thanksgiving sacrifice for a favourable answer given (st 3). A striking feature is the way God is asked to save *by your name*. God's name is seen to possess a peculiar *power*; and so when the prayer is answered the psalmist promises to *praise your name for it is good.*

In slave labour camps the world over, oppressors seek to dehumanise people by reducing them to mere numbers. A name is powerful: it gives dignity and personality, it stands for the person, it opens up the possibility of inter-personal relationships. But God's name is in a class apart: its revelation is already an invitation to friendship, and throughout the Bible, and especially in the psalms, it is regarded as being filled with his power and life and energy and even his presence.

But in the New Testament we find God with a human face and a human name; 'you are to name him Jesus' (Matthew 1:21). There is no other in which we can be saved (Acts 4:12); by it sins are forgiven (Acts 10:43) and baptism conferred (Romans 6:3). It carries such power, such weight, with the Father, that we are promised that prayer in this name is assured of a favourable response (John 14:13). Indeed, Christians are actually defined as those who invoke the name of Jesus (1 Corinthians 1:2). And so on behalf of all those who cry out to God for help in their troubles – and even more for those who do not know how or to whom to cry in their misery – we recite this psalm in Jesus' all-powerful name; and indeed that name *is good*.

## EVENING PRAYER
### PSALM 48(49) Didactic

The prelude to this psalm is impressive, some might say pretentious, with its appeal for a hearing from *all who dwell in the world*. But it is not unusual for didactic psalms, dealing as they do with the great issues of life, to begin in this way. The psalmist, like the sages and wise men so revered in the Near East, will *speak words of wisdom*, and if his heart is *full of insight*, it is because what he has to offer is more than human wisdom. But what does the psalmist mean by anouncing: *with the harp I will solve my problem*? For the Israelites music was an inspired art, a kind of communication with God. The psalmist strums his harp to seek divine help in his wrestling with the baffling secrets of life. The message is addressed above all to the *low* and *high* – a warning to the *rich*, a promise of hope to the *poor* (§1 st 1-2).

Having faced enemies *who trust in their wealth* and are filled with pride, he does not fear them, for he has come to understand (and so ought they) that *wealth* is not to be trusted. The simple fact is that no one, however wealthy or reknowned, can pay the *ransom* that would buy off death, that great leveller of *wise men and fools* alike (§I st3-5). The situation is summed up in the refrain (§I st 6 and see §II st 5): death prizes the rich from all they possess: they have no surer future than the animals who are fattened only to be slaughtered.

Perhaps it is the reference to cattle that leads the poet to liken the rich and self-confident to a flock of *sheep* and death itself to a *shepherd*, leading them unerringly to a destination where all *their outward show vanishes* and where their worldly *glory does not follow* them. But he now goes further: if that is what becomes of them, how different the fate that awaits him (and others like him). He must die of course, but *God will ransom him from death* (a thing that is beyond human achievement: see §I st 4) and take his *soul to himself*. If earlier he raised the question: *Why should I fear?* (§I st 3), now he has his answer (from God): *do not fear*; just remember the ultimate fate of the wicked compared with that of the just.

As we draw towards the end of the day, this psalm leaves us with much to dwell upon. It might be described as the psalter's equivalent to the story of the rich man and Lazarus in Luke 16:19f: in every age God's people need to be warned of the dangers which accompany great wealth. But the psalm goes further: its reference to *ransom* puts us in mind of our Lord's assertion that he has come "to give his life as a ransom for (the) many" (Mark 10:45); and its suggestion – one of the mountain tops of Old Testament hope – of life beyond the grave, at least for the just, prepares the way for the New Testament revelation of resurrection of the dead and eternal life.

**CANTICLE – Revelation 4:11; 5:9,10,12.** (see Week 1 Tuesday, page 77)

# WEEK 2 WEDNESDAY

## OFFICE OF READINGS

### PSALM 38(39) Lament

Even a cursory reading of this psalm reveals the conflicting emotions of its author, as he tries to come to terms with the brevity of human life, with bewilderment and trust, resentment and touching loyalty. It was loyalty, the fear that hasty words about God in the wrong company (*when the wicked man stands before me*) might be misinterpreted, that had inclined him to keep silent (§I st 1). But in the end he could hold out no longer: his *tongue* simply *burst into speech*. He is prepared to say exactly what he feels, to express his anger and work through his feelings. Present afflictions lead him to reflect on the impermanent nature of human beings. They have no more substance – even those who apparently *stood so firm* – than a *mere breath*; they pass by in this life like a *mere shadow* flickering on the wall; and what is true of them is true of *the riches* they hoard (§II st 2-3).

Against such a backcloth, the psalmist's act of faith and surrender to God are most impressive: *in you rests all my hope*. And he begs that he may be forgiven, lest through his sins and complaining he should become *the taunt of the fool*. Nonetheless he is still bewildered by God's heavy-handedness towards us, and the divine punishment of death which eats away, like *the moth*, at all we treasure. But he cleverly turns his plight into a reason why his prayer should be answered. Since his stay in this world is as short-lived as that of an overnight *guest,* surely the Lord ought not to be *deaf to my tears*.

His final request for God to *look away* so that he can breathe freely again is reminiscent of Peter's "Depart from me" (Luke 5:8f). God knows how to deal with such prayers which, however mistaken, are spoken with obvious sincerity. But how fortunate we are, for Jesus is risen and we look forward with joyful hope to that ecstatic moment when God, far from *looking away* from us, will welcome us face to face into his presence.

# WEEK 2 WEDNESDAY

**PSALM 51(52) Lament**

Not for the first time (see psalm 1), we meet a psalm which presents two contrasting pictures. The first is of the wicked person, an absolute *champion of evil*, who has a tongue as destructive as *a sharpened razor,* who trusts in *wealth*, who has become *powerful* by crime, and who loves *evil more than good*. What a fate awaits such people. *God will destroy them*: they seem so secure, but he will *uproot* them. Even the just will be awestruck at what happens, and then fear will give way – in rather unChristian fashion, it may be thought – to laughter (st 1-4).

The psalmist, speaking now in the first person, reveals the very different fate awaiting those who are just. They are like an *olive tree*, one of the longest living of all trees, which is not only still *growing* (because still full of sap) but also planted in the precincts of the *house of God* where it is safe. Their trust is *in the goodness of God*, whom they *thank for evermore* (st 5-6). In less violent colours Jesus himself paints contrasting pictures of those who, despite all appearances, are set for disaster (because they have built on the 'sand' of trust in self) and those who will stand firm (because they have built on the 'rock' of trust in him) (Matthew 7:24-27).

# MORNING PRAYER

**PSALM 76(77) Lament**

One of the attractive features of the psalms is their directness and honesty. The psalmist says what is in his heart not what he feels he ought to say. Like many a believer before and since, the author has known what it is to cry *aloud to God* apparently in vain, to search for him during sleepless nights and fail to find him; but he dares go further and admit that he has wrestled with the most terrible possibility of all: *Has* God's *love vanished for ever? Has his promise come to an end?* (st 1-4).

# WEEK 2 WEDNESDAY

But this very expression of doubt in prayer became a turning point. As he recalls the past, the psalmist realises that there is no god *great as our God* for it was he who delivered his people from Egypt. With poetic skill, he portrays *the waters* trembling and *moved with terror* before their Lord at the Sea of Reeds, the thunderous *voice* from the *skies* and the flashing *arrows* of lightning that heralded his appearence on mount Sinai. He recalls too, God's loving guidance of his people *like a flock* through the desert – though, he gently adds, *no one saw your footprints* (st 5-8). The hour of darkness has surely passed.

In our bleakest moments, when we are perhaps assailed with fearful uncertainties, the surest remedy is to *ponder the mighty deeds* of God, above all the death and resurrection of Jesus. They are the tangible proofs of his love and of his power; and with them comes an assurance that our good Shepherd has not deserted us, in fact is still leading us, even if *his footsteps* remain unseen.

### CANTICLE – 1 Samuel 2:1-10
This canticle takes us back to the 11th century B.C. and to Hannah, a barren woman who had long prayed for a child. When at last her prayer was heard, she returned as she had promised to dedicate her little son, Samuel, to the service of God in the shrine at Shiloh. Her song of thanskgiving bubbles over with joy, as she proclaims that *there is no Rock like our God:* he is the utterly dependable one. He *knows all*, he *weighs men's deeds* and he acts accordingly, so that the arrogant are brought low and the lowly are raised up. He is the Lord of *life and death* and it is he who has set the *earth* on its *pillars*.

In the Prayer of the Church the scripture heading to this canticle is taken from the Magnificat, reminding us of obvious similarities and contrasts between the two prayers. There is the joy and gratitude, the acknowledgement of God's might which completely reverses human

# WEEK 2 WEDNESDAY

expectations, the fates of the wicked and the just, and also the contrast between the barren and the virginal *childless wife* who bears a child. Whereas the child whom Hannah carries in her arms is to be merely a prophet, the child in Mary's womb is God's own Son, *his king, his anointed* one who *will judge the ends of the earth.* And it is to that Son, towards whom Samuel and the whole of the Old Testament was leading, that we make our prayer this morning.

### PSALM 96(97) Enthronement Psalm

As has been mentioned, it seems that on one of their annual festivals (perhaps that of Tabernacles) the Israelites would acknowledge God as their King. There may even have been a 'sacramental' re-enactment of his enthronement, to which the people would respond with cries of: *The Lord is King* (or, as we might say, "Long live the King"). And then they would summon the whole *earth,* to its furthest extremities (*all the coastlands*), to join in their rejoicing. The mysterious presence of their God-King is at once hidden, shrouded in *cloud and darkness,* and yet revealed in nature by *fire,* earthquakes *and lightnings* which *light up the world* and melt the *mountains* as though they were made of *wax;* and in history by the defeat of all *his foes.* As in psalm 18 the very heavens are heralds of his victory to *all peoples* (st 1-3).

And so while idol worshippers are brought to shame and *worthless gods* fall prostrate in worship, the people of *Sion* are filled with joy at God's *judgements,* the way he has worked things out in their history. Though their city may be tiny, their God is *Lord above all the earth and all the spirits.* He loves the *just* and protects them, he brings the *light* of salvation and with it *joy* into their lives. To such a God all must respond with rejoicing and give *glory to his holy name* (st 4-8).

# WEEK 2 WEDNESDAY

This morning we pay royal worship to our Saviour King who reigns for eternity. In doing so we also commit ourselves to working for the coming of the Kingdom in the circumstances of our daily lives.

## PRAYER DURING THE DAY
### PSALM 118(119) VIII Didactic

The psalmist has no doubt: his *part* is to keep God's *word*. Even as he says it, he realises that he needs divine help and he begs for it *with all my heart*. In sts 3-4 he seems to say: having reflected *over my ways*, I know that I have failed – ensnared as I have been by *the nets of the wicked* – but I have *returned to your will* without delay; and for that, and for whatever is your will, I will be forever grateful, and seek the friendship of those who share the same outlook.

In words that come straight from his heart he cries out: *Lord, your love fills the earth.* Those words provide us with a prayer which should enable us to face whatever the rest of this day has to bring.

### PSALM 54(55) Lament

Here is the prayer of a worshipper overwhelmed with *cares* and *trembling, fear* and *horror*. He is unable to sleep; his very life is in danger; in words that now form part of a popular aria, he longs for *wings like a dove* so that he may make good his escape from *the raging wind, from the destructive storm.* Movingly, he begs God not to play hide-and-seek with him: *Do not hide from my pleading.*

We are not told the nature of the *foe*, but it sounds as though there has been a break-down of law and order. A vivid picture portrays *violence and strife* parading everywhere, even patrolling *on the city walls*; the holy city and *its streets* filled with *evil and sin, tyranny and deceit* (§I).

# WEEK 2 WEDNESDAY

All this is bad enough, but the psalmist has something even more grievious to bear: the arch-enemy is none other than *my own companion, my intimate friend*. It is this tragic realisation that leads not only to ardent prayer at *evening, morning and at noon* but also to the conviction that *the Lord will save*. However, there is judgement for those who *will not amend their ways*, and for those whose words seem *softer than butter* but in fact *are naked swords*. Emboldened by this reflection, the worshipper encourages others (just as later St Peter will do, using the same words: 1 Peter 5:7): *Entrust your cares to the Lord and he will support you.* There is profound spiritual insight in these words: we hand over our cares to the Lord. He will not, necessarily, take them away, but will always give us the support we need to continue bearing them. After a final comment on the fate of the wicked, the psalmist who began this prayer with such dire cries for help ends on a stirring note of trust in the Lord (§11).

As we pray this psalm, the thought of Jesus' sufferings comes unbidden to mind. Evil is entrenched in the holy city itself so that a fair trial becomes impossible; the longing to get away from *the destructive storm* ("Father, if you are willing, take this cup from me" Luke 22:44) and the torment of being betrayed by a friend, whose kiss of greeting is as deadly as a naked sword. Finally, we recall the entrusting of everything to the Father in hope ("into your hands I commit my spirit" Luke 23:46).

However, there are many people who wish they had *wings like a dove* to escape from their current troubles: from husbands or wives who have been deserted by their marriage partners, and children who find it almost impossibly difficult to go on nursing aged parents, to priests and bishops who are overwhelmed by the burden of responsibility they carry, and men and women who have been betrayed by their 'best friends'. All these, and thousands like them, are sharing in the sufferings of Jesus and can be supported by our prayer today.

# WEEK 2 WEDNESDAY

## EVENING PRAYER
### PSALM 61(62) Confidence

In this psalm, as in so many others, one senses the sea-sawing of emotions in the psalmist's heart. He has been through a bad time but at last has come to recognise that it is *in God alone* that he can find that serenity of soul which will enable him to cope with his difficulties. A series of images – *rock, stronghold, fortress* – points to God's unshakeable strength (st 1). Then the thought of his enemies comes flooding back to mind. Cowards as they are, they have banded together against him and they will stop at nothing; they are determined to *destroy* him, they happily indulge in lies and play the hypocrite, their "God bless you" being a cover for the curses in their hearts. The psalmist feels he has become like *a tottering wall* or *fence*, liable to collapse at any moment (st 2-3).

And so once more he takes up the opening sentence of the psalm but this time as a word of encouragement to himself rather than as a statement (st 4). And it works so effectively that the "tottering wall" becomes a powerful support to the congregation, as he shares with them his renewed conviction that God is the dependable One; he is *safety and glory, rock and refuge*. In comparison with him, all others, whether *common folk* or *great men*, are as light-weight and insubstantial as *a breath*. So too are power and *riches* (st 5-7).

With a final affirmation of God's dependability, the psalm comes full circle by means of a 'numerical proverb', such as is common in the Bible: *God has said only one thing: only two do I know*. It is meant either to emphasize the number of times the truth has been repeated or else to suggest two aspects of the one God – his *power* and his steadfast *love*, a power and love which ensure that all persons will receive their just deserts (st 8).

This quiet confidence in God and a spirit reminiscent of that of the Sermon on the Mount (see Matthew 6:25-30) make this psalm a source of comfort for all who struggle.

### PSALM 66(67) Thanksgiving

Though gratitude for a succeful harvest occasioned this psalm (see st 5), it is not satisfaction of the people's material needs but a desire for God and the extension of his reign that dominates their prayer. And so they begin with the plea, echoing the priestly blessing of Numbers 6:24f, that he will *be gracious and bless* them and that his *face* will shine with love upon them. As a result, the *saving help*, consisting of knowledge of him, will spread to *all nations* (st 1), a thought picked up by the refrain (st 2) and repeated twice more (st 4 & 6) in the course of the psalm. Fired by the prospect of God's world-wide reign, they boldly call upon all *the nations* to rejoice, because his rule will be one of *justice and fairness*. He will *guide* them, as a shepherd guides his sheep.

Again the refrain rings out; and then, after a brief reference to the abundant harvest with which *our God has blessed us*, thoughts turn once more to hope of an even greater blessing, hope which will overflow to people at t*he ends of the earth* who will reverence *our God* as their God too.

This psalm which forms part of our evening prayer today is also one of the alternatives for the Invitatory psalm at the very beginning of the day. Morning and night, in giving thanks to God for his blessings, we must not forget that "the fields are white, ready for the harvest"(see John 4:35) and the whole Church is called to be a missionary people, unable to be satisfied until all *the peoples praise you, O God.*

CANTICLE – Colossians 1:12-20 (see Week 1– Wednesday, page 85 )

# WEEK 2 THURSDAY

## OFFICE OF READINGS
### PSALM 43(44) Lament

The Hebrew people have suffered so often and so deeply that it is not suprising that one third of the psalms are laments. Yet there is very little whining self-pity or bitterness in them. Psalm 43 illustrates the point. It falls naturally into three sections.

§1. Past glory: Faced with some national catastrophe, the people recall the traditional *story* which they had heard from their *fathers*. It is the story of a nation whose glory is due not to its own heroic exploits or its stock-pile of weapons but entirely to the action of God and his strong *right arm*. It is he who, like a farmer, planted them, after first clearing the ground by uprooting the *nations* which stood in their way, which is why they *praised your name without ceasing*.

§2. Present disaster: And so what has happened? It is because *you no longer go forth with our armies* that disaster has overtaken us. And what disaster! Defeated, slaughtered *like sheep,* dispersed among pagan nations, mocked and taunted, we have been sold by our God *for nothing*. One senses the underlying question: how can this unbelievable situation be explained?

§3. Probing into the future: An answer seems all the more improbable because Israel's present plight cannot be attributed to their having *forgotten you,* or *been false to your covenant*, or *strayed from your path*; nor, they movingly add, to their having *stretched out hands to another god*. Yet at this point of greatest demoralization the psalm moves forward with a remarkable phrase which brings us to the threshold of the New Testament: *it is for you*, Lord, that these tragedies overtake us. St Paul himself quoted this verse (Romans 8:35f) to illustrate the fact that nothing can separate us from the love of God: "These are the trials through which we triumph, by the power of him who loved us". And so the psalm culminates in a passionate and daring prayer that God will at last *awake*, that he will not *hide* his *face* any longer. The Lord who seems to be asleep, as one day the apostles would discover on the Lake of Galilee (Mark 4:35f), will *stand up* and overcome the fiercest storm because of his steadfast covenant *love*.

We are to pray in this bold language as we view the sufferings in the world, the starving, the war weary. We are to beg the King to come to our help, to give peace to his people.

## MORNING PRAYER
### PSALM 79(80) Lament

Towards the end of the 8th century B.C. Israel was under threat from Assyria, and this psalm, which seems to date from that time, is a petition for the Northern Kingdom, possibly prayed in the Temple at Jerusalem by the southerners on behalf of their brothers and sisters in the north. It is dominated by two striking images:

The first (st 1-4): God as the *shepherd of Israel*. His *flock* is *Joseph's* tribes, that is to say, *Ephraim* and *Manasseh,* which together with the associated tribe of *Benjamin* are virtually synonymous with Israel. The prayer is that the bright presence of God, enthroned on the sphinx-like *cherubim* whose outstretched wings cover the Ark, will be seen in their midst; and that he will *rouse up* his *might* and *come to our help*. The people's response (to be repeated at st 4 and 10) is that he will *bring* them *back,* in the sense either that he will deliver them from their misfortunes or that he will bring them to repentance. But his *face*, far from being lit up with joy for them, is darkened with a *frown: tears* are their food and drink, while neighbours *taunt* and *enemies laugh* them *to scorn.*

The second (st 5-10): Israel as the *vine* which God *brought out of Egypt*. How lovingly he has cared for it throughout its history: in the

Exodus and settlement in Canaan, he *drove out the nations* and *cleared the ground* so that his vine might take root. It grew until (by poetic licence) it overshadowed the mighty *cedars* and even the *mountains,* and its branches stretched out *to the Great River* Euphrates. All this leads to the burning question: *why,* then, has he now left it unprotected, so that it can be plundered, *ravaged* and *devoured* at will? In the absence of an answer they can only plead with him to *turn again* towards *his vine and protect it;* and ensure that those who have *destroyed* it may themselves experience *the frown of your face –* disaster. And yet they seem to sense that the current trouble is at least in part of their making: in asking for divine protection for *the man you have chosen* (probably, their king), they promise: *we will never forsake you again.* And the psalm ends with the refrain, prayed now with faith and hope renewed.

Whatever its original significance, the expression *the man you have chosen* takes on a deeper meaning for Christians who recognise in Jesus not only God's chosen one, but also the Good Shepherd and the true Vine (the one who fulfils all that Israel was meant to be). And just as the divisions among God's people (in the northern and southern kingdoms) was one of the great tragedies of their history, so the continuing tragedy of Christian history is the disunity which persists among us. This morning, as we repeat the plea: *God of hosts, bring us back,* what could be more appropriate than that we should make this psalm an earnest prayer for Christian unity, remembering who it was that spoke of there being "only one flock and one shepherd" (John 10:16) and compared his followers to a single vine whose many branches draw sustenance and life from the one sap? (John 15)

### CANTICLE – Isaiah 12:1-6
Chapter 12 of the book of Isaiah rounds off a section which looks forward to a new exodus when God will have gathered his people

together from the nations. It is just six verses long, and all of it, but for a few words, appears in this canticle. It begins with gratitude that the divine *anger has passed* and *comfort* been restored. And recalling God's saving work, the singer takes on his lips the cry that was first raised at the exodus from Egypt: *the Lord is my strength, my song, my saviour* (see Exodus 15). The reference to *the wells of salvation* (st 3) suggests the situation in which it was first sung. A well was regarded as an appropriate place to recount the mighty works of God since its life-giving waters stood as an obvious symbol of his saving power.

Thanksgiving moves into praise, praise into the desire that his *glorious deeds* be made *known to all the earth*, and the spread of his fame into rejoicing within Israel because *the Holy One* is in her midst (st 3b -5).

It was beside a well that Jesus revealed himself to the Samaritan woman (John 4:26). As the heading in the Prayer of the Church indicates, he also invited "the thirsty" to come to him and slake their thirst (John 7:37-38). The occasion of this invitation was the feast of Tabernacles with its daily water ceremony, in which priests carried silver pitchers from the pool of Siloam and poured the contents over the altar in the Temple as a plea for rain. Moses may have brought water from a rock (Exodus 17:1f); Jesus, who stands in their midst, is soon to offer them living water – the water of the Spirit who is to be released when he returns to his Father.

We, who share the final exodus accomplished by his death and resurrection, know that he *the Holy One* is in our midst and that he has poured out the Spirit upon us. How right that, in our prayer this morning, we should sing the ancient exodus song and *shout for joy and declare the greatness of his name*, and thereby *draw water from the wells of salvation*.

## PSALM 80(81) Didactic

This psalm begins where the canticle left off: with an appeal for shouts of *joy* and *triumph* to the God of the exodus. The joyful singing is to be accompanied by an array of musical instruments: the tambourine-like *timbrel, the sweet-sounding harp, the lute* and the ram's horn *trumpet* (the shophar) whose powerful notes announce the *new moon* and, fifteen days later, the full-moon (the occasions for celebrating the New Year and the beginning of the feast of Tabernacles, respectively). The festival is a divine 'command performance', imposed by God on *Joseph* (Exodus 23:14f) on that far-off day, now being 'renewed', when *he went out against Egypt* (st 1-3).

The psalm takes on a different tone as a divine spokesman delivers to the assembly a message received from *a voice I did not know* (the mysterious voice of God). Significantly, the message is couched in the second person – *you, your shoulder, your hands* – to show that, through worship, the constraints of time and space have been brushed aside and the saving work of God is present now. The One who delivered his people *from the burden* of labouring under the Egyptians, who *answered* them, *concealed in the storm cloud* and who *tested* them and found them wanting in the desert; that same One is with them today. For he is ready to sate their deepest hunger (st 4-6).

Then, wistfully, he proclaims the sad truth: *my people did not heed my voice,* and so they were left *to follow their own designs.* The implication is clear: do not follow that example. For his part he is still ready to save them and defeat their enemies, but they must respond by walking in his ways. Then they will enjoy *finest wheat* and *honey from the rock*, a poetic description of the choicest fare (st 7-9).

"Christ accomplishes 'the work of redeeming mankind'...not only when the Eucharist is celebrated and the sacraments adminstered, but also in other ways, especially by praying the Liturgy of the

Hours" (General Instruction on the Prayer of the Church, §13). As we pray this Prayer today, Jesus is present, continuing his redeeming work among us now. He longs for us to *heed his voice* and *walk in his ways*, so that we may be filled with the good things that he has in store for us.

## PRAYER DURING THE DAY
### PSALM 118(119) IX Didactic

From time to time we, like the psalmist, become alive to the fact the Lord has *been good* to us in so many, many ways. But we dare to ask for more: for *discernment*, so that we may become more sensitive to what he wants of us, and for *knowledge*, so that we may become more intimately united with him. Maybe, again like the psalmist, we have to confess that there have been times when we have *strayed* (and if we haven't, it is thanks to his mercy), and we were *afflicted* by guilt; but that was *good* for us because it brought us to our senses. Others may sneer and even slander us, as we *strive to keep your word*; but the simple truth is that doing your will matters more to us than the most glittering and costly rewards.

### PSALM 55(56) Lament

A notable feature of this psalm is that in the midst of cries for help against enemies who, *all day long, fight proudly* and openly (st 1) or lurk *in ambush* secretly(st 3), there is a touching act of confidence in God: *when I fear I will trust in you*, because my trust rests not on myself but on the *word* of God (st 2). The Lord has *kept an account* of his *wanderings* and *tears*, and that assures the psalmist that his enemies *will be put to flight*. And so he takes up again his act of trust: what can *mortal man* do to me when *God is on my side?* (st 4-5) Knowing that his prayer is answered, he promises to keep *the vows* he made in time of adversity and presents thank-offerings to God, for now he has emerged from the darkness and goes forward in union with God towards *the light of the living*.

After translating this psalm, St Jerome gave it the heading now found in the Prayer of the Church. It 'shows' us Christ suffering, Christ who "offered up prayer and entreaty, aloud and in silent tears...and his prayer was heard (and) he became for all who obey him the source of eternal salvation" (Hebrews 5:7-10). But Jesus Christ still suffers, still weeps in the lives of so many people: the oppressed, the deserted, the fearful. Our prayer is that they may be enabled to leave the darkness behind and, aided by *the presence of God*, walk tall in *the light of the living*.

**PSALM 56(57) Lament** (see Week 1 Thursday, page 89)

## EVENING PRAYER
**PSALM 71(72) Lament**

This splendid royal psalm conjures up a vision which could be realized by no human potentate, however great or good, but only by Jesus Christ the King of kings. It begins with a blessing which shows that the king is to act as God's viceroy: grant *your judgment* and *your justice* so that he may prove himself the champion of *your people* and, significantly, of *your poor*. Thus, may true *justice* reign, may *the poor* and *the needy* be protected, and the very *mountains* give birth to that harmony between people, nature and God which is called *peace*, shalom(§I st 1-2). The reign of this king is to be as enduring as *sun and moon*; because of his closeness to God, he will be like *rain,* bringing fruitfulness to the whole realm. And just as his reign is to be endless, so also his dominion is to be boundless, from *the Great River* (the Euphrates, or perhaps the river of Paradise which was believed to run through Sion) to the ends of the earth. Kings will come from *Tharsis and the sea coasts* (the western extremities of the world), from *Sheba and Seba* (in Arabia to the south east) to express their allegiance by the gifts they bring in *tribute* (§I st 3-6).

Once more it is made clear that the king's success is dependent upon his practical concern for *the poor* and *the needy: justice,* right relations among people, will be reflected in nature. Where there is such a king, there will be cries of *long may he live*, and the precious *gold of Sheba* will be his and there will be prayer *without ceasing* for him and his enterprises: so that crops are *abundant* even in the unpromising soil at the *peaks of the mountains*, and citizens flourish *like grass on the earth*, and he himself is given fame that will last *for ever* and the promises made long ago to Abraham are, in him, fulfilled (§II st 1-3). The fine conclusion (§II st 4) was added later as a doxology to mark the end of the second division of the psalter (Psalms 41[42]- 71[72]).

The Church uses this psalm at Epiphany in honour of the 'little king' in the manger, visited by wise men who arrived from the East, bringing *gifts*, and "falling to their knees they did him homage" (Matthew 2:1-12, and compare with §I st 6). However, the frequent references in this psalm to the help offered to the poor, the needy and the oppressed remind us of the "great King" who "comes in his glory" and in judgement, announcing that whatever we have done or failed to do for "the least of these brothers of mine", we have done or failed to do to him (Matthew 25:31-45).

CANTICLE – **Revelation 11:17-18;12:10-12** (see Week 1 Thursday, page 96)

# WEEK 2 FRIDAY

## OFFICE OF READINGS
### PSALM 37(38) Lament

This is another psalm which has been numbered traditionally among the seven Penitential Psalms. Its general theme, therefore, is the plight of the sinner. He is suffering from an appalling disease which he, like his contemporaries, attributes to his own sinfulness. He humbly confesses that *through my sin there is no health in my limbs* (§I st 2). But what makes the situation almost unbearable is the fact that his own friends *avoid* him *like a leper,* presumably because they too regard him as having brought the tragedy upon himself. To add to his troubles, *wanton enemies* take advantage of his plight to begin a smear campaign against him. While submitting in silence, *like the deaf who cannot hear* and *the dumb* who are *unable to speak*, he appeals earnestly to God as the only one he can *count on* and touchingly begs him *do not stay afar off* (§II & §III).

Whatever the circumstances which orginally produced this psalm (it may have been a 'standard' psalm, available in the temple to any who found it suitable for their own plight), it takes on fresh meaning this Friday as we contemplate the sufferings of Jesus. Here is one who carried *a weight too heavy to bear*; not simply the weight of the Cross, but the weight of our sins. Though sinless, he was contaminated by our sinfulness to such a degree that he experienced our guilt, towering higher than his head. *There is no health in the limbs* of the Crucified one. His *frame burns with fever*, he is *spent and utterly crushed* and *those closest to* him *stand afar off* (as Luke 23:49 explains, using this text almost word for word), *lying foes* surround him and mock him, even as he lies dying. But his trust in his Father does not waver. He can indeed say that this is *the result of my own folly*, but it is the folly of Divine Love.

# WEEK 2 FRIDAY

## MORNING PRAYER
PSALM 50(51) Lament (see Week 1 Friday, page 98)

### CANTICLE – Habakkuk 3:2-4,13,15-19
Little is known of the prophet Habakkuk but he seems to have lived towards the end of the 7th century B.C. The central question he addresses is how God's patience towards evil can be squared with his holiness. His answer is that God is totally free to deal with the wicked in his own way and in his own time. The book ends in chapter three with a prayer, in beautiful poetic language, from which this canticle is taken. The prophet is filled with *awe* at the thought of God's mighty *deeds* of the past and begs that they may be seen again *in our days*. He recalls the triumphal progress as God led his people from Egyptian slavery into their own land, *coming forth* from the direction of Mount Sinai – *from Teman* (to the south of Judah) and *Mount Paran* (to the south west) – and setting *the earth* ablaze with *his brilliance, rays* of light (thunderbolts?) flashing *from his hands* (st1-3).

The prophet envisages God marching out again to save *the one you have anointed* (the people of Israel). The defeat of the enemy is an awesome prospect and he finds himself trembling at the thought of it. But fear soon gives way to gratitude, and he concludes with what has been described as one of the most amazing acts of faith in the Old Testament. No matter what may happen, despite disaster all around him, despite failed crops and *empty* cattle *stalls*, Habakkuk will still *rejoice in the Lord*, confident that he is *my Saviour* and that he will enable him, like a *deer*, to reach *the high places*, well out of harm's way (st 4-6).

We too can sometimes be impatient, wondering why it is that God does not do his mighty deeds *in our days*, why he does not act more quickly and decisively to conquer evil. And yet in prayer we grow in the conviction that the all-holy God, who longs for conversion of the wicked rather than their destruction, does things in his time and in his way, and that justice will triumph in the end.

### PSALM 147 (147B) Hymn

*Jerusalem*, the heart of God's creative and redemptive work, is urged to *praise the Lord*. It owes everything to his loving care: its strength and vitality, its peace and prosperity (st 1-2).

Then the psalm centres upon God's *word*. Its creative power is shown in the events which it effortlessly produces: *snow, white as wool* covering the ground, *hoar-frost* scattered about *like ashes* and *hailstones like crumbs* of bread. He needs only to touch the waters and they freeze, only to breathe upon the ice and *the waters flow* again (st 3-4).

But his word is also revelation: through his *laws and decrees* he discloses himself to his chosen people. It is by allowing his word to govern their lives that they show that no other nation has been treated by God as they have (st 5).

The Prayer of the Church has a heading which suggests that in Jerusalem we are to recognise "the bride the Lamb has chosen", i.e. the Church. Jesus has guaranteed her strength by setting her on a rock so that the "gates of the underworld can never hold out against (her)" (Matthew 16:18). He *has blessed* her with children in the sacrament of baptism. On the first Easter day he *established* her in the fullness of messianic *peace* (John 20:20); and he has provided for her the *finest wheat* of the Eucharist. He is himself the *Word*, sent out by the Father, who by the power of his *breath* (the Spirit) *melts* hearts that have grown hard and chill. He himself is the fulfilment of the Law and we are called upon to make him the model of our lives. Never did he deal thus *with other nations*. Let us praise the Lord.

# WEEK 2 FRIDAY

## PRAYER DURING THE DAY
### PSALM 118(119) X Didactic
What a splendid act of faith with which to brighten up our day: *It was your hands that made me and shaped me!* We are totally his. We want *to learn* and understand his *commands*, for he has our interests at heart, and *his decrees are right.*

If we have failed him, then like the psalmist let us trust in his merciful *love.* The father of the prodigal said that his son "was dead and now he is alive" (Luke 15:32). So too when I experience God's love I know that *I shall live.* Others may try and seduce me with their *lies* but *your faithful* ones will *rejoice* in me because *I trust in your word.*

### PSALM 58(59) Lament
Like most laments, this one begins with an expression of the psalmist's needs – *Rescue me, protect me, save me from powerful, blood-thirsty* enemies – and an appeal to the God who has proved himself warrior king of Israel to *Awake* – and when he awakes, there is trouble for Israel's foes (st 1-2). This is followed by a fine act of faith, as the psalmist turns to God whom he acknowledges as his *strength* and *stronghold*, and the one *who shows him love.* The same prayer will return at the end of the psalm (st 6), but in the meantime there is a renewed call for help and a confident promise that, as a result of God's intervention, *each morning* the psalmist will *sing* of God's *strength* and *acclaim* his *love* (st 4-5).

Is it not possible that a troubled brother or sister somewhere in the world will be acclaiming God's love tomorrow morning because we prayed this psalm on his or her behalf today and our prayer was heard?

# WEEK 2 FRIDAY

## PSALM 59(60) Lament

What a terrible thing to feel that God has deserted you! That is what the singers of this psalm must have experienced, as they spoke of God rejecting them, of the whole *earth* seeming to *quake* and give way beneath their feet, of their being intoxicated, as it seemed, with *a wine* that was spiked, of God himself giving the *signal* to retreat. Yet still they cling to their belief that they are *your people, those who fear you* and even *your friends*; and so they beg him to reply by raising that strong *right hand* of his which no-one can resist (st 1-3).

God's response, given through a priest or prophet, is immediate and surprising. He asserts his lordship over the Promised Land and his right to parcel it out to his people: he gives them the towns of *Shechem* (meaning 'neck' because of its central position on the pass that links the Mediterranean coast to the Jordan) and *Succoth,* on either side of the river; *Gilead,* a territory to the east of the Jordan, stretching north from the Dead Sea, and *Manasseh,* a large area spanning either side of the river. The two principal tribes, *Ephraim,* in the north, and *Judah,* in the south, become respectively the *helmet* and the *staff* (sceptre) of the warrior king. A different fate awaits the old enemies of Israel, *Moab* in the south-east and *Edom* in the south, the first, partly because of its bowl-like configuration around the Dead Sea, being described as God's *washbowl,* and the second claimed as his own by the ritual act of throwing his *shoe* upon it. And finally he sings triumphantly *over the Philistines* along the south west coast-line.

The people can scarce take in such bold assurances: is *Edom,* notoriously secure in its mountainous surroundings, to fall into their grasp? Some of the former despair seems to seep back, but then it vanishes as, acknowledging their own helplessness, they turn to him and ask for his *help.*

160

# WEEK 2 FRIDAY

This psalm is not without its relevance for us today. Some people are filled with anxiety as they look to the future of the Church – because it has changed too much, or because it has changed too little. And the remedy is hope. The hope that springs from the two-fold truth so neatly captured in this psalm: though *the help of man is vain yet with God we shall do bravely*. The mighty Lord is still in charge.

## EVENING PRAYER
### PSALM 114(116) Thanksgiving

St Teresa of Lisieux found difficulty in praying the first lines of this psalm because they seemed to suggest that our love for God depends upon what we can get out of him. However, so great are the psalmist's joy and relief at God's response to his *appeal* that he feels *love* of the Lord welling up in his heart and, with the honesty typical of the psalmists, he knows he has 'to tell it as it is': I love you because you've heard me. He had been in a tight corner, *the snares of death* and *the anguish of the tomb* snatching at him menacingly. Perhaps it was a deadly illness or some other dreadful experience which took the light out of life and made it seem hardly worth living. In any event, his instinctive reaction was to call out with child-like confidence upon *the Lord's name* (st 1-2).

Now he bursts into praise as he recalls *how gracious* the Lord has been. His *compassion* was the more extraordinary because, as the psalmist puts it, *I was helpless so he saved me*. A strange reason for saving any one, it might be thought, and yet if offers us great hope: our very weakness draws God's help. When *the Lord has been so good*, the psalmist can be *at rest*. And his resolution henceforth is to *walk in the presence of the Lord* so long as he remains *in the land of the living*.

We have personal experience of appeals that have been heard, compassion that has been shown us beyond all our deserving, favours granted when we were *helpless*. Recalling such things in our faith history, we too are filled with gratitude and, like the psalmist, seized with a great *love*.

### PSALM 120(121) Confidence

This is one of the 'songs of ascent' (see page 20) and if these songs were used, as is commonly believed, in the course of the thrice annual pilgrimage to the Temple, then it is not difficult to follow the mind of the singer of this song. He gazes up at the high mountains which surround Jerusalem, fearfully perhaps, dreading what dangers may lie hidden there, or hopefully, longing to seek refuge in their protective fastness. Then he raises his eyes still higher, dwelling upon the skies above, and he realises that his protection *shall come from* no one less than *the Lord who made heaven and earth* (st 1-2).

At this point we seem to eavesdrop as he enters upon a dialogue with himself (or with a pilgrim companion?). In response to his query, he tells himself that there simply is no *guard* to compare with the Lord. (That word *guard*, repeated six times over, gives a 'stair-like' quality to the psalm as it mounts to an exalted understanding of the protective goodness of God). He is a guard who never rests, never leaves his post, never goes off duty, neither *sleeps nor slumbers*. Day and night, he is *at your right side*, like an advocate, or as a *shade* from the fierce rays of the Palestinian sun or the harmful influences associated with *the moon*. Looking up at the mountains, and beyond, the psalmist's thoughts become more daring as he reflects upon the full extent of God's protection: he *will guard you from* every *evil*, in every *going and coming* of life, *both now and for ever*.

The movement and rhythm of this psalm, discernible even in translation, puts one commentator in mind of a woman comforting her child by gently rocking it to and fro as she lulls it to sleep. In any event, this lovely psalm has much to tell us about the wonderful mothering care of God. Near the front door of their homes many modern Jews have a mezuzah, a metal cylinder containing a parchment with texts from Deuteronomy (6:3-9; 11:13-21), which they touch each time they enter or leave the house, at the same time reciting the final stanza of this psalm.

**CANTICLE – Revelation 15:3-4** (see Week 1 Friday, page 105)

# WEEK 2 SATURDAY

## OFFICE OF READINGS
### PSALM 135(136) Hymn

This prayer, in the form of a litany, would have been familiar to Jesus and he may well have recited it at the Last Supper. We are to visualise a priest or choir chanting, verse by verse, the story of God's goodness, and the congregation replying again and again with the thunderous response: *for his love is without end.* After a typical invitation to *give thanks to the Lord for he is good,* §I points to creation as tangible proof of this divine love. The Lord loves us and this is shown by the fact that he *made the skies,* that he *fixed the earth firmly* amidst the subterranean waters, that he *made the great lights* of *sun* and *moon and stars;* for this faithful love shown in deed he is deserving of thanks.

But the Lord entered into Israel's very history in startling fashion at the exodus, *arm outstretched, with power in his hand,* and it is this mighty deed which is unfolded in §II. The destruction of *the first-born of the Eygptians* may seem an improbable sign of God's love. However, in addition to what was said earlier about the *difficult psalms* (see page 25), it is helpful to note the commendable honesty with which the Israelites recount the event. It did in fact involve the loss of life, even of innocent life; but that was an inevitable part of the Lord's total rescue operation, and it is in the overall event that his love is reflected.

§III recalls that the Exodus was followed by years in the desert during which God again showed his love by leading *his people*; by enabling them to secure victories, which became proverbial, over *the Amorites* to the east of the Jordan, and the kingdom of *Bashan,* further north close to the Lake of Galilee; and by giving them *their* promised *land.*

The final stanza not only sums up all that has gone before but brings promise of God's continuing faithfulness, and so the psalm ends, as it began, with the call to thank him for *his* great and unending *love.*

Each person who prays this psalm is able to continue the litany by adding his or her own special reasons for giving thanks. Each one of us has a personal history in which God has time and again shown his love. But as a Christian community the psalm has a special significance for us. The Creator God has come to live among his creatures; he has conquered all the Pharaohs which threaten us, he has through death and resurrection led us out into freedom, he has prepared a place for us in the promised land of heaven. As St Paul says, all the events of the exodus are but "figures", faint foretellings, of the still more wonderful works accomplished for us by Jesus Christ (see 1 Corinthians 10:6). It is supremely in him and in his life's work that we find conclusive evidence that God's *love is without end*.

*During Advent, Christmastide,Lent and Paschal time, psalm 135 is replaced by the following:*
**PSALM 105(106) Lament**
It may seem strange that a lament should begin with *thanks to the Lord*. However, it quickly becomes clear that §I st 1-3 are by way of preparation for a confession of sin. Sinfulness is the more terrible when set against the truths professed: the enduring *love* of God, the unworthiness of any creature to tell his *mighty deeds* or give him fitting *praise*, the happiness of those *who do what is right*. And then (st 2b-3) the psalmist slips in a personal prayer of his own, as though to say: Count me in too. He asks God to look down favourably *out of the love you have for your people*.

The remainder of the psalm tells the sorry story of Israel's infidelities from the exodus to the entry into Canaan and beyond. However, this historical flash-back is not meant to divert attention from the singers of the psalm. The fact is that *our sin is the sin of our fathers*; we have behaved as badly as those who went before us. They were forgetful, *paid no heed, forgot the greatness of your love*, even had the temerity to defy *the Most High*. One moment *they sang his praises*, the next they were putting him *to the test in the wilderness*. He gave them *the favour they asked* and they paid the price for it (presumably a reference to the story of the quails and its aftermath, see Numbers 11). They became *envious of Moses and of Aaron* and rebelled against them.

In §II the catalogue of sin continues: the worship of the golden *calf at* the foot of *mount Horeb* (Sinai), which was tantamount to *exchanging the God who was their glory for the image of a bull that eats grass* (Exodus 32); their forgetfulness of all that God had done for them *in the land of Ham* (Egypt), so that only the powerful intercession of Moses, who *stood in the breach before them*, saved them from disaster (Exodus 17:1-7); their point blank refusal to march into Canaan, *the land of promise*, with the result that that whole generation was left to die in the desert (Numbers 14:1-23); worse still, their apostasy, when they *bowed down* (in worship) *before the Baal of Peor* (a mountain in Moab) and this time it was *Phinehas* who saved them from the fate they deserved (Numbers 25); and, finally, their provocation of God at *Meribah*, when even Moses failed to live up to expectations, by angrily striking out at the rock (Numbers 20:1-13).

§III vividly and terribly describes how Israel succumbed to the pagan cults of Canaan. Instead of fighting against evil they *learned to act as they* (the pagans) *did*. They offered human sacrifices in which their own children were the victims. *They defiled themselves* by having sexual relationships with cultic prostitutes and thereby *broke their marriage bond with the Lord*. And so at last he is pictured as handing them over to *the nations*: all their defeats, including perhaps the fall of both kingdoms, was the punishment they had drawn upon themselves, and yet – a lovely touch – the psalmist insists that, *in the greatness of his love*, God ensured that they were *treated with mercy* by their captors. And so they have courage to call upon him now that he may *bring us together from the nations*, among whom we have been scattered, to thank and praise *your holy name*. This psalm is the last in the fourth book of the psalter (89[90]-105[106]), and, like the other books, this one ends with a doxology §III st 9.

The people of Israel, as this psalm testifies, were well aware of the importance of history. But if they were conscious of the sins commited by their forefathers and now repeated by themselves, they were even more conscious of the merciful love of God. The greatest of the wonderful works of God is that *time after time*, despite their constant backsliding, God *paid heed to their distress, so often as he heard their cry*. One of the salutary lessons of history taught by the Church is that she is always in need of reform and renewal, always in need of a confession of her sinfulness, for, by and large, *our sin is the sin of our fathers*; whether as Church or as individuals, we constantly rise and fall, constantly stand in need of forgiveness. As we pray this psalm today we might remember that the Church and indeed the whole world stands in need of people like Moses (see §II st3) who, through prayer, will stand as intecessors before God on behalf of all their brothers and sisters.

## MORNING PRAYER
### PSALM 91(92) Thanksgiving

Later Judaism, probably with an eye to 'the week of creation' (Genesis 1 -2:4), allotted seven psalms to the seven days of the week. This psalm was linked with the Sabbath. That was the day the Lord rested, having viewed all that he had made and declared it "very good". *To give thanks to the Lord* for his handiwork – *in the morning* and even *in the watches of the night* – is also *good*; it is like *music* to the ear of the *Most High*. Indeed, gratitude was expressed, literally, in music, with *lyre, lute* and *harp* combining in the symphony of praise (st 1).

To give thanks to God is not only to be *made glad*, but also to be filled with awe at the greatness of his *works* and the profundity of his plans. One aspect of his *deep designs* is the way in which *the wicked*, who seem to prosper, are destined *to be eternally destroyed,* whereas God himself is the Transcendant One, *eternally on high*. However, all this is beyond the understanding of *the fool*, the person without faith's vision and so without understanding of why or how he or she ought to give thanks (st 2 -3).

In contrast to his *foes*, the psalmist has been endowed by God with the proverbial *strength* of the *wild-ox* and re-dedicated to the divine service by an anointing *with the purest oil*. To put it another way, he will stand as boldly upright as *the palm-tree* and as tall and majestic as *a Lebanon cedar*. He, and others like him (at this point, singular changes to plural) are assured of long life, like trees which rest undisturbed in the precincts of the Temple. More than that, though old age may come upon them, they will still be fruitful, still able *to proclaim* God's goodness. Finally, the psalmist, as though appending his signature to all that has been said, ends with a personal testimony to the rock-like goodness of God (st 4-5).

The fourth weekday preface says, "Our desire to thank you is itself your gift". So this psalm which is placed on our lips today is in itself a blessing from God. "Our prayer of thanksgiving adds nothing to your greatness" yet it "makes us grow in grace'" and fills us, as it filled the psalmist long ago, with gladness and joy.

### CANTICLE – Deuteronomy 32:1-12
Towards the end of the book of Deuteronomy comes this splendid Song of Moses, the first part of which forms today's canticle. It

begins in solemn fashion, with *heavens* and *earth* called upon to take account of the message about to be delivered and learn how the Lord is vindicated (st 1). His teaching is *'like the rain', 'like the dew', 'like rain drops', 'like showers'* – it refreshes and it transforms.

The burden of the message is that while God has always been like a *Rock*, sure, dependable, unwaveringly *faithful*, the people *whom he begot* have become, unlike their *father, crooked, false, perverse* (st 3). And so, in a manner typical of Deuteronomy, they are now called upon to *remember, to recall* past events, which any of their *elders* could tell them about: the way *the Most High* so fixed *the boundaries of the nations* as to make clear that *Israel's sons* were his special *possession*. He *found* them in *fearful, desolate* desert *wastes*; *surrounded* them with care; lifted them up; preserved them like treasure, delicate *as the apple of his eye*. The conclusion is a beautiful picture; he swooped down like a giant *eagle*, took them upon *his outstretched wings* and guided them, like a mother eagle teaching her little ones how to fly.

The heading for this canticle in the Prayer of the Church suggests that the loving care which God showed his people of old has taken on fresh meaning through the life of Jesus, whose great desire is to gather all people, like a hen drawing her chicks to her breast.

## PSALM 8 Hymn

This glorious hymn is framed by an acclamation of praise, voiced in st 1 and repeated in st 6. It suggests that *mortal man* cannot be understood without reference to God, for in him is the beginning and end, the origin and destiny, of every human creature. The divine *majesty* evokes praise not only *above the heavens* but also in the child-like on this earth (see our Lord's use of this verse in Matthew 21:15-16). Such praise is the antithesis of the rebellious behaviour of *enemy* and *foe* and reduces them to *silence* (st 2).

To discover God's magnificence, says the psalmist, you have only to look up to *the heavens* – his handiwork; to the arrangement of *the moon and the stars* – his artistry. What would he have said had he been aware of the breath-taking discoveries of modern astronomy? And, in comparison with God, what is *man?* How can such a God *keep* such a creature *in mind*, and, more than that, in his *care?* (st 3)

The psalmist offers no answer, but, instead, makes the incredible assertion that the human creature has become *little less than a god,* has been *crowned* with *glory* and *honour* (attributes usually associated with God himself), has been entrusted with God-like dominion over all creation. And all of this is of God's own making (st 4-5). But more striking still, the psalmist seems to say in the final stanza, is the fact that only man, of all visible creation, knows how to raise his voice in praise of God (st 6).

This hymn manages to offer a combination of reassurance and challenge: reassurance at the thought that God has bestowed such an incredible dignity upon us human beings; challenge in the realisation that we are called upon to recognise that dignity even in, perhaps especially in, those who seem anything but *little less than a god.*

## PRAYER DURING THE DAY
### PSALM 118(119) XI Didactic

There are few of us who have not experienced from time to time the feelings expressed by the psalmist: we *yearn* and we *hope*, as we wonder *when* (or even if) the Lord will keep his *promise* and send us his *saving help*. Yet despite the tedious, exhausting waiting, despite the plotting and planning of *foes*, the psalmist, at any rate, refuses to give up – or give in. He will be true to God's *commands*, his *law*, his *precepts*, no matter what the cost.

We have now reached the half-way mark in this long psalm. If we are finding the constant insistence upon God's commands a little wearisome, we might remember that Jesus once said: "Anyone who does the will of my Father in heaven, he is my brother and sister and mother" (Matthew 12:50). After that, I supect that we will want to join the psalmist in praying: if you show me *your love* (your practical help), *I will do your will*.

## PSALM 60(61) Lament

The opening stanza of this psalm betrays profound distress; it is the cry of one who feels as though he is at *the end of the earth*, with an unbridgeable gulf lying between him and God. In all probability he is in exile; from the depths of grief his thoughts are raised to the One enthroned *on high*, the One who has always been a *tower against the foe*. The prayer grows in intimacy and confidence as it proceeds. The psalmist wants to share God's own *tent for ever*, wants to seek refuge under his protective *wings*; and is sure he will receive *the heritage of those who fear you*: his prayer will be heard (st 2-3).

The petition for *the king* (st 4) is unexpected. It may simply reflect the belief that the future well-being of the nation is inextricably linked with that of its monarch; or perhaps the whole psalm was composed by, or at least for the use of, a king. However, there is also the possibility that the petition was added later with a Messianic significance. In any event, it is a prayer which finds its richest fulfilment in Jesus Christ our king, who sits *enthroned before God*, his Father, for ever. Our eternal well-being is totally dependent upon him; it is he who leads us back from exile; and because of him we *shall always praise your name* and *day after day* continue to give thanks – just as we do in this psalm today.

# WEEK 2 SATURDAY

**PSALM 63(64) Lament**

One would love to know the circumstances which bring forth so agonised a cry for help. But all we can know for certain is that the psalmist, faced with *a band of the wicked*, begs to be spared the paralyzing *dread* that would undermine resistance and also to find a hiding place with God (st 1).

In the next three stanzas the behaviour of the wicked is contrasted with that of God: they have aimed their words *like arrows*, and he *has shot them with his arrow*. They shot *at the innocent ... suddenly*, and he has imposed upon them *sudden wounds*. They used *their tongues like swords*, and, through his intervention, *their own tongue has brought them ruin*. They said *'Who will see us?'*, but he has revealed their evil-doing to the world so *all who see them mock*.

And so a psalm which began with anguish ends with a wholesome *fear* of God's mighty *deeds*, which in turn leads to joy, confidence in him as a *refuge*, and the desire, shared by *all upright hearts*, to give *glory*. On occasions when we are distressed by the apparent complacency of those who enjoy secret scandal-mongering, this is a prayer which will renew our confidence and even encourage us to raise our voices in praise of God.

# WEEK 3 SUNDAY

## EVENING PRAYER I
### PSALM 112(113) Hymn

This hymn is the first in a series (112[113]-117[118]), known as the *Hallel* (Praise) psalms, which was used at major festivals, as well as at the family Passover celebration. It begins with a call to the *servants of the Lord*, which in this context means not only the priests and levites but the whole assembly, to raise their voices in praise of *the name of the Lord*. The psalmist's vision is truly universal. He longs for that name to be blessed throughout all time (*now and for evermore*) and throughout the entire world (*from the rising of the sun to its setting*) (st 1).

Two reasons for such praise make a striking contrast with each other: on the one hand, his transcendent greatness *(above all nations* and *above the heavens),* and, on the other, his wondrous condescension (he *stoops from the heights to look down*). And when the Lord looks down, he does so with a glance that is both compassionate and effective, so that the transcendent One is also the One immanent and active in human history (st 2).

Two traditional examples are given of his gracious "stooping down": *from the dust* (literally, the dung-heap; you can't get much lower than that) he lifts up the *lowly*, exalting him to princely status, and for *the childless wife* (a most shameful condition for an Israelite woman) he provides the joy of a real *home*, alive with the presence of *children*.

The extraordinary graciousness of God is a principal theme of the New Testament. It shines out particularly in the two events that stand at the beginning and end of the Gospels. At the beginning, we see *the childless wife* who "was found to be with child through the Holy Spirit" (Matthew 1:18) and who, in her gladness, proclaimed "the greatness of the Lord...because he has looked down upon his lowly handmaid" (Luke 1:46,48), and, at the end, the Man of Sorrows who went down into the tomb but was lifted up *from his misery* in the princely glory of Resurrection. But in praying this psalm we also remember that Jesus has made himself dependant upon us for the continuation of his work among *the lowly* and *the poor,* the marginalised and the outcasts. And by a wonderful divine paradox, in serving them we are also serving him. *Alleluia!*

This is a psalm we might like to learn by heart: it was sung by a young Japanese martyr as he awaited death by crucifixion in 1597. "He had learned this", wrote a contemporary, "at the catechetical school in Nagasaki, for among the tasks given to the children there had been included the learning of some psalms such as these" (cf The Divine Office I, p 144*)

### PSALM 115(116 B) Thanksgiving

This is another of the Hallel psalms (sometimes called the 'Great' or 'Egyptian' Hallel because of its association with the Passover feast), whose original purpose was to offer thanks to God for favours received. The psalmist recalls how in difficult times he had clung to his faith in God, though he had often had occasion to recall that *No man can be trusted* (st 1). Nor was his trusting in vain: now, he is overwhelmed at the thought of God's goodness to him. *How can I repay the Lord?* Even as he puts the question, its answer is clear. He will take into his hands *the cup of salvation* – either to present it to God as a drink-offering or, more likely, to drink from it as part of a thanksgiving meal – he will invoke the holy *name* and, in accordance with *his vows,* will make a votive offering *in the presence of all his people.* He commits himself, in gratitude, to the Lord.

The next words of the psalmist seem to suggest that *the death* of those who remain *faithful* is something *precious* in God's sight. However, the sense may rather be that it costs God dear to see the death of one of his friends (which is why he saved the psalmist?) (st 2-3). What follows expresses the psalmist's determination to show gratitude to God not simply by words, even those of the liturgy, but also by deeds. His real *thanksgiving sacrifice* will be his whole life as *your servant, Lord.* And he concludes by reaffirming that he will be true to the vows he has made; he will fulfil them in the very *courts of the house of the Lord* (St 4-5).

There is a particular poignancy in this psalm when we recall that it was sung by Jesus and his friends in the Upper Room before he went out to his death (Matthew 14:26). Throughout his Passion he *trusted* and remained faithful, though betrayal by friends showed that *no man can be trusted.* At the supper he had raised *the cup of salvation* and in doing so pledged himself as the victim of Calvary. His death remains *precious* for all time, but it is also dreadfully costly – for him, and for his Father. But death was not the end: God *loosened* its *bonds* over his Son, and now Jesus' great sacrifice will be renewed in the midst of the new *Jerusalem,* the Church, until the end of time. As it is renewed in our parish church this Sunday, we, like the psalmist, may well find ourselves wondering how we can ever repay the Lord for his goodness to us.

CANTICLE – Philippians 2: 6-11 (see Week 1 – Sunday, page 40)

## OFFICE OF READINGS
### PSALM 144(145) Hymn
It might be thought that an 'alphabetical' psalm (one whose first line begins with the first letter of the Hebrew alphabet, its second with the second, and so on) will inevitably be artificial and dull. But this psalm gives the lie to such thoughts. Though alphabetical in form, this is a fine, spontaneous outpouring of praise.

# WEEK 3 SUNDAY

§I begins with a declaration of intent: to *bless* and glorify God, the Creator King, *day after day* and *for ever*. The reason is that his greatness is beyond all human calculations. So long as the world shall last, his *mighty*, awesome deeds, his majestic *glory*, but above all his *abundant goodness* and *justice* will be proclaimed (st 1-4). Enlarging upon the notion of the Lord's goodness, the psalmist takes up, almost word for word, the response that Moses received when he asked God to reveal to him what he was really like (Exodus 34:6): he is *kind*, brimming over with *compassion, slow to anger, abounding in love*. And this Father-God's tenderness and compassion extend to the whole of creation (st 5).

And so, in §II, all his *creatures* and, pre-eminently, all his *friends* acknowledge with gratitude his royal splendour, his glorious *reign*, his unending *kingdom*.

§III looks back to §I st 5, highlighting some of the ways in which God's kingly power and fatherly solicitude are revealed. It is seen in support for those who stumble, in a helping hand for those who are stooped beneath life's burdens and in *food* from a wide-open *hand* for all creatures who look to him expectantly (the reference to God's generous provision has made this psalm, or at least this verse of the psalm, a traditional form of grace before meals). It is seen too in closeness and readiness to listen to those who pray sincerely, and in protective care for *all who love him* (together with a less happy fate for the *wicked*.)

All this amounts to an overwhelming proof of God's love and faithfulness, and so, with renewed fervour, the psalmist returns to where he began – but this time with the prayer that *all mankind* will unite with him in his song of praise *for ages unending*.

# WEEK 3 SUNDAY

Today the psalmist's prayer is answered once again as we take on our lips this wonderful ABC of praise, raising our minds and hearts to a God who is King of all creation and at the same time a compassionate and loving Father. In Jesus Christ we have seen mightier deeds, more bewildering signs of God's compassionate love than the psalmist could ever have dreamed of.

## MORNING PRAYER I
### PSALM 92(93) Hymn

A tribute to a *king*! But this is no ordinary king. He robes himself not in purple and ermine but in *majesty* and *might* and *power*. To his footstool, *the world*, he has given a stability reflecting that of his *throne* in heaven. And now the hymn addresses the divine King directly, acknowledging his eternal sovereignty: he always was, and he was always king (st 1-2).

At creation (as at the exodus) he vanquished the watery chaos which reared up against him, roaring with a voice of *thunder*. A notable feature of this poem, the doubling and even trebling of expressions, is here used to wonderful effect: one can almost see and hear the breakers surging forward, lifting ever higher and higher and higher (st 3). But he is gre*ater* and *more glorious* than the pounding *waters*; he reigns supreme (st 4). His *decrees* (i.e. his Word, his revelation, his commands) are no less trustworthy than the material universe he has made. For all time, *holiness* alone can provide a fitting palace-home for such a King as this.

No doubt the Israelites regarded the Temple at Jerusalem as the holy dwelling place of the divine King. That temple, however, was not destined to last *until the end of time*. And so a new significance is given to the words of St Paul: "Didn't you realise that you were God's temple? ... the temple of God is sacred; and you are that temple" (1 Corinthians 3:16). It is we, the followers of the Lord in every generation, who are called upon to provide a holiness befitting the King who dwells within us.

**CANTICLE – Daniel 3:57-88,56** (see Week 1 Sunday, page 47)

**PSALM 148 Hymn**
Like the canticle which precedes it, this psalm calls upon all creation to join in a great symphony of praise to God, its Maker and Sustainer. The call goes out first of all to the heavens (st 1-3), then descends to the earth (st 4-5), extends to all humankind – high and low, male and female, young and old – (st 6) and finally reaches his chosen people, *the sons of Israel.* Such praise is due because it was at his word of command that all things sprang into being, endowed with the laws which govern their nature and functions, but also because his unique and majestic *splendour* has been made manifest.

It is most appropriate that we should pray this ecstatic song of praise – a great cosmic "alleluia", as Pope John Paul II describes it – on this the Lord's day, for we are the new people of God, the ones whom *he exalts* through the dying and rising of his Son. We are the ones who are called to be *saints* and *the people to whom he comes close* at our Sunday Eucharist.


## PRAYER DURING THE DAY
**PSALM 117(118) Thanksgiving** (see Week 1 Sunday, page 48)

# WEEK 3 SUNDAY

## EVENING PRAYER I
### PSALM 109(110) Didactic (see Week 1 Sunday, page 52)

### PSALM 110(111) Hymn
Gratitude, says a French proverb, is the heart's memory. The author of this psalm believes that he can best give thanks *with all* his *heart* in the company of others, rather than in solitude. Using the twenty two letters of the Hebrew alphabet as skeleton for his thoughts – this is another alphabetical psalm – the poet speaks briefly of *the works of the Lord* which are so *majestic and glorious*. God himself has decreed that his *wonders*, all of them proof that he *is compassion and love*, should be kept alive in the heart's memory (especially through the great festivals: Exodus 23:14-17)) (st 1-2).

Once again, the mighty events of Israel's history are recalled – the exodus and the feeding of the tribes in the desert, the conquest of Canaan, the giving of the commandments and the covenant at Mount Sinai. But more than that, through worship those events are in some way made present, so that the worshippers once again experience God's justice (his power to make people just, pleasing in his sight) and his *truth* (his utter faithfulness). In the presence of this thrice-holy God, one is filled with fear, not the cringing fear of the slave, but the reverential fear – mixed with wonder and gratitude – of the creature before his Creator (st 3-5).

Perhaps our psalmist was a teacher; in any event he cannot resist the opportunity to make his point that where such fear exists, there is *the first stage of wisdom* (the practical art of living in God's world). And he draws the striking conclusion that his prayer of gratitude admits him into the chorus of praise that *shall last for ever* (st 6).

This psalm is used on the feast of *Corpus Christi*, but it is appropriate for any Sunday. Today we have taken part with the *assembly* of our brothers and sisters in a great act of thanksgiving. The Eucharist could truly be described as 'the heart's memory' of the Church. Indeed, it was founded with the explicit injunction: *Do this as a memorial of me*. It is *food to those who fear him*, it is the new *covenant* in his blood (1 Corinthians 11:24-25). "The eucharistic memorial is no mere calling to mind of a past event or of its significance, but the Church's effectual proclamation of God's mighty acts" (ARCIC: Eucharistic Doctrine §5 – Windsor 1971). This act of praise and thanksgiving will continue *until he comes again in glory*, when it will give place to the song of everlasting praise and thanks.

**CANTICLE – Revelation 19:1-2, 5-7 or 1 Peter 2:21-24**
(see Week 1 Sunday, page 56)

# WEEK 3 MONDAY

## OFFICE OF READINGS
### PSALM 49(50) Didactic

One of the most famous scenes in the Old Testament is the confrontation between the prophet Nathan and David, the king who betrayed God by adultery and murder. The prophet tells the story of a rich man who kills his poor neighbour in order to take possession of his ewe lamb. The king explodes with wrath: that wicked man, he roars, must die for his crime. "You are the man" says the prophet (2 Samuel 12).

This psalm may remind us of that scene. §I shows the *God of gods*, dwelling in dazzling splendour in the midst of Sion and summoning *the earth*, from east to west, to come before him. *Fire* and *tempest*, typical signs of the divine presence, surround him and *the heavens and the earth* are called as witnesses. It seems that the stage is set for him to pass judgment on the heathen nations. But suddenly the tables are turned: the finger is pointing at *his people*. It is they, *my people,* who are arraigned before him, the people who entered into solemn *covenant* with him on Mount Sinai, a covenant sealed *by sacrifice* (Exodus 24:3-8).

Before charges are brought, God addresses the people in words (*Listen my people...I am your God*) similar to those used in their daily prayer, the *Shema* ("Hear, O Israel, the Lord your God is one Lord ..." Deuteronomy 6:4f), as well as those which introduce the Ten Commandments; ("I am the Lord your God ..." [Deuteronomy 5:6]). The remainder of §II shows how 'religious' folk have failed to live up to their daily prayer and to the first great commandment of the decalogue. It is not the manner or the number of their *sacrifices* which are at fault, but rather the unworthy notions they have about God; after all, he does not need their sacrifices, nor is he dependant upon his people, like some poor relation. Indeed, the truth is exactly the opposite: *all the beasts* and *all the birds* belong to him; if he did really stand in need of a meat dish, he wouldn't have to come to them; they cannot do him any favours. What is required therefore, as the final stanza of the section shows, is that they should offer *a sacrifice of thanksgiving*, thereby recognising their dependance upon him, and make the appropriate *votive offerings*, thereby acknowledging publicly that he has answered their prayers. These are the ways in which they affirm his position as Lord and theirs as his creatures.

§III is concerned with *the wicked*, who while reciting the *commandments* and the *covenant* formula (note the link between this section and the first stanza of §II) ignore the law of God in daily life. Mention is made of three ways in which *my words* (the commandments) are ignored – theft, adultery and slander. The wicked associate with, or at any rate connive at, those who commit such sins. But they need not imagine that God is like them. They may *never think of God*, but he has his eye upon them: like a lion, he will *seize* them and then there will be no escape.

The final words of this powerful indictment draw together the two groups and show what is required of each: by *a sacrifice of thanksgiving* the 'religious' truly honour God; and by acting uprightly the 'wicked' are assured of God's *salvation*.

This psalm is so close in outlook to the Gospel that as we pray it we may well find that the finger of accusation is pointing at us. Its three parts may be summed up in three of our Lord's statements – §I: "When a man has a great deal given him, a great deal will be demanded of him" (Luke 12:48); §II: "True worshippers will worship the Father in spirit and in truth" (John 4:23) and §III: "It is not those who say to me, 'Lord, Lord'. who will enter the kingdom of heaven, but the person who does the will of my Father in heaven". (Matthew 7:21)

# WEEK 3 MONDAY

## MORNING PRAYER
### PSALM 83 (84) Hymn

We have already seen how the Israelites sang pilgrim songs as they made their way up to Jerusalem for the great festivals. This psalm is a perfect example: the note of *longing and yearning*, affection and desire, is there from the start. God's *dwelling place* has a unique loveliness, an extraordinary attractiveness, about it, so that the psalmist is filled, *heart and soul*, with joyous anticipation of coming into the presence of God, *the living God*. It is like the instinct of the birds which brings them back to their *home* beside the very *altars* of *my king and God*. Lucky birds! the psalmist seems to say (st 1-3).

There is beatitude, happiness, for the officials who spend their lives *in your home* in perpetual praise. But there is happiness too for those who make the pilgrimage journey; already they experience God's *strength*, already in their *hearts* they are treading the final stage of the sacred highway which leads *to Sion*. They may have to pass through *the Bitter Valley* – a reference not perhaps to a geographical location but to the hardships and difficulties, especially the thirst, encountered on the journey – but, with the faith that moves mountains, *they make it a place of springs;* they enjoy *the autumn rain,* a favour which pilgrims prayed for at the autumnal festival. And as they draw closer to their goal, far from weakening, they discover fresh reserves of strength (st 4-5).

The psalmist's voice is now raised in a plea that God will *give ear*, in particular that he will turn his *eyes* towards *your anointed*, the king, for the welfare of the people is closely linked with that of their sovereign (st 6-7). Again the psalmist reflects on the wonder of being in the Temple. To be merely at *the threshold* of God's house (and so exposed to the elements) is preferable to being ensconced in the home of *the wicked*. God is at once protective *rampart and shield* and giver of *favour and glory* to all true followers (st 8). And then a final resounding beatitude: O, the happiness of the one *who trusts in you!* (st 9).

This wonderful song, which springs from the heart of a mystic, is like a parable of our Christian life. We are a pilgrim people, with a homing instinct for the new Jerusalem of heaven; yet there is no situation in which we cannot find a way to God. We may feel envious of those who can give themselves to uninterrupted prayer, but they, like us, have their pilgrimage journey to make. At times the way is hard, each one us has his or her *Bitter Valley* to face, but our king and God never deserts us, he turns the impossible into the possible, he gives us new strengh. As Jesus expressed it, "happy the man who does not lose faith in me" (Luke 7:23).

### CANTICLE – Isaiah 2:2-5
The psalm we have just considered flows naturally into this canticle. Isaiah, with poetic exaggeration, envisages a time when the hill of Sion (Jerusalem) will tower above every other and *all the nations* will stream towards it, longing to learn the *ways* and *walk in* the *paths* of Israel's God. Then, by his intervention, the human dream of universal peace will come true when all nations *beat their swords into ploughshares* (words enshrined today in the precincts of the United Nations).

As we pray this canticle, maybe the hill that comes to mind is that 'hill far away' on which there stood 'an old rugged cross' (George Bennar). Calvary is little more than a hillock but in moral stature it is loftier than any mountain. Ever since Jesus was 'lifted up' there, he has drawn all to himself. The latter days of Isaiah's prophecy may not finally come until the end of time, but the future begins today. And we contribute to that future when by loving and peaceful lives we draw others towards Jesus and his Cross, saying: *Come, let us walk in the light of the Lord.*

# WEEK 3 MONDAY

## PSALM 95 (96) Hymn

If the psalm of today's Office of Readings featured God coming as Judge of his people, this one features his people coming to acknowledge him, and summoning *all the earth* to acknowledge him, as king. *A new song* is called for, which is perhaps another way of saying: let us sing once more to this God whose newness is inexhaustible. The good news of *his help, his glory and his wonders,* which are freshly experienced *day by day*, is to be proclaimed *among the nations* (st 1 -2).

*The heavens*, which are of his making, bear testimony to *his power* and to his superiority over the non-gods of *the heathens* (st 3-4). Such a God is worthy of praise. And just as his people were three times called upon to sing to the Lord (st 1), so now the fam*ilies of peoples* are three times called upon to *give the Lord glory*, and even to worship *in his temple* (st 5 – 6). Also just as the proclamation of his kingship (*God is king!*) is to be proclaimed *to the nations*, so the whole of nature – *heavens and earth, sea and land* – are invited to rejoice in God as king and judge (st 7-9).

Day by day, and several times a day, we pray: Thy Kingdom come. Here is a psalm which reads like the answer to our prayer. At first, it is a handful of faithful ones who proclaim: *God is king,* but then all the nations take up the cry, and finally dumb nature thunders with joy as it too is caught up in "the same glory and freedom as the children of God" (Romans 8:21).

## PRAYER DURING THE DAY
### PSALM 118 (119) XII Didactic

We can never be reminded too often of the sureness, the reliability of God's *word*; whether thought of in terms of revelation or of commandments, it is at least as dependable as *the heavens* and *the earth* which he has created. In the face of *affliction* the psalmist has found it to be a sure defence and a giver of *life* (st 1-3a).

The final stanza and a half take on added meaning for us who have accepted the Word-made-flesh. Jesus said that if we love him we must keep his commandments; in the measure, therefore, that we *seek* his *precepts* we ask that he may save us, for – wonderful thought – we are *yours*. Though others may try to lead us astray, we want *to ponder on your will* and put it into practice. While all that falls under our experience has its limitations, there is no limit set to God's great *command of love*. "Love", wrote St Peter Chrysologus, "knows nothing about judgment, is beyond reason, and is incapable of moderation". We are called to *boundless* love.

### PSALM 70 (71) Lament

The paradoxical *Be a rock of refuge for me...for you are my rock* (§I st2) is suggestive of the New Testament prayer: "Lord, I do believe, help thou my unbelief", and in fact this psalm seems to fluctuate between complete trust in God and fear that the unthinkable might happen and the psalmist might be abandoned.

He knows that he can look back on a life-time of trust in the Lord, ever *since my youth*. Indeed, he acknowledges that even *from my mother's womb* he was dependent upon God, who proved *a strong refuge* and filled his lips with praise. However, now he is *old* and failing in strength and faced by enemies who try to take advantage of him, and so his ardent prayer is that God may not forsake him. Rather, may it be his enemies who are *put to shame* and *covered with confusion*.

Heartened by these reflections, he continues with an outpouring of trust and praise (§II). Though unable to forget present troubles – again he begs not to be forsaken now that he is *old and grey-headed*

# WEEK 3 MONDAY

– his predominant thought is to praise God, and *proclaim his wonders all day long*, not least those involved in putting his enemies in their place.

It is good to find that the psalter has this ready-made prayer to offer us for occasions when we are despondent at the thought of the advance – or actual presence – of old age, and the limitations and even humiliations it brings. (We can pray it the more confidently because through his prophet the Lord has assured us:"In your old age I shall be still the same, when your hair is grey I shall still support you" (Isaiah 46:4)). But every age has its problems and there is no time in life when we cannot pray with the psalmist that our trust may endure – confident, as he is, that our God is without compare (for *who is like you?*).

## EVENING PRAYER
### PSALM 122 (123) Lament

This is another of the lovely psalms of ascent. St 1-2 reveal the attitude of the psalmist as he raises his eyes to God *in the heavens*, with the humble submission and ready obedience of a slave or a *servant*. St 3 is a petition for help on behalf of the people in their affliction at the hands of the wealthy and arrogant.

A peculiarly attractive feature of the psalm is that it might serve as a commentary on prayer. Like *slaves*, eyes fixed on *their lords*, ready to respond the moment he gives the signal, we in prayer place ourselves in the presence of our gracious Lord – quietly, expectantly, ready for whatever he may ask of us. Or we are like the little *servant* girl who stands at the end of the dining hall; apparently doing nothing, yet all the time intent upon her mistress, waiting to hasten forward and do her bidding. Of course she may not be called upon to

# WEEK 3 MONDAY

do anything, except to remain at her post, alert, fulfilling her duty. To pray is to be totally at God's disposition; it calls for the self-effacement involved in making him the focus of our attention and leaving him to be in charge and *show us his mercy* in whatever way he may decide.

**PSALM 123 (124) Thanksgiving**
The opening line of this psalm is the invitation given to the assembly by its leader (a priest or a cantor), calling upon them to join in singing *Israel's song.* And, with much enthusiasm, that is what they proceed to do. They give thanks to God for their wonderful deliverance. Using graphic picture words, they compare their experience to that of escaping from the jaws of a monster, who *would have swallowed us alive,* or from the waters of a raging torrent, that would *have engulfed us.*

The leader adds another picture to theirs. The escape was like that of a *bird*, which disentangles itself from the net *of the fowler.* Clearly the *help* which made such an unbelievable escape possible can only have come from *the Lord*, the one who had power to make *heaven and earth.*

As we draw towards the end of another day our task is to thank God for the times that he has saved us from our 'enemies' during the past twenty four hours, but above all to reflect with gratitude that "For all the names in the world given to men, this (Jesus) is the only one by which we can be saved" (Acts 4:12) from our most fearful enemy and achieve freedom.

**CANTICLE – Ephesians 1:3-10** (See Week 1 Monday, page 66)

# WEEK 3 TUESDAY

## OFFICE OF READINGS
### PSALM 67 (68) Thanksgiving

This splendid song might be described as the psalmist's *Bayeux tapestry*: a vivid verbal record of the triumph of the Lord. However, the record is not confined to words; the evidence suggests that the psalm may have accompanied a ritual re-enacting of the divine victory. It begins with words similar to those used, in ancient times, as the Ark was lifted up at the start of a desert march (Numbers 10:35), an indication that originally it was used in a processional context. The victorious *God*, symbolized by the ark, is returning in triumph to his temple. *His foes* have good reason to fear. They are dealt with as decisively as *smoke that is blown away* or *wax that melts before the fire* (a fate that may have been illustrated by the curling smoke of a sacrifice and the melting wax effigies of the Lord's enemies). But for *the just*, his *presence* brings exulting and dancing. There is to be song and music and rejoicing *in the Lord*, as the assembly forms a *highway* (a processional route) for him who, not for the first time in the psalms, uses the clouds as his chariot (§I st 1-2).

After greeting him as the befriender of all in need, such as *the orphan, the widow, the lonely,* and the *prisoners* – a very different end awaits the rebellious – the psalm recalls two of his great exploits: the leading out of his people from bondage to freedom (an echo of his redeeming work at the exodus) and the providing of the annual rains (an echo of his creative work involving the subjection of watery'chaos') (§I st 3-5).

The precise sense of much of §II is uncertain, yet the general theme is clear enough. Like a successful army general, God releases a communique of *good tidings* – the defeat of his enemies, who are now in full flight. Then the scene swiftly changes to the home front where *the women* are sharing out *the spoils* and bedecking themselves with *silver and gold* and precious *jewels* which glisten *like snow* on a dark mountain side. 'Dark mountain' seems to be the sense of *Mount Zalmon* (§II st 1-2).

As the procession wends its way up Mount Zion, the people sing of how God has *chosen to dwell* – and *for ever* – on this small hill, while other much more magnificent mountains, such as those in the *Bashan* range, can only look on *with envy*. The huge procession resembles the *thousands upon thousands of chariots* that God has at his disposal and the innumerable *captives* that follow in his train, as he makes his triumphal journey from far-away *Sinai* to this his *holy place*. Such reflections evoke a hymn of praise to *this God of ours*, who has proved himself *a God who saves*, a God *who bears our burdens*, but also a God who *holds the keys of death* – and is not slow to use them for *those who persist in their sins!* The final st of §II, in which none of his enemies is allowed to escape by seeking refuge in the high mountains of *Bashan* or in the *depth of the sea*, may not come easily to our lips, but at least it represents an honest recognition that war is a horrible and bloody business.

§III again focusses on the procession with its *singers*, its young women playing *timbrels*, and no doubt dancing too, and finally its *musicians*. With the eye of faith, the onlookers *see* in this victory parade the *solemn procession* of God himself to his *sanctuary*. (The psalmist calls upon *Israel's sons* to *bless the Lord*). As the procession moves by it is clear that the whole people is represented by the presence of two tribes from the north (*Zebulun* and *Napthali)* and two from the south (*Benjamin* and *Judah*) (§III st 2-3).

God is called upon to demonstrate now the *might* he displayed in his former victories, so that pagan *kings* may acknowledge him with *their tribute*, especially those of Egypt (disparagingly compared to a *wild beast that dwells in the reeds*) and even of far-off *Ethiopia,* modern Sudan.

# WEEK 3 TUESDAY

And so the stage is set for a final call to all the *kingdoms of the earth* to raise their voices and *praise the Lord* and *acknowledge* his *power*, so wonderfully revealed by his thunderous *voice*. But it is *Israel* above all, and more especially *his holy place* in the *temple*, which is the focus of his *glory*. It is from there that he assures his people of *strength and power*.

St Paul bathes this psalm in Christian light when he pictures Jesus as a warrior who, having got rid of the Sovereignties and Powers (the forces of evil) now returns victorious, parading his enemies behind him in his triumphal procession (Colossians 2:15); he has *gone up on high* and by doing so has made possible the granting of gifts to men (Ephesians 4:8). Thus, the broad outline of the psalm recreates the epic victory of our Lord, who has won the decisive victory and ascended into heaven, leading the whole of redeemed humanity with him in order to give us a place with him (God) in heaven (Ephesians 2:6). With even greater enthusiasm than the psalmist, we have reason to cry out that Jesus *bears our burdens*, that *this God of our is a God who saves* and that, by his resurrection, he has shown that he *holds the keys of death*.

## MORNING PRAYER
### PSALM 84 (85) Lament
In difficult times it is natural for believers to recall the goodness God has shown them in the past and perhaps 'remind' God of the same. And that is how the singers of this psalm begin. They speak of the way God once *favoured* his *land* and his *people*, by reviving their *fortunes* and forgiving their *sins* (st 1). On that basis, they pray that he will take the initiative once more, freeing them from current difficulties, restoring their lives, giving them visible evidence of his continuing *mercy* (loving kindness) (st 2-3).

From the midst of the assembly a voice is raised, presumably that of a prophet, bringing exciting news: God has spoken and he has a message of *peace* for all *those who turn to him in their hearts*. He himself will be their Saviour, and *his glory*, the sign of his presence, *will dwell in our land* (st 4). And when it does, wonderful things happen. God's covenant *mercy* (steadfast love) and utter *faithfulness* converge, *justice* (the right ordering of things) and *peace* (wholeness, plenty, well-being) kiss each other; and *faithfulness* (total commitment) springs up *from the earth* (from human hearts) in response to his *justice* (saving love) which *looks down from heaven* (st 5). The Lord will pour out his goodness and, in response, *our earth shall yield its fruit*. Meanwhile, *Justice* will clear the way before him and *peace* will arise wherever he treads (st 6).

The Church's Christmas liturgy makes use of this psalm, especially its final stanzas: God's saving deeds of the past have led us to expect great things from him, but the coming of Jesus exceeds all human expectations; in him we have seen God's *glory in our land; in him God's mercy* and *faithfulness* are united, in him *justice and peace* are made possible. God's saving goodness has stooped down from heaven and our earth has produced its perfect fruit: Jesus, the Saviour, who brings peace to men of good will, *to all who turn to him in their hearts*.

## CANTICLE – Isaiah 26: 1-4,7-9,12

This canticle forms part of *the apocalypse of Isaiah* in which he looks beyond present circumstances to a Jerusalem gloriously renewed by God's final intervention in human history. Taking our cue from the previous psalm, we might take the canticle in an ecclesial sense. God has intervened through Jesus Christ: his church is a str*ong city* with *walls and bulwarks*, ("the gates of hell will not prevail against it": Matthew 16:18) which exists only to bring his *salvation* to the whole human race. Citizenship is open to upright people who have *faith* (st 1). God himself keeps in *perfect peace* all who fix their thoughts on him with trust. Indeed, he is as sure as a *rock* that cannot be shaken and he will *make smooth the path of the righteous*, not in the sense that he will give them an easy time but rather that he will guide them along the right way (st 2-3).

As he thinks of these things, the prophet *yearns* for God's coming; and *in the night* of this world, we too pray for the dawn when his kingdom will come and with it *righteousness and peace*.

**PSALM 66 (67) Thanksgiving** (see Week 2 Wednesday, page 147)

## PRAYER DURING THE DAY
**PSALM 118(119) XIII Didactic**

Once again the psalmist speaks of his attachment to the law – *It is ever in my mind* – and of the *insight* and *understanding* it brings, as well as of his enduring faithfulness to the Lord and determination to avoid *the ways of falsehood*. Such devotion to the law may strike us as excessive until we recognise that for the psalmist 'law' also had the meaning of instruction: his ultimate concern is to understand God's teaching. Viewed in that light, his thought is close to that of many a passage in the New Testament, such as this one from the letter to the Colossians: "..since the day we heard about you, we have not stopped... asking God to fill you with knowledge of his will through all spiritual wisdom and understanding. And we pray this in order that you may live a life worthy of the Lord and may please him in every way: bearing fruit in every good work, growing in the knowledge of God, being strengthened with all power according to his glorious might so that you may have great endurance and patience, and joyfully giving thanks to the Father..."(Colossians 1:9-12).

Praying the psalms in a Christian spirit often, as in this instance, gives them an even richer meaning than they had before.

**PSALM 73 (74) Lament**

On 9 November 1938, *Kristallnacht* (the night of broken glass), the Nazis began their open persecution of the Jews. When Dietrich Bonhoeffer looked for a way to describe the horrors that were unleashed that night, he turned to this psalm, through which, centuries before, Jews had tried to convey the anguish of persecution. Though it is impossible to pin-point the events which occasioned it, there is no escaping its underlying emotions of bewilderment and outrage. It has an immediacy of style (see §I and the end of §II) which gives the impression of an eye-witness report.

The unbelievable has happened: God who once called a people to be *the sheep of* his *pasture* has now *cast* them *off*. Can it be *for ever?* Poignantly, he is asked to *remember that you chose them, you redeemed them, you made your dwelling* on mount Sion, and is invited to come and see for himself the pillaged *sanctuary*. The temple, *your house of prayer*, has been desecrated by enemies who came storming in, shattering its silence with their *uproar*, profaning its holiness with their pagan *emblems*, destroying its wooden doors *with hatchet and pickaxe* and – *O God*, exclaims the psalmist, as though still horrified at the thought of what happened – committing to the flames *the place where you dwell* (§I,1-3).

It is terrible enough that the enemy should be hellbent on destroying every vestige of God's presence *in the land*, but, far worse than that, God himself is silent; there is no prophet to say *how long it will last*. Just as at the beginning of the psalm a two-fold *why?* expressed unbelief at God's desertion, so now a two-fold *why?* expresses uncertainty as to when it will come to an end: no-one knows when he will at last draw forth his strong *right hand* which is *hidden* in his robe (§I,4-5). And yet at this moment of near-despair, the psalmist suddenly takes off in a new direction, recalling that *God is our king always and everywhere* (§I,6).

Present troubles are seen in perspective when viewed through the eyes of faith. It is God *who divided the sea* of Reeds, destroyed the fiendish enemies of his people, crushing the seven-headed monster, *Leviathan,* (probably, Egypt, described in Ezekiel 29:3 as "the great crocodile wallowing in the Nile") and handing over the carcase as food, and *opened springs* of water in the desert (§II,1-2). But, as well as Warrior-King, he is also Creator-King, who provides day and night, *summer and winter,* who sets *a bright sun* in the heavens and boundaries to the earth (§II,3).

The psalmist begs for help, no less insistently than before (note the three-fold *remember* and the repeated use of *your*), but now upheld by the belief that the redemptive and creative power of God will be more than a match for the *scoffing, senseless people* which *insults your name* (§II 4-6).

This powerful psalm might be prayed in two ways:

i) it might call to mind the suffering of Jesus, with its frightening description of handing over to the enemy, of mockery, stripping and destruction, and of God himself holding back his *right hand* while his *dove* is at the mercy of *the hawk*;

ii) it might also serve as a reminder that in the midst of all our troubles we are supported by the faith of the whole Church. Thus the psalm becomes a prolongation of that prayer at Mass in which we beg God to "look not on our sins" (and the punishment they deserve)"but on the faith of your Church".

## EVENING PRAYER

**PSALM 124 (125) Confidence**

This Evening Prayer begins with another of the psalms of ascent. As the pilgrims approach Jerusalem, the very sight of the holy city puts them in mind of God and of their relationship with him. Because they *trust* in him, they are as secure as *Mount Sion*, which, according to popular belief, would stand firm *for ever*. Still more, the *mountains*, which hem the city in and make it virtually impregnable, are an impressive symbol of the way in which God protects his people on every side (st 12).

The confidence which these reflections inspire leads naturally to the assertion that *the sceptre of the wicked* (the dominion of evil) will never be allowed to flourish in *the land of the just* – for that might tempt them to lose faith and *turn to evil*. This is followed by a prayer that God will show his goodness to the faithful and drive away *the crooked,* so that Israel may enjoy *peace.*

Here is a psalm which might have inspired St Patrick's *breast-plate*, with its confidence in a God who surrounds us on all sides – with me, within me, behind me, before me, beside me, beneath me, above me and in all whom I meet.

**PSALM 130 (131) Confidence**

Another of the psalms of ascent, breathing the same spirit of confidence as the one we have just prayed. (see page 20).

**CANTICLE – Revelation 4:11; 5:9,10,12 (see Week 1 Tuesday, page 77)**

# WEEK 3 WEDNESDAY

## OFFICE OF READING
### PSALM 88 (89) Lament

It may seem strange to style this long psalm a lament since it reads much more like a hymn of praise and gratitude. However, what we have today is only its first part (§I-§III); tomorrow, in Office of Readings, we shall see that it is a prelude to an appeal for help (§IV-§V).

The whole psalm takes its stand on the sacred *covenant* which God made with *David* (§1 st 2)) and on the divine *love* and *truth* (faithfulness) – these two key words, repeated again and again, express God's unconditional love – which guarantee that the promise of old will be kept *for ever*. Moreover, God's fidelity is reinforced by his matchless kingship, which is acknowledged with awe in heaven by *the holy ones* (the angels) and proved in the world by his taming of the raging *sea* and *the monster Rahab* that dwells there (perhaps a double reference: to creation, when God mastered watery chaos, and to the exodus, when he mastered Egypt, sometimes nicknamed Rahab). God's kingship is displayed by the whole of creation, to earth's extremities, *the North and the South*; and proclaimed *with joy* by lofty mountains, such as *Tabor and Hermon*. But his *mighty arm* is not that of a tyrant, for *justice and right* are the foundations of his throne and *love and truth* are his courtiers (§I st 3-7). The psalmist proclaims the blessedness, *the bliss*, of all who *acclaim such a king*, who daily walk in his presence and *find their joy* in him; their own earthly *ruler is in the keeping* of this supreme King (§I st 7-9).

Now the psalmist returns to the covenant, as if to suggest that the choice of *David* and the promise that went with it were part of God's plan since the creation of the world. The implications of the divine initiative are explored. The office of kingship is from God, it is he who anoints the king with *holy oil*, who gives him strength and an empire stretching from the *Sea* (of Reeds) to *the River* Euphrates, who grants him the privilege of calling upon God as *my Father*, who treats him as *my first-born* and who gives endless assurances of *love* and *fidelity* for ever (§II). And as though this were not clear enough, God insists that even if David's successors should prove unfaithful and be punished for their wrong-doing, *I will never take back my love: my truth will never fail* (§III).

There is an ancient Russian Orthodox tradition of telling jokes all day on Easter Monday – even in church – to symbolize the supreme joke that God pulled on Satan by raising Jesus from the dead. Looking back at the sad history of the Davidic dynasty which seemed to be finally blotted out in the sixth century B.C, we might fear that, despite all this psalm says, God did indeed go back on his word. But of course the laugh is on us – and to our eternal benefit. In Jesus, Son of David, the psalm has a fulfilment beyond all human expectations. He is indeed a king forever, Lord of heaven and earth, the anointed one, a *first-born* who in a unique way can call upon God as *my Father*. As we pray this psalm, how happy we should be to *acclaim such a king*, to *walk in the light of* his *face* and to find *our joy every day* in his *name*.

## MORNING PRAYER
### PSALM 85 (86) Lament
This cry for help pours out a series of reasons why God should intervene, as if to ensure that at least one will reach its target. There is the poverty and need of the suppliant, his faithfulness and trust, the fact that he is *your servant*, his perseverance in prayer *all day long*, and the humility with which he lifts up his *soul* to him whom he recognises as *my God* (st 1-2). There is also God's own goodness, his readiness to forgive and the fact that he is *full of love to all who call* (st3). Inspired by such reflections, the psalmist's thoughts centre upon God's greatness. He is simply without compare, in himself and in his *work*, so that any so-called *gods* are of no consequence. He

alone will win the worship of *all the nations* (st 4-5). And if that be so, what is to be said, except *Show me your way* (the psalmist's equivalent of our Lord's: "Not my will but thine be done") and put in the *heart* of my being a reverential *fear* for you and all you stand for (st 6).

It is a prayer which gives fresh spirit; the psalmist promises *praise* of God *wih all my heart* and *for ever*. He gives thanks for that great *love* which has already snatched him *from the depths of the grave* – perhaps because he has been given this assurance through a Temple prophet, or perhaps because he is re-living a past experience (st 7). In any event the psalm once more makes mention of *the proud* and *ruthless men* who beset him; and this, in turn, becomes a prayer of confidence, resting on that wonderful self-description that God delivered to Moses – "God of tenderness and compassion, slow to anger, rich in kindness and faithfulness" (Exodus 34: 6). And finally, relying once more on the fact that he is God's *servant*, he boldly asks that he may be given *a sign* (a miraculous deliverance?) that will bring consolation to himself and *shame to his enemies* (st 8-10).

Psalm 85(86) is not only part of Morning Prayer today but also of Evening Prayer for Mondays. At the beginning of each day, as at its end, we have so many needs to bring before the Lord; we may or may not be able to lay claim to the trust and the faithfulness, the humility and the perseverance of the psalmist, but of one thing we can be sure – all that the psalmist had to say about God are as true now as they were then. A *God of mercy and compassion, slow to anger..abounding in love and truth* – what a thought on which to begin – or end – the day.

## CANTICLE – Isaiah 33:13-16

Those who are *far off* and those *who are near* are all invited to recognise the *might* of God. *Fire* is the sign of his presence but also the symbol of his holiness, a holiness which fills *sinners* with fear and gives rise to the question: who, even among the just, can hope to live with such *devouring fire?* The reply is: those who are virtuous in deed and in word, who have no truck with oppressors, whose *hands* and *ears* and *eyes* shun what is *evil*. Such people are like a hilltop city, which has the powerful *defence* of steep *rocks* and the supply of food and access to *water*, which are vital in the event of siege by enemies.

It is good for us to be reminded from time to time of the fiery nature of our God. His blazing holiness, as Isaiah discovered (Isaiah 6), can overwhelm us with a searing awareness of our sinfulness. And yet, through his Son, Jesus, this all-holy God assures us that if we strive each day to follow the advice of the canticle, by being doers of the word, there will be a place for us in his kingdom; we shall be as safe as a fortified city *on the heights.*

### PSALM 97 (98) Enthronement Psalm

Like other psalms in honour of God, the King, this one is magnificent and exhilarating. It begins with the call to *sing a new song* in his honour, a new song, perhaps, because he has been just been enthroned anew in the liturgy, but also because he *has worked wonders*, he has given fresh proof of his royal power in his saving deeds. Nor is it only *the house of Israel*, but *all the ends of the earth*, that have been made aware of his loving faithfulness to his people (st 1-3).

And so the whole world is invited to *shout* and *ring out* its *joy* as it greets its king. Psalm-singing and musical instruments – *harp, trumpets* and *horn* – are to unite in paying royal homage. But that is not all: *the sea*, and all that is hidden in its depths, the wide *world, and all its peoples*, are to *thunder* their praise; *the rivers* – here especially the poet is at work – are envisaged clapping their hands and *the hills* breaking out in spontaneous joy (st 4-5). The source of all this delight and praise is *the presence of the Lord* and his kingdom which are a guarantee of universal *justice and fairness.*

# WEEK 3 WEDNESDAY

This psalm is an antidote to the fear that many people express in regard to the Second Coming and in complete harmony with the prayer at Mass which speaks of our waiting "in joyful hope for the coming of our Lord Jesus Christ". It is also a reminder of the intimate relationship between humankind and the rest of creation and, by implication, of the respect we ought to accord to all God's handiwork. And, finally, it is a welcome assurance that worship of God, our King, need not be – indeed cannot be – divorced from joy.

## PRAYER DURING THE DAY
**PSALM 118 (119) XIV Didactic** (see Week 2 Sunday, page 113)

**PSALM 69 (70) Lament**
This psalm is almost identical with the latter part of Psalm 39(40) – see Week 2 Monday, page 128, except that:

i) in st 1 the appeal seems more urgent, not simply a plea that God may *come* but that he may hurry (*make haste*);

ii) similarly in st 2 the request is that enemies may not merely be appalled but actually *retreat;*

iii) in st 4 the note of urgency is maintained by the substitution of the request: *come to me*, for the statement: *the Lord thinks of me* in psalm 39(40).

By way of comment, there is little to add to the gospel text: "Lord, save us, for we are in peril" (Matthew 8:25). The apostles' cry, as their tiny boat foundered on the Lake of Galilee, is of a piece with this psalm, which can express our urgent need for God's help in all the crises of life.

# WEEK 3 WEDNESDAY

### PSALM 74 (75) Didactic

Where there is a keen awareness of the reality of God and of his activity, there is the spirit of gratitude. And so this psalm, alive to his *wonderful deeds* and ready to *call upon* him for action, begins with a prayer of thanksgiving (st 1). At once, God makes his response (perhaps through a prophet), assuring his people that in his time and in his way he *will judge with justice.* Though earth's foundation may seem to rock under the impact of *the wicked*, he is the one who upholds it, and his command is for an end to *insolent* boastfulness and flaunted *strength* (st 2-3).

In reply to the divine oracle, the psalmist (or a priest, maybe, on behalf of the people) anounces that, search where you will, there is no final judge *but God himself.* And then a vision opens up of God administering the *cup* of judgment, which the evil *drink to the dregs* (st 4-5).

At the prospect of *the wicked* being reduced to weakness and *the just* being exalted in strength, the worshipper is confident that he *will rejoice for ever* and express his joy by singing *psalms to Jacob's God* (st 6).

At times we hear it said despairingly that "There's no justice in this world", so it is good to have assurance that justice, true and perfect justice, will ultimately be done.


## EVENING PRAYER
### PSALM 125 (126) Lament

Ecstatic joy (mouths *filled with laughter* and *songs* on the *lips*), incredulty (*it seemed like a dream*), amazement on the part of heathen enemies (*What marvels the Lord worked for them*) and rejoicing on the part of Israel (*Indeed we were glad*) – such were the emotions roused in times gone by when God restored his people's fortunes by enabling them to return from exile, or to escape some other national disaster (st 1-2). And they are called to mind now as his people come to Jerusalem (this is another of the psalms of ascent), because once again they are in need and are appealing for his help.

*Deliver us, O Lord*, they plead, either by a response coming with the swiftness of *streams* which miraculously transform parched land, or with the painstaking slowness of the farmer who must go out day after day (you can almost feel the drudgery of it in the repetition of the phrases *they go out* and *they come back*) to plant his *seed* before he can finally return *full of song* carrying the harvest *sheaves* (st 3-4).

This psalm brings home in delightful picture-language the sovereign freedom of God in answering our prayers. He may respond immediately, spectacularly; or he may do so imperceptibly – either in the sense that nothing seems to happen for a long time, or in the sense that the outcome seems to depend more upon us than upon him. However, it is hard to pray this psalm without thinking of the most momentous change in fortunes, that moment when we reach the heavenly Jerusalem and we shall be changed (1 Corinthians 15:36); then our mouths will be *filled with laughter* and on our lips there will be *songs* and *tears* will be no more. However, it will not be *like a dream*; it will be the great reality, the human dream come true.

## PSALM 126 (127) Didactic

Without the Lord all is *in vain*. This truth is applied to three areas, which are at least as important for us as they were for the psalmist and his contemporaries: building, security and family life. In building your *house,* your home, your community, all will be pointless unless *the Lord* builds with you. In preserving your *city*, your country, your possessions, protective devices will fail to keep you safe *if the Lord himself does not* keep *watch* (st 1).

# WEEK 3 WEDNESDAY

Similarly, you may have to *toil for the bread you eat*, but working all the hours that God sends you, as though everything depended upon you, is equally pointless. Moreover, it is senseless, for God *pours gifts* on those he loves during sleep, (a reference to the recouping of their energy, as well as to the nightly dew, so vital for the life of plants and crops) (st 2). It leads the poet to think of a most wonderful *gift from the Lord* – the children without whom *a house* is incomplete and yet whose creation rests in God's hands. Indeed, a rare *happiness* is enjoyed by *the man* who has many children, especially many *sons*, for they will accompany him to the city gates, where popular courts are held and disputes settled, so that, with this small army of witnesses, he will be as well defended against *his foe* as would a warrior with a quiverful of *arrows* (st 3-4).

In days of insurance cover, security locks, neighbourhood watch schemes and in vitro fertilization, this psalm is still able to stop us in our tracks. In the end God-less activity fails – *without me you can do nothing* (Jn 15:25) – a truth dramatically demonstrated by the fact that on that November day in 1963 when John F Kennedy, president of the most powerful nation on earth, was gunned down, the speech he was to deliver in Dallas concluded with the words: *If the Lord does not watch over the city, in vain does the watchman keep vigil.*

CANTICLE – **Colossians 1:12-20** (Week 1 Wednesday, page 85)

# WEEK 3 THURSDAY

## OFFICE OF READINGS
### PSALM 88 (89) Lament

*And yet* – after the sunny optimism of the earlier parts of this psalm (see yesterday's Office of Readings), these two words strike an ominous note. And suddenly it is all being poured out; the psalmist speaks of rejection, divine anger with the *anointed* one, breaking of the *covenant*, dishonour, *crown in the dust, fortresses* ruined, the *taunt of..neighbours, glory* brought *to an end* – all this despite God's promises, and, worse than that, all this of his doing. He has even *exalted the right hand of* our *foes* (note how *You* is the subject of virtually every aspect of the disaster described in §IV st 1-4)

And so it becomes clear why this psalm, which seemed initially to be a lively prayer of praise and gratitude, is in fact a lament. The psalmist raises to God the pitiful cry that has been made so often down the ages: *How long, O Lord?* And yet, with an unexpected boldness, he is prepared to argue his case with the Lord, reminding him of *the shortness* of human life coupled with the inevitability of *death*, as well as the promises he himself made to *David*, and *the insults* and mockery that have to be borne by *your servant* (§V).

The final line does not belong to this psalm – it has been added as a doxology to mark the end of the third division of the psalter (72[73]-88[89]) – and yet it helps us to see things in perspective. Though the psalmist's prayer (and ours too) may seem to go unanswered, the Lord is still to be relied upon; like Jesus, he is *the Amen* (Revelation 3:14) and is to be *blessed for ever.*

### PSALM 89 (90) Lament

New Zealand university chaplain, Fr E O'Sullivan O.P., records that, when he was seriously ill, students used to recite psalms at his bedside each day and his one vivid memory is of "the calmness in the face of danger, the confidence which seeps into you from the phrases of the Book of Psalms". The confident assertion that God has proved himself *our refuge* through succeeding generations is also an appeal for help. This is an appeal given added poignancy (as in the previous psalm) when the eternity of God (who is *without beginning or end and in* whose eyes *a thousand years are like yesterday*) is contrasted with the pathetic frailty of human beings (who return to their native *dust* (see Genesis 2:7), are swept away *like a dream*, are as ephemeral as *grass*) (st 1-3).

Death is the consequence of human sinfulness (Genesis 2-3). Everything, even *our* (guilty) *secrets* lie open before him. It is as though we had drawn down God's *anger* upon ourselves. Thus the whole of life, which at best is *seventy years or eighty*, is as fleeting as *a sigh*; indeed, it is *emptiness and pain* for the most part. And so the request that we may learn the lesson; there is no *wisdom of heart* in ignoring such basic truth (st 6-7a).

And then, shrugging aside all pessimism, the poet turns from painful reflection to ardent petition, begging God to *relent*, forgo his *anger* and *show pity* to his servants. May God's intervention, coming with the freshness of a new *morning, fill us with your love*, so that we can find *joy to balance our affliction* and *exult and rejoice all our days*. This will be proof of *your work* and a favour that our *children* will enjoy in their turn. And grant us your blessing, for then it is not only *your work* that will meet with success but *the work of our hands*, too (7b-9).

"Perhaps medically, as well as spiritually," writes Fr O'Sullivan,"it would be good for all of us to have that matter-of-factness about death which colours this psalm and others like it." In these psalms we are offered a way of seeing death that no longer frightens us. The psalmist teaches us that in death we surrender into the hands of God our human effort, not troubled about its inadequacy, but leaving it for God to complete: Give success to the work of *your* hands.

# WEEK 3 THURSDAY

## MORNING PRAYER

**PSALM 86 (87) Hymn**

In a few dramatic verses this psalm shows how highly *Sion* was esteemed by the people, and how deeply cherished by the Lord himself. The very *mountain* has become *holy* because he is there. For his own inscrutable reasons he prefers this spot to all *Jacob's* other *dwellings*. In prophetic vision the psalmist has heard and seen *glorious things:* God inviting to *his city* the Gentile nations, many of them Israel's foes, including the ancient persecutors, *Babylon and Egypt;* the enemy that was a constant threat on Israel's border, *Philistia;* the ancient coastal city of *Tyre;* and even distant *Ethiopia.* Not only are they invited to come to Sion but also to acknowledge it as *Mother* (st 1-2). It is *the Lord Most High* himself who ticks off the register of Sion's multitude of *children;* and their response is to *dance* with delight and sing with joy of Sion as the universal *home* of the nations.

This precious psalm of praise can be prayed, first, as a hymn for Mother Church, the new Jerusalem, which is commissioned to go forth to all the nations and guaranteed to endure to the end of time (Matthew 28:20). And second, it can be a hymn for the heavenly Jerusalem, the new Jerusalem...as beautiful as a bride all dressed for her husband...a city lit by the radiant glory of God and the Lamb and in which everyone is a "first-born son" (See Revelation 22 & Hebrews 12:23). Such thoughts might well have us all wanting to sing and dance with joy.

### CANTICLE – Isaiah 40:10-17

Often it is in the dark times that we unexpectedly grow in our understanding of God. That was Israel's experience, too. During the dark days of exile in Babylon, when it seemed that God had deserted them, their faith, far from being destroyed, seems to have been purified, so that the author of this canticle (written about 550 B.C.)

has come to an awesome vision of God. Though part of the canticle is in question form, the questions are rhetorical, as good as statements but with the addition of a touch of irony. On the one hand, he is a God of *might*, a warrior God who has *reward* and recompense at his disposal (st 1); a God who holds *the waters* of the oceans in *the hollow of his hand* and spans *the heavens* between outstretched thumb and little finger, who collects *the dust of the earth* in a bushel measure, weighs the mighty *mountains* and the *hills* like objects on a scale (st 3). He is a God who is dependent on no-one for direction or counsel, for *knowledge* or for *understanding* (st 4), a God in whose presence *the nations*, whether the archipelagoes and distant coasts of the Mediterranean or the giant powers nearby, are as nothing. The mighty cedars of *Lebanon* could not meet his *fuel* needs, nor could *all its beasts* provide a suitable *burnt offering* for such a God (st 5-6).

On the other hand, this towering, mighty God is *like a shepherd*, full of compassionate concern for his *lambs* (i.e. his people), gathering them *in his arms*, carrying them next to his heart and *gently* leading those with special needs (st 2).

This is a song which combines praise and wonder both at the 'richness' of God's power and wisdom (see Romans 11:33-36) and at his gentle attractiveness as the Good Shepherd (John 10:11-16). It is a prayer, which like many others among the psalms, gives substance to Pascal's remark that only God can speak well of God.

### PSALM 98 (99) Enthronement Psalm

Like yesterday's Morning Prayer, today's ends with a hymn to God the king. Its opening words – *The Lord is king* – suggest the cry of obeisance with which the people greet their God as he is liturgically enthroned above the cherubs, which flank the Ark of the Covenant in the inmost sanctuary of the Temple. Meanwhile (to the poet's eye) *peoples tremble* and *earth quakes* before a monarch *so terrible and great.* He is indeed deserving of universal praise, above all because *he is holy,* the totally other (st 1-2) – a theme which runs like a spine down the full length of this psalm. It is a holiness revealed not only in his overwhelming *power* but also in his love for *what is right* and the *justice* and integrity with which he guides history, especially that of his people *Jacob.* In the presence of such an awesome God, who so towers above the worshippers that *Sion* itself serves as *his footstool,* the only appropriate response is to prostrate oneself in worship (st 3-4).

After again referring to God's holiness, the psalmist speaks of *Aaron, Moses* and *Samuel.* If the remembrance of religious heroes of the past is an implied appeal to God, it is also a challenge to his people to imitate them in their pursuit of *his will* and in the keeping of *his law,* for a God of holiness is one who not only *forgives* but also takes *offences* seriously (st 5-7). And so the psalm rises to its predictable climax: an appeal to adore and worship *our God* whose *mountain* home has been made *holy* because he himself *is holy* (st 8).

This psalm, with its constant reference to God's resplendent holiness, his total 'otherness', might serve as a useful antidote to the alleged loss of the spirit of awe and wonder in much modern worship. At the same time, it reminds us that in Jesus Christ we have a Mediator greater than Moses, a Priest greater than Aaron, a King greater than Solomon (Matthew 12:42). It is in him and through him and with him that we – in this Morning Prayer and in all our worship – approach with confidence the all-holy king of glory.

## PRAYER DURING THE DAY
### PSALM 118 (119) XV Didactic
In the sixth beatitude Jesus spoke of the pure of heart (Matthew 5:8), those whose purity goes to the very core of their being. Such people,

and our psalmist was one, are the opposite of half-hearted men: they are single-minded, one-track minded, where the things of God are concerned. They see him and his *word* as their *shelter*, their *shield* and their *hope* (st 1).

Yet they feel the pull exerted by those *who do evil* and they know they themselves need God's constant support. At times they may even have to remind themselves of the fate which befalls those who *swerve from* him (st 2-4). However, for the Christian, there is another side to that coin: our Lord promised that the pure of heart will see God. An eternal reward, the face to face vision of God, awaits those who whole-heartedly serve him.

### PSALM 78 (79) Lament

Like psalm 74(75), which we prayed yesterday, this psalm is filled with both the anguish and the bewilderment of those involved in (or who recall) the destruction of Jerusalem. Anguish at the scale of the massacre in which *blood* ran *like water* in the holy city and at the *mockery and scorn* of the surrounding pagan nations. Bewilderment because it is God's *land* (note the repetition of *your*) that has been *invaded*, God's *holy temple* that has been profaned, God's *servants* whose carcasses have suffered the final indignity of being deprived of burial and dumped as *food* for bird and beast. But there is also the recognition that they have brought the tragedy upon themselves. It is as though their infidelity had aroused the Lord's *anger* and they wonder *how long* it will last; surely not *for ever?* (st 1-2).

And so they are led to plead for his help, acknowledging their own sinfulness but begging that they may not have to bear their fathers' *guilt also* and that – *for the sake of* his own good *name!* – his *compassion* will *rescue* them from their plight (st 3). Then, as though with renewed courage, they pray that those who taunt may be *repaid* and those who groan in their captivity may be reprieved so that for all times those who are *your people* and *your pasture* may *give you thanks* and *tell your praise.*

It may seem incredible that worshippers who began this psalm in such distress could end it in unbounded gratitude and praise. But Luke 15 teaches us, in the figure of the prodigal father, that when God lets his *compassion hasten to meet us* we are raised from the misery our sinfulness has earned and are able to burst forth into dancing and rejoicing.

**PSALM 79 (80) Lament** (see Week 2 Thursday, page 149)


## EVENING PRAYER
**PSALM 131(132) Hymn** (see Week 1 Saturday, page 106)

**CANTICLE – Revelation 11:17-18;12:10-12** (see Week 1 Thursday, page 96)

# WEEK 3 FRIDAY

## OFFICE OF READINGS
### PSALM 68 (69) Lament

Once more it's Friday, the day associated with our Lord's passion and death, and the fact is clearly reflected in today's Prayer of the Church. Its opening psalm is one of the two most frequently quoted in the New Testament. Originally the prayer of an individual caught in deep distress, it is suggestive of the sufferings endured by Jesus and in fact finds its way into the passion accounts of all four gospels.

It begins with a flurry of images – *waters* up to the *neck*, treacherous *mud* under the feet, ground giving way so that there is *no foothold*, great pounding *waves*. But what adds to the fears aroused by adversaries, who are *more numerous than the hairs of the head* and who, in their hatred, resort to *lies*, is the fact that the psalmist feels totally deserted. Praying and *looking for my God* are all in vain (§I st 1-4).

Already we are reminded of the desolation of Jesus in his agony in the Garden. And if he, the all-holy one, could never have prayed the next two stanzas (in which the psalmist humbly confesses his *sinful folly* and begs that others may not be led astray by the tragedy he has brought upon himself), he could certainly assert, with even greater conviction than the psalmist, that the *taunts* and the *shame* and the fearful feelings of alienation that he endures are all being borne for God's sake. They are, at least in part, the result of the murderous anger aroused in his enemies when, out of *zeal for* God's *house*, he had cleansed the Temple (John 2:17). Even his asceticism and penance have earned him public disgrace (§I st 7-8).

Once more there is reference to the *mud* and the *waters* which threaten, but now the prayer they inspire seems to have a new quality about it. There is confidence in God's *great love*, his never-failing *help*, his kindness and *compassion*. And yet the sufferings are real enough. Jesus certainly knew what it was to have a *heart* broken with anguish, to be *at the end of his strength, to look in vain* for comfort from his friends ("Could you not watch one hour with me?" (Matthew 26:40) and, in his burning thirst, to be given *vinegar to drink* (Matthew 27:48) (§II 1-5).

But from the midst of the *poverty and pain* there emerges *a song of praise* and *thanksgiving*, as though the sufferer has already been assured of the longed-for *help* from God. It is a song in which not only the *poor* and the *God-seeking* and *the needy* participate, but all creation too. Indeed, the unexpected turn of events arouses fresh hope that *Sion* will be rebuilt and the Babylonian exiles will return home (an indication of the probable date of this psalm's composition) (§III st 1-4).

It has been persuasively argued that the earliest Christian liturgies celebrating the pasch gave birth to the gospel narratives of the passion and that this was one of the psalms that was read, and perhaps commented upon, on such occasions. If this is so, it underlines the suggestion already made that psalm 68(69)is a prayer peculiarly appropriate for Friday, the day of the Lord's Passion.

## MORNING PRAYER
**PSALM 50 (51) Lament** (see Week 1 Friday, page 98)

### CANTICLE – Jeremiah 14:17-21
The prophet proclaims a time for ceaseless *tears* because in *the city* and in *the field* God's people, personified as *the virgin daughter*, face the disasters brought about by political (*the sword*) and natural (*famine*) disturbances (st 1-2). *Prophet and priest* may have no explanation for these events, but Jeremiah has. He sees them as

punishment for *our wickedness* and so calls upon all to *acknowledge* their sins and beseeches God for his *name's sake* to be mindful of his *covenant* and not allow the holy City (here described as his *throne*) to be dishonoured (st 2-5).

Today we think of Jesus who has has established the new covenant in his blood. For us it is a cause of sadness and even of *tears* that he, the sinless one, should have to suffer (though "I have found no case against him that deserves death" Luke 23:22); but there is also joy in the knowledge that in his wounds *there is... healing* (even) *for us.*

**PSALM 99(100) Hymn** (see Week 1 Friday, page 100)

## PRAYER DURING THE DAY
**PSALM 21 (22) Lament**
This is one of the most beautiful psalms, yet also one of the most terrifying, in the Psalter. Several of its verses are cited in the New Testament passion narrative. Its opening cry – *My God, my God, why have you forsaken me?* – was on the lips of Jesus as he hung upon the cross (Mark 15:35) and so leads us inescapably to think of the events of Good Friday.

The to-and-fro pattern of §I reflects the tortured spirit of the Sufferer, as he turns this way and that, now focusing upon himself and his plight, now outwards and upwards towards God, then back again to himself. He feels *forsaken* even by *my God*, a God so far away, so *deaf to the cry of my distress* (st 1). Yet he knows that God's holiness sets him beyond human comprehension. The people's songs of praise are like a lofty seat on which he is *enthroned; our fathers trusted* in him and were *set free, cried* to him and *escaped*, their prayers were *never in vain* (st 2).

Nonethless, he finds himself like *a worm and no man* (an apt description of the degradation of death by crucifixion); *scorned, despised, derided* by those who *curl their lips and toss their heads* and scornfully enquire why *the Lord* does not come to his rescue *if this is his friend* (Matthew 27:43) (st 3). But, *yes, it was God who* brought him safely to birth, accepted him as his son, looked after him through life. From the swirling fog of pain and doubt, the voice of faith emerges, crying out that God may *come close*, for now there simply *is none else to help* (4).

But then the voice is silenced by the onrush of suffering, nigthmarishly presented in §II, where enemies feature as *bulls of Bashan*, reknowned for their strength and ferocity, ravenous *lions,* snarling *dogs* and powerful *oxen* – a pack of wild animals drawing near for the kill.

The sufferings described are so like those of Jesus that scholars believe that this psalm helped to shape the passion stories of the gospel writers, especially those of Mark and Matthew (cf what was said above, about the influence of Psalm 68(69) on the Gospel passion accounts). We read of *bones* wrenched until they feel *disjointed*, a *heart* in its terror melting *like wax*, a *throat* parched like dried *clay*, gaping *holes* in *hands* and *feet*, a human being who seems to have been *poured out like water, the dust of death* settling upon him. Through the taut flesh of his distended chest it is possible to *count* the very *bones*. Not far away his *clothing* is being divided among the soldiers and, as he hangs there exposed and vulnerable, heartless *people stare at* him and *gloat* (Mark 15:24f).

Just as the voice of faith rose above the sufferings at the end of §I, so it is heard again at the end of §II, but now more insistently: *do not leave me*, make haste to help me, *rescue* me, *save* me. Then, suddenly, incredibly, the psalm twists into an entirely different direction. His prayer will be heard and he will proclaim God's goodness and give him praise (st 6). It is like a bridge pitched between despair and hope, between darkness and light. It leads to the extraordinary hymn of §III in which not merely Isra*el's sons* but *all families of the nations* are seen to be praising him for answering the prayer of *the poor man*, and not merely *all the earth* but even *peoples yet unborn*, and not merely those present and to come but (according to a possible interpretation of *all who go down to the dust*) even those already dead.

What is described in §I and §II has an uncanny resemblance to what happened to Jesus on Good Friday, the prophetic words of §III receive their most remarkable fulfilment in the events of Easter Sunday and beyond. The failure of Calvary was transformed into the glory of the resurrection, death gave way to life, and the Paschal Mystery became the central event of human history and of the Church's worship. This 'death song' of Jesus is not only a moving meditation on his sufferings, physical and mental, but also a word of comfort to those who face undeserved suffering, those who cry out to a God who does not seem to hear, those whose faith is tested almost to the limits of endurance.

## EVENING PRAYER
### PSALM 134 (135) Hymn

The whole community, both priests and Levites (*in the house of the Lord*) and laity (in the forecourts of the temple), are called to *praise the name of the Lord* and to *praise him*. As the parallelism indicates, that *name* is virtually synonymous with himself, and he has shown that he is *good* and *loving*, above all by his choice of Israel as the people of God (§I st 1-2).

But he is also supreme, the only one able to achieve *whatever he wills* anywhere in the universe. He is the Lord of nature (§I st 3-4),

Master of the *clouds, the rain* and *the wind*. He is the Lord of history too (§I st 5-6): in words almost identical with those we met in psalm 135(136) (see p164), the story of the exodus and the settlement in the Promised Land is once more remembered.

§II st 1 emphasizes the permanence of God's *name* (and therefore of his presence) in the midst of the assembly and of the concern he has shown *for his people*. This leads to a twofold conclusion: first, that *pagan idols* are powerless and absurd – and so are *their makers, and those who trust in them* §II, st 2-3) – and second, that the congregation (*the sons of Israel*), the priestly orders (*sons of Aaron and Levi*) and then everyone together (All *you who fear the Lord*) should *bless the Lord* (§II 4). What could be more appropriate than that *the Lord be blessed* from *Sion* where he has his dwelling (§II st5).

The Church, more than the chosen people of old, is called to reject idols of whatever kind and be united in praising and blessing the Creator and Redeemer. As we praise and bless him tonight, are we not doing so on behalf of the whole Church and also on behalf of the whole human race?

CANTICLE – **Revelation 15:3-4** (see Week 1 Friday, page 105)

# WEEK 3 SATURDAY

## OFFICE OF READINGS
### PSALM 106 (107) Thanksgiving

The scene is the temple. The priests call upon the assembly, *gathered* from all points of the compass, to *give thanks* to God for his goodness and enduring *love*. All have experienced how he, like a kinsman who steps in to champion his blood relations, has *redeemed* them (§I st 1-2).

The form the redemption has taken may have differed from one group to another, but a double refrain, repeated four times with minor modification (in §I st4 & 5, st7 & 8; in §II st2 & 3; st6 & 8), shows the links that bind all the groups together. First, *they cried to the Lord in their need and he rescued them from their distress*; and, second, they are invited to *thank the Lord for his love, for the wonders he does for men*.

Among those who have arrived on pilgrimage with grateful hearts are:

1. Those who were lost in *desert* wastes, unable to find *a* habitable *city* and tortured by a hunger and thirst which almost finished them; but then, in answer to their prayer, *the Lord* intervened – and they experienced his loving kindness (§1 st 3-5);

2. Those who were *prisoners*, dwelling *in darkness and in gloom, in misery and chains* – apparently because of their own misdeeds – but again *the Lord* in his love showed that even *gates of bronze* and *iron bars* are no obstacle to him (§I st 6-8);

3. Those who, having brought down upon themselves a near-fatal sickness through *their sins*, turned to God and felt his healing *word* which won them recovery (§II st 1-3);

4. Those who were caught in a terrible storm at sea, which showed forth the power of God but at the same time reduced them to the likeness of men in a drunken stupor; but at least they could pray and, in response, God *stilled the storm to a whisper* (§II st 4-8).

§III is a hymn, recapitulating the essence of what has gone before: our God is a God of surprises, a God whose power is so great that it can turn *streams into a desert* and vice versa, can give barrenness or fruitfulness, can destroy the *princes* of this world and bless and raise up *the needy*. Ultimately, those *who do wrong* will be *silenced*, while *the upright* will *rejoice*. *Whoever is wise* is invited to take to heart the message and to reflect prayerfully on *the love of the Lord*.

As we look back over our own lives, we too can recall situations in which we have experienced his redemption, in which we have known his steadfast love, in which impossible things have happened to us. The thought of God's goodness fills us with happiness, and if, as St James suggests, anyone who is happy should sing a psalm (5:13), then this is the psalm for you and me.

## MORNING PRAYER
**PSALM 118 (119) XIX Didactic** (see Week 1 Saturday, page 109)

### CANTICLE – Wisdom 9:1-6,9-11
By the time this book was written, towards the end of the Old Testament period, Wisdom had become personified as God's companion, as st 3 clearly shows. Having created all things, God in his *wisdom formed* man and woman as lords of creation, but with that honour go immense responsibilities. Human beings are *weak and short-lived*, with limited understanding; *without the wisdom that comes from you* they are *as nothing* (st 1-2).

# WEEK 3 SATURDAY

And so the ardent prayer that God will *send her forth from the throne of your glory* so that she may share in our *toil*, teach us *what is pleasing to you*, and *guide* and *guard us with her glory* (power) (st4).

The portrayal of Wisdom in this canticle hints at the mystery of God himself, as becomes clear in the light of the New Testament, where we are told that Jesus is the Word of God (the original Greek term being close in meaning to wisdom) and also that he is nearest to the Father's heart (John 1:1 & 18). In Catholic piety, Mary is called *Seat of Wisdom* because she brought into our world the Wisdom of God (Colossians 1:16) and is herself filled with his Spirit. As sons and daughters of God's *maidservant*, we might seek her intercession on this day (Saturday is Mary's day) that we in our turn may be filled with that Spirit of wisdom, without which we are *as nothing*.

**PSALM 116 (117) Hymn** (see Week 1 Saturday, page 110)

## PRAYER DURING THE DAY
### PSALM 118 (119) XVI Didactic

For the second time today we meet a section of Psalm 118 (119). Even those who *have done what is right and just* meet with adversity: the psalmist is in that position as enemies threaten. But he is God's *servant*, a point made three times in these lines, and so he begs the Lord to ensure his *well-being* and treat him *with love*. A trifle impatiently he reminds God that *it is time* for him *to act*. But despite everything, he boldly proclaims that whatever may be God's will he accepts as more precious *than finest gold*.

This is a courageous prayer. There are times when we too try to serve the Lord well and yet meet with disappointments. We can afford to be bold in our prayer, asking God to intervene on our behalf, making the point that we are his servants and even begging him to bestir himself. But having made our plea, may his will be done and may we go on striving to *rule* our *life by* his *precepts.*

**PSALM 33 (34) Thanksgiving** (see Week 1 Saturday, page 111)

## EVENING PRAYER I
### PSALM 121 (122) Hymn

One pilgrim voices the emotions of himself and his companions. They had set off with joy in their hearts, knowing that they were on the way to *God's house*, but *now*, he says addressing Jersualem itself, *our feet* are actually *standing within your gates*. We have arrived (st 1)!

Surveying the *compact city* and its sturdy walls, he recalls that it is here that *the tribes of the Lord*, which form one compact people, have their divine appointments, the annual festivals (Deuteronomy 16:16-17), and the Davidic kings their *thrones*. With a play on its name (*Jerusalem* = city of shalom), he calls upon his friends to pray for the *peace* of the city, a peace which will be found in every home and *reign* in every palace (st 2-4).

It is a prayer motivated both by *love of brethren and friends* (who all benefit from the peace flowing from Jerusalem) and love of the Temple itself (which is *the house of the Lord* and the source of blessings for the community) (st 5).

It is a similar love that moves us to pray for the Church (the new Sion), which is built upon the twelve apostles, symbolic of the twelve tribes of Israel. We beg that God will grant her his *shalom*, that fullness of *peace*, happiness and prosperity that will make her more and more perfectly the Sacrament of his presence in the world, until the day when the pilgrimage is over and the new Sion is born, resplendent in all her perfection.

### PSALM 129 (130) Lament

The opening words – *Out of the depths* – suit the start of the pilgrims' physical journey up to Jerusalem (this, like the preceeding psalm, is a psalm of ascent), but also that of the spiritual haul from despondency to confidence, from repentance to assurance of forgiveness, which is the theme of the psalm as a whole. The psalmist cries out to God to *hear* and *be attentive* to his plea, which is based on the fact that God does not *mark our guilt* – if he did, what chance would there be for any of us? Indeed, he might be descibed as the One with whom *is found forgiveness* (st 1-2).

Confidence begins to return at the thought of the Lord's promise (*his word*). As he waits for the Lord, the psalmist compares himself to a lonely *watchman*, who paces to and fro in the cold and darkness of the night, *waiting* for the first gleam of the new day – and the end of his shift. The psalmist's longing is even more intense than that of the watchman, and he, and all *Israel*, can *count on* the coming of the Lord as surely as the *watchman* can count on the arrival of the dawn (st 3).

So let the whole assembly share in the waiting, because the Lord has given abundant proof of his *mercy* and his readiness to free them from *all iniquity* (st 4).

It is unfortunate that in Catholic piety the *De Profundis* (or *Out of the depths*) is associated almost exclusively with prayer for the dead. Though a most appropriate prayer in that context, it has a much wider application. It can be used whenever we find ourselves waiting in the dark in anxious vigil for the intervention of the Lord. In the Middle Ages it was included among the seven Penitential Psalms as an appeal for deliverance from sin. It played a significant role in the conversion of John Wesley, founder of Methodism, when he heard it being sung in St Paul's and found his heart "strangely warmed". Perhaps our hearts will experience a similar awakening as we make this psalm our own in prayer.

CANTICLE – **Philippians 2:6-11** (see Week 1 Sunday, page 40)

# WEEK 4 SUNDAY

## OFFICE OF READINGS
**PSALM 23 (24) Didactic** (see Week 1 Tuesday, page 70)

### PSALM 65 (66) Thanksiving
Israel was never a major nation, but such was the people's appreciation of *the glory* (the power, the weightiness) of God, that they did not hesitate to summon *all the earth to render him glorious praise* and acknowledge the *tremendous* nature of his *deeds*; nor did they ever doubt that their bold universal appeal would be answered (§I st 1-2).

They believed that, despite his awesome greatness, God had revealed himself to them in his mighty *works* – the crossing of the *Sea* (of Reeds) and the river Jordan, the first and last of the founding events of their history as his people. But they also believed that he was revealing himself now, that he was present with his saving deeds in the temple worship, so that people could be invited to *come and see*. For Israel, such an experience is both a source of *joy* and also an assurance that *the* (pagan) *nations* are under God's watchful *eyes* (§I st 3-4). And so once more the cry goes up that all *the peoples* should *bless our God*, and once more the story of Israel's deliverance is rehearsed, a deliverance the more remarkable because the way of salvation had been a painful one, like the testing of *silver* or a going *through fire and through water*. Commentators disagree as to whether st 6 and 7 refer to the exodus or to some more recent event, because the exodus 'pattern' was repeated in Israel's history just as the paschal pattern is repeated in Christian history (§I st 5-8).

As we move to §II, a single voice is raised in thanksgiving. Perhaps it is that of an individual worshipper who has personal reasons for a public act of gratitude, or perhaps that of the king who speaks on behalf of the community. In either case, he has come to fulfil the *vows* made and present the lavish *offerings* promised in the hour of *distress*. If earlier the invitation was to *come and see*, now it is *come and hear*, for as the story of what happened is unfolded, *all who fear God* will be led to glorify him. They will see that a *prayer* has been answered, and that was because it rose from a pure heart – but only God could have preserved it from *evil*.

This is a psalm which can easily be interpreted in terms of the death and resurrection of our Lord. Each Sunday we *come and hear* (in the Liturgy of the Word), *come and see* (in the Liturgy of the Eucharist), the foundation events of our Christian faith. Our Mass is a community prayer of thanksgiving for all that has been done for us, above all through the paschal mystery; it is thanksgiving on behalf of the whole human race and thanksgiving for personal favours received. A prayerful approach to this psalm can be a preparation for or a prolongation of that Eucharist.


## MORNING PRAYER
**PSALM 117 (118) Thanksgiving** (see·Week 1 Sunday, page 48)

**CANTICLE – Daniel 3:52-57** (see Week 2 Sunday, page 117)

**PSALM 150 Hymn** (see Week 2 Sunday, page 117)


## PRAYER DURING THE DAY
**PSALM 22 (23) Confidence** (see Week 2 Sunday, page 118)

**PSALM 75 (76) Hymn** (see Week 2 Sunday, page 120)


## EVENING PRAYER II
**PSALM 109 (110) Hymn** (see Week 1 Sunday, page 52)

### PSALM 111 (112) Didactic

The accusation of being so heavenly-minded as to be no earthly good could not be levelled against most of the psalmists for, like their contemporaries, they did not believe in an after-life. But they certainly did believe in making the most of this life, and their *wisdom* writers – the author of this psalm was one – were eager to show how men and women should live as responsible human beings, aware of the beauties as well as the deficiencies of this world and able to pursue a worth-while course that would be pleasing to God and bring happiness to themselves and others.

So the psalm speaks of the blessedness (the blissful happiness) of *the man who* has a reverential fear of the Lord and *takes delight in all his commands*. Both he and his *children* are the beneficiaries (st 1).

If the promised prosperity seems excessively materialistic – *riches and wealth* – it is accompanied by sterling moral qualities: he is a man of *justice, a light* for other like-minded people. His goodness overflows in other ways too, for he is both *generous* and *merciful*, and always ready to lend without taking advantage of the borrower. The memory of his life will live (*he will be remembered*) *for ever* in his descendants (st 2-3).

There is of course no guarantee that he will be free of cares – it will not always be good news that he hears – but what is guaranteed is that he will be unwavering, fearless, with a heart that is *steadfast* because it *trusts in the Lord*. Just as he is *open-handed* in giving to *the poor*, so he will gather in a rich harvest of *glory*. Finally, in a manner typical of wisdom literature, his life is compared with that of *the wicked*, whose days are filled not with happiness but with anger and grinding of teeth, and whose memory does not last for ever but quickly *fades away* (st 4-6).

# WEEK 4 SUNDAY

We may not share the simplistic theology of the psalmist who sees virtue being rewarded and evil punished even in this life, but our prayer and especially our Sunday Eucharist can inspire us with a deep concern for this world. We are called to make it a better place for those who come after us by overcoming evil and promoting good in ourselves and in our community.

**CANTICLE – Revelation 19:1-2,5-7 or 1 Peter 2:21-24** (see Week 1 Sunday, page 56)

# WEEK 4 MONDAY

## OFFICE OF READINGS

**PSALM 72 (73) Didactic**

Men and women have always been haunted by the problem of evil, and God's people were no exception. It might be said (and some of the psalms do seem to say) that *God is good to those who are pure of heart*, but that is not the psalmist's experience. He has *come close to stumbling* in his faith precisely because he sees *how the wicked prosper* (§I st 1). They are *sound and sleek* and untouched by *sorrows*, and the inevitable consequence is that they sport *their pride like a necklace*, their *violence* like a status symbol, and *their hearts* and *minds* are for ever scheming evil. They are arrogant, scornful of heaven and superior to their fellow men and women on earth. Yet they draw the crowds, who *drink in all* they say. "*How can God know* (or care) what happens to the individual?" they cynically enquire. And the psalmist finds himself repeating the question as he ponders on the good fortune that seems to attend them (§I ).

With amazing candour, he confesses his doubts – he had begun to feel that his efforts had been a waste of time, earning him nothing but suffering *all day long*. Then, aware of his self-centredness, he acknowledges that such thoughts are a betrayal of the community of *faith* to which he belongs. But even that did not solve the problem; there was still a good deal of heart-searching to be done *until* the decisive moment when he entered the sanctuary of God (rather than *pierced the mysteries of God*). It was there through prayer not speculation that things fell into perspective: for all their success *the wicked* are only men of the moment, they are poised on a *slippery* slope, judgment will surely come to them and then they will be as substantial as last night's *dream* (§II).

And if that is a negative view of things, what follows is positive – and magnificent. Having admitted his stupidity – he had behaved *no better than a* senseless *beast* – he now makes a soaring declaration of faith:

amid all his troubles he was in fact *always in your presence*. God was actually *holding* him *by the right hand*. His trust was not so much his clinging to God but God's clinging to him. And this assures him that he will continue to enjoy the guidance of divine *counsel* and that ultimately *glory* awaits him. (For us, and perhaps for the psalmist too, these words set life's trials against the backcloth of eternal life). At the heart of his faith is his present union with God. That is everything; apart from that, he wants *nothing* in *heaven* or on *earth*. His whole being faints with *joy* at the thought that God is his *possession for ever* (§III st 1-3).

The wonderful psalm draws to a close, first, with a brief summary: *To be near God* spells life and *happiness*, to be cut off from him, death. This is followed with the promise to share his new-found joyous faith by proclaiming *all* God's *works* to whoever will listen *at the gates of the city* (§III st 4).

The problem of evil, and more particularly, the problem of innocent suffering, haunts us still. There are no simple answers, but, as we pray this psalm, we find in the struggles and triumphant faith of its anonymous author both reassurance and challenge. The challenge is to acknowledge that in every trial God is still *holding me by my right hand*, that ultimately he is all I want and that he is to be *my possession for ever*. Was it not such convictions that sustained the Innocent Sufferer, who himself entered into the problem of evil and made it his own by dying on a cross and so won for us eternal life?

## MORNING PRAYER
**PSALM 89 (90) Lament** (see Week 3 Thursday, page 205)

**CANTICLE – Isaiah 42:10-26**

In the verse immediately preceeding this canticle, having announced that previous predictions have been fulfilled, God foretells *fresh things*. At once the prophet calls for *a new song* to be sung *to the Lord*. It is to be heard *to the end of the earth*, and *the sea* with its roaring will join in the praise, so will *the coastlands* and *the desert* steppe land and all who dwell there, including the Kedarites in the Arabian peninsula and the Edomites in their capital, *Sela* (Petra, the rose city 'twice as old as time') (st 1-3).

Now the reason for the praise is given: *the Lord*, for so long silent, has at last bestirred himself (like a woman suddenly in labour) and reveals that he is a mighty warrior. Nothing can withstand his power, not even *mountains and rivers*, and he will *lead home* the people, who are as helpless as the blind, smoothing their path before them (st 4-7).

In their weary exile (the canticle was written during the Babylonian exile), the people of Israel want the whole world to join them in praise of God who, they have been assured, is coming to their rescue and will lead them back to their own land in a new exodus. As Christians we are filled with gratitude as we recall how our God, with the compassion of a mother (crying out *in travail*) and the unstoppable power of *a man of war*, has come to our rescue, has made it possible for us to be re-born. But in our prayer this morning we also look forward to the time when our Saviour will come again, when this world's time of exile will be over, when he will make all things new (Revelation 21:5) and when all redeemed humanity and all creation will bow in worship before him.

**PSALM 134 (135) Hymn** (see Week 3 Friday, page 216)

## PRAYER DURING THE DAY
### PSALM 118 (119) XVII Didactic

In Matthew's gospel the Law, like the Prophets, points towards Jesus. He fulfils the law not simply by keeping it but by being its fulfilment, just as he is the fulfilment of prophecies. Thus, it is he "who, in his own person, is our Law, our Way, our Life" (B Haring CSSR). If we pray this long psalm with that in mind it takes on fresh meaning.

It is indeed *wonderful* that Jesus should be my rule of life. *The unfolding* of all that he is and all that he stands for irradiates my life with *light* and helps me, *simple* though I may be, to understand how I should live. And so *I open my mouth* in ready anticipation of his guidance (st 1-2a).

What follows might be summarized: "You love me and I am among *your friends*; so lead me not into temptation and deliver me from evil". Then comes the plea that his *face* may *shine* on me with love and concern. Finally, perhaps with the thought of our Lord weeping over Jerusalem in mind, a confession of *tears* (perhaps a description of what I would like to be rather than of what is) shed over those, including ourselves, who fail to listen and respond to Jesus as we should (st 2b-4).

### PSALM 81 (82) Lament

In one sense it would be helpful to know who the psalmist is referring to in speaking of *the gods*. Are they are the so-called gods of the surrounding nations? Or the angels? Or the judges of Israel who act as God's representatives? However, in another sense, it does not much matter, for the central theme is abundantly clear: *God gives judgment*; and woe to those (whoever they are) who *favour the cause of the wicked*, those who fail to come to the aid of *the orphan, the afflicted and the needy, the weak and the poor* (st 1-2). However important they seem to be, in their ignorance they are simply groping *in the darkness* and undermining the divine *order* of things on which society depends. And so God has given his verdict: You may be *gods*, but you are doomed to destruction (st 3).

In response, the assembly pray for the universal coming of his rule (st 4). For us, a more appropriate response might be to remember:

i) that those who hold any position of responsibility (in the home, in the courts, in school) must answer to God for it;

ii) that Jesus himself has made clear what judgment awaits those who neglect the hungry, the thirsty, the sick, the stranger (Mtt 25).

### PSALM 119 (120) Lament

This is the first of the group of pilgrimage psalms, the psalms of ascent, often referred to in these pages. Its author says that he lives *in Meshech* and *among the tents of Kedar*; but since the former is in the far north, beyond the Black Sea, and the latter in the desert of Arabia, far to the south-east, he must be using these place-names metaphorically. Perhaps they are used to indicate that his fellow Israelites behave towards him like barbarians, and, given the notorious reputation of the nomadic Kedarites, firecely aggressive barbarians at that (st 3). Moreover, their lies and slanderous talk cause him deep hurt. He calls upon God for help, confident that he will answer (st 1). What will his enemies get for their arrow-like words and their fiercely burning lies? He answers his own question – the *arrows* and *red-hot coals* of divine judgment (st 2).

Finally, he reminds God once more that for *long enough* he has worked for *peace* among people whose only desire is for *war*. No wonder he longs to set out for Jerusalem, the city of Shalom (st 4).

# WEEK 4 MONDAY

When we find the world hating us (John 15:18), sometimes in return for our efforts to get rid of the weapons of war and promote peace, we shall find comfort in this psalm. Here we will be encouraged to turn to Jesus, to *ascend* to him in pilgrimage, for he "is our peace" (Ephesians 2:14), the one in whom we shall find not merely respite but everything that we seek.

## EVENING PRAYER

**PSALM 135 (136) Hymn** (see Week 2 Saturday, page 164)

**CANTICLE – Ephesians 1:3-10** (see Week 1 Monday, page 66)

# WEEK 4 TUESDAY

## OFFICE OF READINGS
### PSALM 101 (102) Lament

The opening words are similar to those used in the liturgy before a prayer of petition. They are emphasised here by the plea that the Lord will not *hide* his *face,* but rather *turn* his *ear and answer quickly.* The frightening descriptions which follow seem to refer to a terminal illness with its threat to life. There is burning fever, loss of appetite, sense of loneliness (the *pelican* was regarded as an unclean animal), insomnia and ridicule of enemies (see §I st 2-4a). It is more likely, however, that the reference is to the penitential rites which often accompanied laments – fasting, crying *with all my strength,* wearing of *ashes, tears* – and to the fiery ordeal which is endured by the psalmist and his friends. In either case, a climax is reached with the terrifying cry that the Lord in his *anger* has first *lifted me up* and then *thrown me down,* like a useless thing that has been case aside (§I st 4b).

Yet it is at this moment of apparent despair that the psalmist breaks into a hymn-like song of praise, recognising that for the Lord, who endures *from age to age, this is the time to have mercy.* Equally unexpectedly, the prayer now centres on *Sion* (perhaps another indication that the psalm was not primarily concerned with an individual's sickness but with a national tragedy). Its *very stones,* even its *dust* are loved by the people. A future is foreseen when *the prayers of the helpless* will be answered, when *the Lord shall build up Sion again,* when *the nations shall fear* his *name,* when he himself will *appear in all his glory* and *people yet unborn* will praise him, especially *in the heart of Jerusalem* (§II).

However, another surprise awaits us at the beginning of §III: once more the complaint is made that God, *whose days last from age to age,* has cut short the life of the psalmist (and the people?) *in mid course.* Yet if this is a moment of darkness, it soon passes and the psalm ends (§III st 2) in a serene and glorious acknowledgement of

God's creative activity, his eternity, his changelessness, with the obvious implication that here is a God on whom we can depend.

Perhaps the most shocking aspect of this fifth Penitential Psalm has always been its portrayal of God as one who picks up his people only to cast them down again like a play-thing. It is reminiscent of Gloucester's "As flies to wanton boys, are we to the gods" (*King Lear*) or even the scene in Christopher Nolan's *Under the Eye of the Clock* where the dumb paralysed lad is wheeled into church and, in his anger with God, makes a defiant, obscene gesture at the large crucifix on which Jesus hangs. The psalms teach us that there are times in life when we have to wrestle with God, to let out the suppressed anger, tell him what we think of him – as the psalmists do – even if what we have to say sounds like blasphemy. Perhaps only then will we discover that being honest does not separate us from God but brings us closer to him.

In the letter to the Hebrews (1:10-12) the final stanza of this psalm is addessed by God to his Son. In fact the whole psalm seems to have messianic overtones. §I refers to our Lord's desolation and suffering as he was picked up and thrown down in his passion, §II to his confidence in the coming of the kingdom and his own return *in all his glory* and §III both to his natural shrinking from death when he had reached only *mid-course* (a mere 30-odd years instead of three score years and ten) and the Father's affrmation of his Son's divine nature and promise that what he has accomplished will outlast *the earth and the heavens*.

## MORNING PRAYER
### PSALM 100 (101) Lament
High ideals were set for the king of Israel for he was seen as the embodiment of his people – God's people. It seems likely that this

psalm was used as a declaration of intent by a monarch at his enthronement or on the anniversary of his accession. It begins with words which refer to the covenant: God's *mercy* (loving kindness), and to the first duty of a sovereign towards his people: *justice* (the establishment of right order and peace). With the Lord's help (*O when* will he come?), he resolves to *walk in the way of perfection* (st 1).

This implies on the one hand that he will avoid anything *base* or lacking in integrity, he will silence slanderers and have no time for the arrogant (st 2-4); and on the other that he will care for *the faithful*, make friends of those who follow *the way of perfection* and allow only honest men to dwell in his *house* (as ministers?) (st 5-6). He will be zealous *morning by morning* in dispensing justice, to ensure that *all who do evil* will be rooted out of *the city of the Lord* (st 7).

It has been argued that the royal psalms were never intended simply for the king but for the whole people since they were all called to take responsibility for the true kingly duties. If in Christian tradition Jesus is the fulfilment of these royal psalms, we dare not forget that through baptism we have become a *royal priesthood* (1 Peter 2) with the corresponding responsibilities. It is a truth we need to reflect on *morning by morning*.

## CANTICLE – Daniel 3:3,4,6,11-18

We saw on page 47 how the third chapter of Daniel tells the story of three young men who, thrown into a white hot furnace for refusing to worship the idol set up by the king, strolled unscathed among the flames. As they walked free, they sang three prayers. This, the first of them, sung by Azariah, is in the form of a lament on behalf of the Jewish people. It begins however by blessing and praising the *God of our fathers* and acknowledging that all the disasters that have befallen the people are due to their sinfulness (st 1-2).

# WEEK 4 TUESDAY

Then comes the petition that, *for your name's sake*, you will not forget *your covenant* or, mindful of the great ancestors *Abraham, Isaac* and *Jacob, withdraw your mercy* or forget your promises (st 3-4). The people have been reduced to a sorry state, without leaders, without sacrifices or place in which to offer them. But what they do have is *a contrite heart*, and Azariah begs that in God's sight that may be worth countless animal sacrifices and that they may find strength to *wholly follow* their Lord.

He is so confident that his prayer will be answered that what began as an appeal (*may we...*) now becomes a declaration, a declaration that we might make our own as we pray the canticle this morning: throughout this day, Lord, *with all our hearts we* will *follow you, we* will *seek you face.*

## PSALM 143 (144) Hymn

Once again this morning we are invited to pray a royal psalm, a psalm which in its ideas and wording has affinities with several others in the psalter. The king praises God as his *rock*, as his tutor in the art of *war*, as his *love*, his sure defence, his *saviour*, the one who has placed him in charge of his people (st 1-2).

In comparison with this great God, any human being (even a king) is *merely a breath*, a fading *shadow*. That leads the king to ask God the obvious question: *what is man that you care for him?* Without waiting for an answer – the question may well have been rhetorical – he urges God to intervene, with all the usual accompaniments of his saving presence – *mountains* wreathed *in smoke*, the *flash* of *lightnings* and deadly *arrows*. His *alien foes* are described with equally stylized expresssions (st 3-4). The prayer ends with the confident assertion that he will *sing a new song*, accompanied by the *ten-stringed harp*, to celebrate the latest saving act of the Lord by which *David* (i.e. the current king) has been set *free*.

In Jesus, we see not only the son of *David*, the king who through his death and resurrection wins a victory over his enemies even more remarkable than that described in the psalm, but also the Son of God through whom God himself has reached down from heaven and saved us. In him and through him, every *mortal man* is seen to have a dignity and a worth which his human frailty belies. How could we not want to raise our voices in *a new song* to thank our God for his keeping us ever in mind and in his loving care?

## PRAYER DURING THE DAY
### PSALM 118 (119) XVIII Didactic

Our commitment to God is not a once-for-all affair: it is in need of constant, even daily, renewal, if we are to remain faithful. Like the psalmist, we need to remind ourselves of the rightness, and *justice* and *absolute truth* of God's *will*. It is a matter for *anger*, or at least for sadness, when people ignore it, because God's law has been *tried* and tested in the lives of believers throughout human history and has been proved deserving of our embrace (st 1-2).

We live in a world where we may be *despised* or suffer *anguish and distress* because we try to respect divine law (think, for example, of the opposition faced by those who defend human life from conception to death). That is not going to shake us: *your law is truth*, utterly reliable; it is *eternal*, never-changing, like yourself. By keeping it, we too shall enjoy eternal life (st 3-4).

### PSALM 87 (88) Lament

The psalms are not only for sunny days – or sunny personalities. The author of this psalm is one whose psychic darkness and distress are only too evident. There is no other psalm in the Psalter which can compare with it in its unremitting gloom. Yet, like Job, the psalmist continues to *call for help by day* and *by night* (§I st1), and *all day long* (§II st2), and again next *morning* (§II st 4).

Many of its phrases read like classic descriptions of depression. There is a heart *filled with evils*; the sense of being sucked into a dark *tomb*-like hole and *imprisoned* there; a feeling of guilt, of having aroused God's *anger*; isolation and loss of self-esteem. One feels valueless and unloved (*You have taken away my friends and made me hateful in their sight*). There is complete loss of interest in things that formerly brought pleasure, a blackness which seems to blot out all memory of past joys or future happiness (*my one companion is darkness*), and worst of all for the person of faith the fear that one is abandoned by God, who no longer hears or cares (*Lord, why do you hide your face?*).

Though the words of §II st2b-3 might suggest a terminal illness, they are also applicable to the person who reminds God that, so long as his/her depression (*the dark land of oblivion*) lasts, there is no way in which the divine *love* and *faithfulness* can be made known. Even that slight hope of persuading God to help, quickly disappears, the *flood* waters return and, unlike other laments, the prayer ends without the promise of a happy outcome: *my one companion is darkness.*

This is a psalm that can be used not only by those, and on behalf of those, who have to face what Churchill called his 'black dog' (of depression) and by those trying to cope with bereavement or a terminal illness, but also by those who hit a bad patch, when life loses its sparkle, when they feel alone, rejected, when they struggle with tempations against faith. Jesus himself experienced something of our darknesses and despairs in the course of his passion. And that thought encourages us to keep on praying – even in the dark; for the light will surely come.

# WEEK 4 TUESDAY

## EVENING PRAYER
### PSALM 136 (137) Lament

One of the most traumatic events in Israel's history was the exile in *Babylon*. The bitter anguish of the people is reflected in every line of this psalm. As they *sat* by Babylon's tree-lined water-ways, their thoughts had turned to their beloved *Sion*, now smashed to the ground by pagans, and the Temple which in its desecration left them fearful that God had abandoned them. Songs of lamentation came to an end and the harps, which had accompanied them, were *hung up* on nearby *poplars* as the exiles were cruelly taunted by their captors to sing *one of Sion's* (joyful) *songs* (st 1-2).

They had responded with indignation and defiance; it was inconceivable that they should *sing the song of the Lord* (a psalm in praise of God), and so expose him to ridicule, in this heathen land. In such circumstances, the psalmist (note the change from *we* to *I* which adds to the vividness of what follows) would rather his *right arm wither* than that he should strum the strings of his harp, he would rather his *tongue cleave* to his *mouth*, like the tongue of a person dying of thirst, than that one of Sion's sacred songs should pass his lips. In his loyalty, he will never forget *Jerusalem*; indeed it will remain for ever the first of *all my joys*.

Using a phrase from this psalm, scholars often speak of 'the songs of Sion', a cluster of beautiful hymns which share the common aim of praising and exalting the holy city of Jerusalem [Psalms 47(48), 75(76), 83(84), 86(87), 121(122) and 133 (134)]. It is viewed not simply as a city but as the dwelling place of God and the focus of his activity. And so even in the 'Good Friday' of the exile, the people show an incredible belief in an 'Easter Sunday' to come: neither the destruction nor the taunts of enemy guards can shake their loyalty.

# WEEK 4 TUESDAY

The Prayer of the Church wants us to think of the Church as we pray these psalms. There will be times when, either through the persecution of enemies or the sins and shortcomings of her own members, she looks anything but the Sacrament of God's salvation in the world and the place *par excellence* of our meeting with him. Yet we are called to remain loyal, knowing that a day will come when we shall enter a heavenly Jerusalem, a city where there will be no temple, not because it has been destroyed by enemies but because now God himself dwells with us and makes his home with us in a new world (Revelation 21) where we see him face to face.

### PSALM 137 (138) Thanksgiving

This psalm begins like a *Gloria* of gratitude, the psalmist wishing to *thank* God, seated 'in the highest' (*in the presence of the angels*), and to *bless* him and *adore* him *with all* his *heart*. It expresses gratitude for a petition that has been answered and for God's *faithfulness and love* which constantly exceed expectations (st 1-2).

The poet imagines *all earth's kings* (together with their people?) coming to worship the Lord when they learn *of the Lord's ways*, for though so *high* he *looks down* with compassion *on the lowly ones*, such as the psalmist himself, delivering them from every *affliction* and saving their lives. And so he pleads confidently that the *hand* which made him and which stretched out to his defence will never abandon him (st 3-5).

Each of us who prays this psalm has his or her own prayer of gratitude to make, a thanksgiving for favours received throughout the course of the day. And as we look back over our lives we realise that God's *faithfulness and love* have always attended us, often surpassing all our hopes. We think of his mighty *hands* which made us, which in his Son Jesus stretched out to save us, on whose palms our names have been carved (Isaiah 49:16), and we plead that in his eternal love they will never *discard* us, so that we may *thank* and *bless* and *adore* him *with all* our *heart* for ever.

**CANTICLE –** **Revelation 4:11;5:9,10,12.** (see Week 1 Tuesday, page 77)

# WEEK 4 WEDNESDAY

## OFFICE OF READINGS
### PSALM 102 (103) Hymn

Referring to Psalms 102(103) and 103(104), Derek Kidner writes: "In the galaxy of the Psalter these are twin stars of the first magnitude" (Psalms 73-150 – Inter-Varsity Press). This one rejoices in God as loving Saviour, as Psalm 103(104) rejoices in him as loving Creator (see page 115).

After a self-exhortation to *give thanks to the Lord* and *never forget all his blessings*, the poet turns to the blessing that is to be the main theme of his song – divine forgiveness, and the healing and renewal it brings. To be forgiven is to walk on air, to soar like a powerful eagle, as all *Israel's sons* had reason to know. In the exodus and the desert wanderings of his people, God showed how wonderfully he acts on behalf of *all who are oppressed* (§I).

Even when they had betrayed him by worship of the golden calf (Exodus 32:1-24), he still revealed himself as full of *compassion and love, slow to anger and rich in mercy* (Exodus 34:6). The glorious fact is that he does not nurse grievances, *he does not treat us according to our sins;* instead, he shows the most astonishing spirit of forgiveness. The poet illustrates God's graciousness by means of three fascinating word-pictures.

He seems to be searching for the greatest dimensions he can find, as he points, first, up to the sky high above and says: 'That's how enormous God's *love* is; it stretches from here to there!', then, after gazing to the horizons of the *east* and the *west*, he adds: 'And that's how *far* he casts away *our sins.*'

However, even those two child-like cameos fail to do justice to the incomparable love and mercy of God. And so the poet adds a third, taken this time from family life: God can be relied upon to forgive because he is *a father* and has a father's endless *compassion* for his wayward children. Moreover, he understands our fragility for *he knows of what we are made – dust* of the earth; and he knows how short-lived we are – as ephemeral as *the flower of the field* (§II).

The thought of human transience serves only to highlight the *everlasting* nature of *the love of the Lord* and of the covenant mercy he shows to those who are faithful to him. At this point the psalmist's thoughts turn to God's *kingdom* and he calls upon all the heavenly courtiers to join in the hymn of praise and gratitude. His faithful ones are to *give thanks*, so too are *all his works* (the whole of creation), and finally – as at the beginning of this wonderful song – he himself is to join in the majestic chorus of praise.

The thoughts behind this psalm bring us close to the threshold of the New Testament. It is through Jesus, the friend of sinners, that we learn that our God is indeed a Prodigal Father (Luke 15), in comparison with whom the best of earthly fathers are evil (Matthew 7:11), in whose sight the very hairs of our head are numbered (Matthew 10:30), whose care for the flowers of the field which so quickly fade is an assurance of his far greater care of us, his children (Matthew 6:28f). He is also king, but his is a kingdom in which there is more joy over a repentant sinner than over those who have no need (or think they have no need) of repentance (Luke 15:7). *My soul, give thanks to your Lord.*

## MORNING PRAYER
### PSALM 107 (108) Lament
Do not be surprised if you feel that there is a familiar ring to this psalm: it is in fact an amalgam of two others which we have already discussed: st 1-2 come from Psalm 56(57) and st 3-6 from Psalm 59(60) [see Week 1 Thursday, page 89 and Week 2 Friday, page 160]

# WEEK 4 WEDNESDAY

**CANTICLE – Isaiah 61:10-62:5**

The third major section of Isaiah – chapters 60-66 – was written after the exile at the end of the 6th century. It envisages a wonderful transformation of Sion as it emerges from the ashes of destruction. *The Lord* has arrayed it as magnificently *as a bride* or groom on their wedding day; the divine gardener has ensured that the plants of *righteousness and praise* will *spring up* there (st 1-2). After long years of silence, he raises his voice in what has been described as a song of 'splendid impatience', declaring that the vindication of the city will shine forth like *a burning torch* for all *the nations* and *all the kings* to see (st 3-4).It will become like *a royal diadem* in his hands. More than that, it will no longer be called *Forsaken* or *Desolate* but *My delight in her* and *Married*, because God himself will restore unfaithful Israel and take her once again as his *virgin* spouse (st 5-7).

This splendid song has an obvious application to the Church which St Paul decribes "as a chaste virgin (given) to this one husband" (Jesus) (2 Corinthians 11:2) and to the new Jerusalem, the Church in glory, which St John sees "as beautiful as a bride all dressed for her husband" (Revelation 21:2). However, it becomes a still more moving prayer when it is applied to the individual Christian: it is I who *rejoice* and *exult* because the Lord *delights* in me and has decked and adorned me *with the garments of salvation*. The love of *bridegroom* for *bride* is but a shadow of his love for me.

**PSALM 145 (146) Hymn**

Like the author of Psalm 102(103), the author of this psalm begins by summoning his own *soul*, his inmost being, to *prayer*. The summons is followed by a promise: he means to offer God the *music* of his *praise all* the *days* of his life (st 1).

The remainder of the psalm is didactic in tone, contrasting the impermanence and unreliability of human beings with the power and the faithfulness and the compassion of God. It is folly, the poet implies, to trust even the *princes* of this world – the powerful, the successful, the influential. Like the rest of humanity, they received from God the *breath* of life and when that breath is withdrawn they return to the native *clay* from which they came (Genesis 2:7). But it is wisdom, and happiness, to hope in and *be helped by* the God of Israel, for he is the mighty Maker of *heaven and earth* and *seas* (st 3). He is also the utterly faithful One and his limitless loving-kindness reaches out to all *who are oppressed: the hungry, prisoners, the blind, the stranger, the widow and orphan, and all who are bowed down* with affliction. *The just* need have no fear, they are beloved of God; not so *the wicked*, God will see that their *path*, their way of behaviour, will get them no where (st 4-6a).

And so this psalm that began with a personal resolution to praise God, now broadens out as the poet ponders on the eternal *reign* of God which will be recognised in his city, Sion, *from age to age* (st 6b).

In the synagogue of his home town, Jesus revealed his identity by claiming that the prophecy of Isaiah 61:1-2 "was being fulfilled today even as you listen" (Luke 4:22). He might equally well have pointed to the fulfilment of this morning's psalm: which clearly shows a preferential option for the poor. We are invited to share his concern so that the people of today may learn that Jesus is at work in our world.

## PRAYER DURING THE DAY
**PSALM 118 (119)XIX Didactic (see Week 1 Saturday, page 109)**

**PSALM 93 (94) Lament**
It is perhaps a sign of the sanitized nature of modern religion that many of us are offended by a prayer which begins with an appeal to

the Lord, which twice addresses him as *avenging God*. The psalmists do not share our sensitivity: they see God as the final court of appeal and, faced with the apparent *triumph* of wickedness, do not hesitate to call upon him to fulfil his awesome task. When *evil-doers* are able to *bluster and boast* with impunity, when they *crush your people*, especially the weak and defenceless, it is time for you to act (§I st 1-3)! Their mocking taunt of God – that he *does not see*, that he *pays no heed* – is an indication of their crass stupidity: as though the maker of *the ear* could himself be deaf or the maker of *the eye* blind; as though the controller of *nations* could be no match for current enemies, or the source of all human *knowledge* himself be ignorant. The simple fact is that God has the full measure of his human creatures and their *thoughts*: they are no more substantial than *a breath* (§I st 4-5).

The psalmist now switches attention from the folly of the wicked, and the disaster that awaits them, to the blessedness (*Happy the man...*) and inner *peace* of those who allow themselves to be instructed by the Lord. Though *his people* may be crushed (see §I st 3), he *will not abandon* them and will prove himself to be a just judge (§II 1-3). The psalmist offers a personal testimony: there is only one *who will stand up for me* and *defend me* and that is the Lord, who has no time for the crooked *judges of this world*. When tested to the point where *I think 'I have lost my foothold'*, I become aware of his loving *mercy and consolation* sustaining me (§II 4– 5).

After acknowledging God as *rock* and *stronghold*, the psalmist is confident that an answer will be given to the appeal made at the outset; and so the emphatic, no-nonsense conclusion: *our God will destroy* the enemy (§II 6).

The upheavals in Eastern Europe after decades of oppression remind us that there are still innumerable people who long for justice to be done, wrongs to be righted, God's cause to prevail. We ought to find no difficulty in praying the *How long?* of this psalm on their behalf or of pleading that God will finally sort out the boastful blusterers who oppress the weak and defenceless, who attempt to *crush your people.*

## EVENING PRAYER
### PSALM 138 (139) Didactic

In the language not of philosophy but of poetry – and splendid poetry at that – the psalmist sings of God's incredible intimacy with us, his creatures. It is a three-fold intimacy which makes us like an open book before him.

First of all, there is the intimacy of knowledge; not only an all-embracing knowledge (*Behind and before you besiege me*), alive to whether I rest or rise, *walk or lie down*, but a piercing, searching knowledge that reaches down to the depth of my being, able to *discern my purpose from afar* and my thoughts *Before ever a word is on my tongue.* Such knowledge is bewildering, *too wonderful* for my comprehension – even a little frightening (§I st 1-2).

Secondly, there is the intimacy of presence, so that even if I wanted to get away from him I could never shake him off, neither in *the heavens* above, nor in the depths of *the grave. If I were to fly with the dawn* (viewed as a winged creature) to the *furthest* horizon, I should find that I was still in *your right hand.* And if I were to try to lose myself in *the darkness*, well, you have no need of a light to see by. (§I st 3-5)

Thirdly, the intimacy of power: God's knowledge and his presence stem from the fact that he is my creator: he *knit me together in my mother's womb.* This stunning thought leads the psalmist to cry out in gratitude *for the wonder of my being*, and for all God's wondrous *creation* (or, following another possible and well-known translation, an exclamation of awe: "I am fearfully and wonderfully made"). Though the process of my being *fashioned and moulded* took place *in secret* (*the depths of the earth* may refer to the hiddeness of the womb or to the Earth-Mother from whom, according to an ancient popular belief, all human beings come), there is nothing about me – *body* or *soul* – which was a secret from you. And just as you knew me from the beginning of my days in the womb, so even then my whole life's story was written *in your book* (the psalmist's way of speaking of God's providence) (§II 1-3).

To fathom the vastness and complexity of God's knowledge, I would need to be *eternal like you*; and so, with the psalmist, I turn to him in prayer, begging him to *search and test me* through and through, and ensure that I take *the path* that leads to *life eternal* (§II 4-5).

The 'All-seeing Eye of God' has sometimes been used as a threat, an uncomfortable reminder that we are being watched and that the Lord might pounce at any moment – and what would happen to us then? Perhaps, at the beginning of this song, the psalmist experiences similar misgivings, but, in the end, happily submits to the searching and testing of God. With much better reason, we should be confident that, if God's eye is all-seeing, the gaze he fixes upon us is like that of parents who look long and lovingly upon their child. They may find it hard to let their little one out of their sight, lest any harm befall. God dare not allow us out of his sight, for that would mean oblivion for us. Jesus tells of a God who counts the hairs of our head (Matthew 10:30) and who, in his boundless love, makes the best of earthly parents look evil (Matthew 7:11). It is because he loves us so dearly, because we are precious in his sight, because within him we live and move and have our being that our all-knowing, all-present, creator God draws close to us in intimacy.

**CANTICLE – Colossians 1:12-20** (Week 1 Wednesday, page 85)

# WEEK 4 THURSDAY

## OFFICE OF READINGS
**PSALM 43 (44) Lament** (see Week 2 Thursday, page 148)

## MORNING PRAYER
### PSALM 142 (143) Lament

An English woman, imprisoned in Indonesia for thirteen months, described on radio the conditions of her imprisonment. She had seen many of her companions tortured and lived in a state of constant fear. Though not particularly religious, she had felt the need to pray, and the prayer that had brought her greatest consolation was a psalm she had learned by heart as a child. It was the psalm which the Church invites us to pray this morning.

I can hear that woman appealing to God – as one who is *faithful* and *just* – to *listen*, to *turn his ear*, to *give answer*; and not to judge her harshly for, like the rest of humanity, she cannot stand on her own merits (st 1). In frightening terms, she cries out in *the darkness* and desolation of her cell. She feels *crushed*, isolated, forgotten by the outside world, like one who is *dead*. A numbness settles upon her *heart* (st 2). She tries to re-live happier days and, more importantly, to reflect on God's mighty deeds of the past. Her outstretched *hands*, her thirsting *soul* are a plea for his help (st 3). She begs him not to play games with her any longer by hiding his *face*, for she feels near to death, but to *make haste and answer* (st 4).

Hope begins to return: she prays that *the morning* will really be a new day for her, that God will give her a sign of his *love*. She begs too that in difficult situations (when facing interrogation at the hands of her *enemies*, for example), he will make known to her *the way* she *should walk* and *teach* her *to do* his *will*. Aware of her own weakness and liability to stumble, she asks that God's *good spirit* may be her guide *in ways that are smooth.* She is confident that for his own *name's sake* and in accordance with his faithfulness, he will respond to her appeal(st 5-7).

St Paul bids us weep with those who weep, mourn with those who mourn (Romans 12:15). Here is a psalm (the last of the Penitential Psalms) which gives us the opportunity to unite ourselves with the 'Good Friday people' of this world, all those men and women who prepare to face yet another day of imprisonment, isolation, even torture.

## CANTICLE – Isaiah 66:10-14a
On their return from exile, God's people are assured that the new *Jerusalem* will be like a mother and they like children nursed at her breast. But as the canticle proceeds it becomes clear (note the change from third to first person) that the mothering of the city is but a reflection of his own.

In her *Autobiography* St Therese of Lisiuex tells of the joy this text brought to her: "Never were words so touching; never was such music to rejoice the heart" – for it confirmed her in her *Little Way*: she could afford to go to the Lord as a child, for he would lift her up in his arms. The same heartening news awaits us as we set out on this new day.

## PSALM 146 (147A) Hymn
God has a maternal concern for us, as the canticle has just suggested. However, we approach him not only to seek his help but also to *praise* him because of his goodness and love and, more fundamentally, because that is his *due* (st 1).

He is to be praised, as the psalmist says, for his saving work on behalf of his exiled people and *the broken-hearted.* His ability to marshall and name, and so command, each one of the innumerable *stars* in the sky is evidence of his *almighty* power and his fathomless wisdom. So too is his raising of *the lowly* and humbling of *the wicked* (st 2-3a).

All this calls for *psalms* of thanksgiving (we have already noted how closely linked are praise and gratitude), especially in view of the way he sends the winter *rain* to transform the barren *mountains* with *grass* and *plants* and thereby meet *man's needs*. And he cares not only for human beings but also for *the beasts*; he even responds to the croaking of the *young ravens*. Yet this mighty God looks for no benefit from the prowess of *horses* or the self-esteem of warriors, but finds his humble *delight* in those who reverence him and *wait* patiently for his unfailing *love* (st 3a-4).

This psalm presents a glimpse of a God who *brings back* and *heals* and *binds up all* our *wounds*, who is ruler of the starry heavens and provider for humans and beasts alike, a God who is more than mighty enough to protect the small people and destroy *the powerful ones,* and yet who seeks nothing more than the reverence and trust of his friends. This is indeed a God worthy of our praise.

## PRAYER DURING THE DAY
### PSALM 118 (119) XX Didactic

Even, perhaps especially, for one who remembers *your law*, life is seldom easy. The psalmist calls out for help in his *affliction*, confident that God's *mercies* are limitless for those who observe *your commands* (st 1-2). And so he has not much time for those who sneer at *your promise* – indeed, to speak frankly, he regards them *with disgust* – and for his own part has always striven to give unswerving loyalty to the divine *will* (st 3).

# WEEK 4 THURSDAY

We may feel reluctant to speak as confidently as the poet of our responsiveness to God – and still more reluctant to join him in passing premature judgment on *the faithless* – but at least we are in total agreement with him that God's *word* is grounded in utter *truth*, his *decrees* and promises are of *eternal* value (st 4). And so we renew our resolve to be faithful, with God's help, this day.

## PSALM 127 (128) Didactic

On a flight to the Holy Land a group of rabbis began to chant the psalms of ascent the moment their plane crossed the frontiers of Israel. Albeit in more comfortable circumstances, they were doing what their ancestors had done over the centuries as they made their way *up* to Jerusalem. Among the psalms they sang were two which appear in today's Prayer During the Day.

Psalm 127(128), in a manner reminiscent of Psalm 118(119), declares that true happiness is the reward of those who reverence *the Lord* and *walk in his ways*. Such conduct is rewarded by food for the table, fruit from the womb and fellowship with a loving wife (*fruitful vine* may suggest sexual attractiveness as well as fertility, just as *shoots of the olive* may call to mind the care and tending that goes into the rearing of a family) (st 1-2).

However, the worshipper is not only the head of a family but also the member of a people, and so his thoughts turn to the city, which he is now approaching, and to the whole nation, to which he belongs, as he prays first for *a happy Jerusalem* and then for *peace* in *Israel* (st 3-4).

This attractive little psalm, so far removed from us in time and circumstances, still carries an important lesson. We are not isolated individuals but part of a larger whole: called to be holy not merely as individuals but as a people united by God. And so, whether we are married or single, priests or members of a religious congregation, our service of the Lord and *the labour of our hands* have repercussions for the Church and for the whole of humanity.

### PSALM 128 (129) Confidence

The assembled pilgrims are called upon, perhaps by a priest, to sing *Israel's song*. It is a song of sufferings endured since her history began (*from my youth* in Egypt), terrible sufferings leaving scars and weals that might be likened to the *long furrows* left in the fields by *ploughmen*. But more than the story of Israel's sufferings, it is the story of the Lord's faithfulness and his destruction of *the wicked* (st 1-2).

Israel has her enemies still and the psalmist prays that they too may be *shamed and routed*; that they may prove as short-lived as the wild grass seeds which fall upon the flat Palestinian roofs, where they sprout in the thin layer of mud and quickly wither for lack of depth. And so Israel's enemies will be like a *reaper* who has no harvest to *fill his arms* or make *his sheaves*, and does not receive the usual *blessing* given to harvesters by passers-by nor make the customary response (st 3-4).

This psalm reminds us of the terrible ordeals endured and extraordinary resilience shown by Israel throughout her history and should lead us to embrace our Jewish brothers and sisters in our prayers. But it will also put us in mind of that Servant of the Lord who offered his back to those who smote him (Isaiah 50:6), asked pardon for those who persecuted him (Luke 23:34) and by his stripes won our healing (Isaiah 53:5).

# WEEK 4 THURSDAY

## EVENING PRAYER

**PSALM 143 (144) Lament**

For §I and §II, st 1 see Week 4 Tuesday, page 237. The remainder of the psalm elaborates on the fearsome *foes* who were defeated in the king's victory (§II st 1-2) and then pleads that the God who secured that victory will bless family, fields and flocks, and ensure lasting peace. The psalmist longs to see *our sons* flourishing like sturdy *saplings*; *our daughters* as elegant as the *columns* of *a palace; our barns filled with crops; our herds* of sheep and cattle fertile; and, perhaps above all, no more ruins, *no* more *exile* and *no sound of weeping in our streets.* If the psalmist seems to be unduly concerned with the material *blessings* hoped for from God, the final line of the psalm makes it clear that the blessing to be prized above all others is that which comes from relationship with God, the happiness experienced by *the people whose God is the Lord.*

We who honour a God-made-Man, a God who became fully involved in our world, should have no fear of praying for our family, our material needs and for peace. Indeed, our Lord has told us that we should ask, and keep on asking, if we wish to receive (Luke 11:9-13).

**CANTICLE – Revelation 11:17-18;12:10b-12a** (see Week 1 Thursday, page 96)

# WEEK 4 FRIDAY

## OFFICE OF READINGS
**PSALM 54 (55) Lament** (see Week 2 Wednesday, page 144)

*During Advent and Christmastide the following psalm is used:*
**PSALM 77 (78) Didactic**
Today we embark upon one of the longest psalms in the psalter; in fact the only one that can outdo it in length is the famous Psalm 118(119). Its opening stanza sets the scene. The psalm is addressed to *my people*, presumably by an inspired leader (a priest, perhaps, or a prophet) at one of the great festivals. Its purpose is to *reveal to them hidden lessons from the past*, in other words to make plain the pattern of their national history; and it is being presented in the form of *a parable*, drawing lessons for the future by a comparison with events of an earlier age. (Jesus himself describes his own teaching in parables as a fulfilment of this stanza: Matthew 13:35). It is God's *command* that these events, made known to us by *our fathers*, be passed on to *the next generation*, and they in their turn *tell their sons*.

What history reveals is, on the one hand, the remarkable goodness and faithfulness of God (*the marvellous deeds he has done, the law he established*) and, on the other, the wickedness and unfaithfulness of his people (*a defiant and rebellious race ... whose heart was fickle...whose spirit was unfaithful*) (§I st 2-6).

An illustration of this is to be found in *the sons of Ephraim*. Members of the principal of the three northern tribes which broke away from the rest of Israel, they had become a symbol of unfaithfulness. The reference to their fleeing in battle may be not a factual but rather a poetical way (remember, the psalms *are* poetry) of pointing to the shame which they brought upon God's people by their infidelity. And the source of their infidelity, the psalm insists, is their forgetfulness of *the things he* (the Lord) *had done*, their failure to learn from history.

# WEEK 4 FRIDAY

That history began with *the wonders...in Egypt* (*Zoan* is Tanis, an important city in the north of the Nile delta), God's dividing of *the sea* (picturesquely described as making *the waters stand up like a wall*), his leading them *by day...with a cloud* and *by night with ...fire*, his providing them with water from *rocks in the desert* (§I st 7-10).

*Yet still*, unbelieveably, the very people who had witnessed such wonders *sinned against* him, *defied* him, *put him to the test, even spoke against him* in the course of their desert wanderings, until *the Lord was angry* with them for their lack of *faith* and their failure *to trust in his help.* Even then he was prepared to answer their prayers for food, sending them *bread from heaven* (food fit for *angels*). But still they remained unrepentant and so he *struck down the flower of Israel* (§II).

What has just been recounted is a summary of their history: God is good to them but they have *no faith in his wonders, they go on sinning*; he punishes them, then they *remember* and begin to *seek him*; but their repentance is superficial, *mere flattery.* At this point, when we might have expected God to punish them even more terribly than before, we are suddenly and wonderfully reminded of his *compassion*, of the way *he held back his anger.* His people may forget, but he remembers; in particular, he remembers that they are *only men* (and women), whose lives are as impermanent as *a breath* (§III).

It would be naive to pray this psalm and imagine that it had nothing to teach us. We too have short memories, though God has done even greater *wonders for us*, feeding us in the Eucharist with *bread from heaven.* We too, as individuals and as Church, have brought trouble upon ourselves through our sins; and our repentance all too often is the stuff of which crocodile tears are made. Like those who have prayed this psalm before us, we too find our only hope in *the compassion* of our gracious God.

# WEEK 4 FRIDAY

## MORNING PRAYER
**PSALM 50 (51) Lament** (see Week 1 Friday, page 98)

### CANTICLE – Tobit 13:8-11, 13-15
Though *historically* the book of Tobit is somewhat bewildering, *theologically* it is of a piece with the 'Songs of Sion' which we have met through the weeks of Prayer of the Church. Tobit looks forward to a day when *Jerusalem, the holy city*, will be restored, its Temple rebuilt and, magnet-like, will draw towards it *many nations* – and therefore Gentiles as well as Jews. *Generations* to come who worship God there, will be richly blessed and enjoy *peace*.

In fact the vision never materialized in Old Testament times, but Tobit was one of those who kept it alive until its fulfilment in Jesus Christ and his Church. But even in the Church there is only partial fulfilment, an 'already' and a 'not yet'. She is still not all we should like her to be. Perhaps there are times when we share the strong sentiments of Dorothy Day, who wrote: "As to the Church, where else shall we go, except to the Bride of Christ, one flesh with Christ? Though she is a harlot at times, she is our Mother." But in her we also have a sign of what is to be: the final Holy City, the Bride "without spot or wrinkle" (Ephesians 5:27), as she will be in heaven. Only then will the promises of prophets, and the hopes of Christian people, finally be realized.

**PSALM 147 Lament** (see Week 2 Friday, page 158)


## PRAYER DURING THE DAY
**PSALM 118 (119) XXI Didactic**
These days we are perhaps more conscious than in times past of the dangers of legalism, but the psalmist has not fallen foul of those

dangers. For him, the *law* (the *Torah*) includes the way in which God has revealed himself though Israel's history and the convenant of love which he has made with his people. The *commands* and the *precepts*, which are also part of that *Torah*, are the inevitable outcome of God's special relationship; we cannot respond to another's love (above all the unconditioned love of God) without its affecting the way we live our lives. And so when the psalmist says that, in face of the Torah, his *delight* is like that of *one who finds a treasure* (in the ancient world a farmer would sometimes find in his field a jar of coins or jewels which had been hidden for safekeeping by a previous householder), or that *your law is my love*, it is clear that his interest is not simply in a text but in a Person. Indeed, he says that he prays to that Person *seven times a day*, which probably means that he prayed constantly.

"Keep my commandments," Jesus tells his friends,"...just as I have kept my Father's commandments" (John 15:10). The heart of Jesus' life, and therefore the heart of the Gospel, is the Father. Jesus had come into the world for no other purpose than to do his will. Of us he asks nothing more, but that is already everything.

### PSALM 132 (133) Didactic

At a festal gathering of the people of Israel in Jerusalem – this is another of the songs of ascent – the psalmist is overjoyed at the *unity* that exists among *brothers* and brings to his poet's mind two vivid pictures (st 1).

The first is of an anointing ceremony, such as that of *Aaron* the high priest, when *precious oil*, like an outpouring of divine blessings, is poured lavishly, Middle-Eastern style, over *the head* so that it cascades down to *the beard* and then to *the collar* of the priestly *robes* (st 2).

The second is of the divine gift of the morning *dew*. It falls refreshingly upon mighty *Mount Hermon*, reknowned for its heavy dew, but also descends upon *the heights* of tiny mount *Sion* (st 3a).

Where the Lord grants the *blessing* of unity, it brings with it the promise of happy lives for succeeding generations – *for ever* (st 3b).

St Augustine may have exaggerated when he remarked that this poem inspired monastic foundations; but it certainly should encourage all who are engaged in work for the cause of unity – whether in the family, or among Christians, or among the nations. Is there perhaps a veiled reminder that unity, at every level, is not only gift coming down from above "from the Father of all light" (James 1:17), like the *dew*, but also fruit of the work of human labour, like *precious oil*? Unity is a combined achievement of divine generosity and human striving.

### PSALM 139 (140) Lament

In sharp contrast to the previous psalm, this one speaks of those who, far from living like brothers, are *violent, plan evil in their hearts*, promote *strife* and have tongues as poisonous of those of *an adder* (st 1).

The worshipper pleads for the Lord's help against such vicious people as they plot and *plan* their insidious work (st 2). He advances reasons for God's intervention. First, his own personal relationship with *the Lord*: he is *my God*; second, his past experience of God as *my mighty help*; and third the fact that *the wicked* must not be allowed to *succeed*. The psalm ends with the confident assertion that *the Lord*, the perfect Judge, will ensure *justice for the needy*, while *the just*, his friends, will *praise* his *name* (st 3-4).

# WEEK 4 FRIDAY

The situation depicted in this psalm – the apparent success of evil, the deliberate planning of wickedness, the slander, the vicious speech – is by no means unknown today, even if it usually appears in milder forms; and an essential part of the response is also the same: a resort to God in prayer. He is on the side of *the needy* (all those who try to uphold his cause against heavy odds) and, in a way that even the psalmist could not have understood, his friends will *live in his presence, both now and for ever.*

## EVENING PRAYER
**PSALM 144 (145) Hymn** (see Week 3 Sunday, page 175)

**CANTICLE – Revelation 15:3-4** (see Week 1 Friday, page 105)

# WEEK 4 SATURDAY

## OFFICE OF READINGS
**PSALM 49 (50) Didactic** (Week 3 Monday, page 181)

*During Advent and Christmastide the following psalm is used:*
**PSALM 77 (78) Didactic**

The great psalm which we began yesterday continues today by recalling the *pain* caused to the Lord by the people's waywardness. In particular, by their forgetfulness of *the day* of the exodus when he had shown his saving power in most remarkable fashion (§IV st 1-2). Some of the most spectacular *miracles* and *wonders* of that day, culminating in the death of *the first born in Egypt*, are now rehearsed (§IV st 3-7). And the preacher skilfully contrasts the Lord's dealings with the Egyptians (believed to be the descendants of *Ham*) on whom he *turned the heat of his anger*, with his care of *his people* whom he *guided as his flock, led safely* through *sea* and *desert* until the *holy land* (of Palestine) was reached, the occupying *nations* driven out and *Israel's tribes* duly settled there (§V, 1-3).

But *still* they failed to respond, they proved themselves *as faithless* as those who had gone before them, as unreliable as *a bow* which fails *the archer* on the day of battle. They roused him to jealousy by joining in the obscene rites of Canaanite pagan worship (§V, 4-5). And so his *fury* was now turned against his own people: he *rejected* them, *forsook Shiloh* (the town in Ephraim which had been his chief sanctuary in Israel), allowing *the ark*, which was the seat of his presence there, to be taken *into captivity* by the Philistines and his people to be *devoured* by the ravages of *war* (§V st 6-8).

And yet things are not what they seem to be. God has not forgotten his people, and now he arises as though just awakened *from sleep* or, more daringly still, as though still suffering from a hang-over. *His foes* were routed and, with sovereign freedom, *he chose the tribe of Judah* and *the hill of Sion* in the south, to replace *the tribe of Ephraim* (son of Joseph) and *the tent of Joseph* in the north; there he (not king Solomon) built *his shrine*, the Temple, just as he had made *the heavens* and *the earth*. Similarly, *he chose David*, a shepherd boy, to become *shepherd of his people*. And, in a somewhat idealized picture, king David is portrayed as fulfilling his royal task with blameless heart (§VI).

There is a sense of an unfinished story as we reach the end of this psalm. But that is as it should be, for the psalmist wants future generations to learn and remember the lesson of history. It is significant that when Jesus left to us his most precious gift of the Eucharist, he bade us:"Do this in memory of me". The Eucharist is both a recalling and a making-present of the past, a means of ensuring that we remember the whole reconciling work of Jesus by his death and resurrection. Similarly, the praying of the Prayer of the Church, which is a preparation for and a continuation of the Mass, is yet another way in which we keep alive the memory of all the Lord has done for us.

## MORNING PRAYER
PSALM 91 (92) Didactic (see Week 2 Saturday, page 167)

### CANTICLE – Ezekiel 36:24-28
This, the last of the Old Testament canticles in the Prayer of the Church, stands as a fitting finale to all that has gone before. The prophet in exile looks to a future when God will *gather* his people *from all the countries* and *cleanse* them from their *uncleannesses* and all their *idols*, replacing their *heart of stone* with a *heart of flesh*. He will fill them with his *spirit*, so that they will have the inner power to live in accordance with his *statutes* and *ordinances*. Then, at last, *you shall be my people and I will be your God.*

# WEEK 4 SATURDAY

It might be argued that this wonderful prophecy was never fulfilled; but a New Testament prophet assures us that it is to be fulfilled in a way that surpasses all that Ezekiel could ever have hoped for (Revelation 21:3). Already, in the sacraments, we have been washed in *clean water*, freed from the *idols* which draw us into sin, filled with the Holy Spirit, empowered to respond to God. So long as we remain a people in exile, the idols still beckon, the uncleaness can quickly creep back, our hearts all too easily become hardened and unresponsive. And so we need to cry out to God to continue his saving work within us. At the same time, in a spirit of hope, we look forward to the end, to that day when all God's people will be safely gathered together in their *own land*, the home of their Father, and *They shall be his people, and he will be their God.*

**PSALM 8 Hymn** (see Week 2 Saturday, page 169)


## PRAYER DURING THE DAY
**PSALM 118 (119) XXII Didactic**
Throughout the four-week cycle of the Prayer of the Church, scarcely a day has gone by without a section of this great psalm on our lips. Today, as we reach its final section, we must surely admire its passionate concern for God and his law, as well as the unflagging energy of its young author.

He ends his massive poem still praying to remain faithful to God's *commands* but also to *proclaim your praise* and to receive *your saving help* (st 1-3). If at times his concern with the law has led us to wonder whether he might not have the makings of a Pharisee, our minds should be set at rest when we find that his last words are an admission of his own shortcomings: he is *lost like a sheep* and needs the Divine Shepherd to *seek* him and bring him safely home (st 4).

# WEEK 4 SATURDAY

One of the outstanding spiritual writers of our times, the late Father Thomas Merton, wrote that Psalm 118 (119) "is a litany of praises extolling the peace that is found in the will of God. This psalm, which might at first seem dull and juridical... turns out, on long acquaintance, to be one of the most contemplative of all."

**PSALM 44 (45) Hymn** (see Week 2 Monday, page 129)

# NIGHT PRAYER

## AFTER EVENING PRAYER I OF SUNDAYS AND SOLEMNITIES

### PSALM 4 Confidence

As another day draws to its close, the psalmist makes an act of trust in God. Past experience (*from anguish you released me*) shows that *the Lord hears me whenever I call him* and brings an assurance that he will once again *have mercy* and respond to prayer. He sees the startling contrast between his own happy lot and that of those whose *hearts* are *closed* to God but open to the pursuit of *what is futile and false*. If only they would reverence God, avoid *sin*, quitely reflect, pursue *justice* and have *trust in the Lord.* (st 1-4)

Everyone is seeking *happiness*, but the psalmist knows where it is to be found; and so he begs God to let his *face*, radiant with love, *shine on us*. He meditates on the *greater joy* that God has given him – more to be prized than material things, such as an *abundance of corn and new wine*, the fruits of the two Palestinian harvests, grain and grape – which is a conscience at *peace* and the ability to drop off to *sleep*, confident that you are in the keeping of One who spells perfect *safety* (st 5-7).

In addition to the references to bed-time (see st 4 & 7), there is much in this psalm which makes it an ideal Night Prayer. It is good to look back on the day that has gone, thankful to God for goodness shown and *favours* granted, but also to be able to look forward to coming sleep with peaceful heart, knowing that we *dwell in safety* in the arms of a God who is with us through every darkness, including the darkness of sleep and even the darkness of death. Indeed, there is no *greater joy* than this.

### PSALM 133 (134) Didactic

This is the last of the psalms of ascent. The pilgrims have reached their destination and, as a night falls (or perhaps as the pilgrimage draws to its close), they call upon the priests and levites, *who serve the Lord* day and night in the Temple precincts, to *lift up* their *hands* towards the Holy of Holies, and the divine Presence there, and *bless the Lord* throughout the watches of the night (st 1-2).

Human hands, raised *to bless* God, also bring down God's blessing upon human creatures. The blessing of the mighty Maker of both *heaven and earth* will keep them safe during the night – or during the return leg of their pilgrimage journey (st 3).

The praying of this psalm of *adieu* to God is a fitting way for us to end our day, one more day on our pilgrimage. From the gospels we learn that our Lord sometimes spent a whole night in prayer (e.g.Luke 6:12). In his Body, the Church, he continues that prayer not only through those who get up, while others sleep, to raise their hands in prayer to God, but also through the Church's liturgy which is being celebrated at every hour of day and night in some part of the world. In that unending praise we have been engaged as we prayed the Prayer of the Church this day.

## AFTER EVENING PRAYER II OF SUNDAYS AND SOLEMNITIES
### PSALM 90 (91) Didactic

This is not so much a psalm as a piece of spiritual counselling. Perhaps originally a temple priest addressed it to a pilgrim who had sought his advice. Tonight he offers it to us: after so many centuries, his wise words have lost none of their validity.

As one who has long sojourned in the Temple and experienced God as *shelter and shade*, he declares that the Lord is *My refuge, my stronghold, my God* – the threefold *my* emphasising the intimacy of their relationship (st 1).

He goes on to assure us that it is the same God who is our defender, freeing us from any *snare* set to entrap us, providing us warm, protective shelter like the *wings* of a mother bird and removing every fear. You may face *the terror of the night* (the time associated with evil forces), or *the arrow* of the *day* (even daylight hours have their dangers), or *the plague* that stalks as evening *darkness* falls once more, or *the scourge* of the epidemic that rages *at noon* (the hour when evil spirits are said to roam), but – notice how positively it is put – *You will not fear*. It isn't difficult to adapt this stanza to periods of life rather than hours of the day, so that *the terror of the night* becomes the threat of ageing; *the scourge at noon*, the mid-life crisis; *the arrow by day*, the problems of growing up; *the plague in the darkness*, approaching death. Life may be risky but the command remains: *You will not fear* (st 2-3).

If God's protection is as gentle as that of a mother bird, it is nonetheless as sturdy as a warrior's armour. *His faithfulness* is as nimble as a small *buckler*, as all-embracing as a large *shield*; others may fall to *right* and left, but you will be safe; you have only to compare the lot of *the wicked* with that of those who trust in God to realise that *Upon you no evil shall fall*. While we may find unacceptable the tradition that retribution falls upon evildoers even during life, it is undeniable that no lasting evil shall fall upon those who trust in God. He has even given the command that *his angels* should *keep you in all your ways*, carrying you like a child in *their hands* lest you should dash *your foot against a stone* – a constant danger along the rock-strewn roads of Palestine. And so you will be able to *trample* underfoot all the evils that threaten – colourfully pictured as *lion* and *viper*, *young lion* and *dragon* (st 4-7).

The fine poetic words of the priest now come to an end: in the final stanzas he acts as spokesman for the still more exhilarating words of God himself. To the man or woman who *clings to me in love*, who through intimate union with me *knows my name*, God makes wondrous promises: *I will free* them, *I shall answer* their prayers, *I will save* them and I will crown them with *glory*. They will have *length of life* and abundant proof of *my saving power* (st 8-9).

At the end of the day it would be hard to find a more uplifting psalm, assuring us as it does that our trust in God is not misplaced, that in all the trials of life he is close at hand, that his motherly care never deserts us, his angels are beside us. If the devil's misuse of the psalm stands as a warning that trust in God must not be used as a cloak for testing God (Matthew 4:5f), the true depths of its meaning must surely have escaped even the psalmist himself. It is only with the coming of Jesus that we see how God's promises are fulfilled. If we cling to him in love, if we abide in him (the word, which suggests staying overnight with him, is particularly appropriate in a Night Prayer) we shall be protected and supported in this life, and hereafter we shall enjoy an eternal *length of life* and with it an appreciation of the wonderful *saving power* of our dear God. With such consoling thoughts we can go to bed in peace.

**MONDAY**
**PSALM 85 (86) Lament** (see Week 3 Wednesday, page 198)

**TUESDAY**
**PSALM 142 (143) Lament** (see Week 4 Thursday, page 250)

**WEDNESDAY**
**PSALM 30 (31) Lament** (see Week 2 Monday, page 123)

**PSALM 129 (130) Lament** (see Week 4 Sunday, page 222)

# NIGHT PRAYER

**THURSDAY**
**PSALM 15 (16) Confidence** (see Week 2 Sunday, page 113)

**FRIDAY**
**PSALM 87 (88) Lament** (see Week 4 Tuesday, page 238)

# Appendix 1
# LIST OF CANTICLES

(1 Timothy 3: 16 This canticle which is used only at Evening Prayer I on the feast of the Epiphany is not dealt with in this book.)

# Appendix 2
# A NOTE ON THE PSALM NUMBERS

*The numbering of the psalms sometimes causes confusion. There are two different numerations in use, the original Hebrew one and the one in the Greek translation made 200 years or so before the time of Christ. The Greek translators noticed that the Hebrew psalms number 9 and 10 are in reality one long 'alphabetical' psalm, i.e. the first letters of each verse, when taken in sequence, make up the complete Hebrew alphabet. They decided, therefore, to correct this anomaly by numbering the whole psalm as 9. But they also introduced other changes – 114 and 115 were made into one psalm, while psalms 116 and 147 were each divided into two. The net result is that the numbering of the Hebrew version is for the most part one in advance of the Greek. For practical purposes all that need be remembered is that the Prayer of the Church, like many other liturgical books, follows the Greek numeration, and places the Hebrew numbering in brackets. Thus, the psalm "The Lord is my shepherd' is headed Psalm 22 (23), i.e. number 22 in the Greek and number 23 in the Hebrew. The same arrangement has been adopted throughout this book.*

# Appendix 3
## LIST OF PSALMS

| PSALM | PAGE | PSALM | PAGE | PSALM | PAGE |
|---|---|---|---|---|---|
| 1 | 30 | 18(19)A | 91 | 36(37) | 95 |
| 2 | 31 | 18(19)B | 45 | 37(38) | 113 |
| 3 | 33 | 19(20) | 55 | 38(39) | 101 |
| 4 | 192 | 20(21) | 56 | 39(40) | 92 |
| 5 | 43 | 21(22) | 156 | 40(41) | 74 |
| 6 | 42 | 22(23) | 86 | 41(42) | 90 |
| 7 | 46 | 23(24) | 51 | 42(43) | 96 |
| 8 | 123 | 24(25) | 66 | 43(44) | 107 |
| 9A(9) | 42 | 25(26) | 73 | 44(45) | 93 |
| 9B(10) | 50 | 26(27) | 60 | 45(46) | 75 |
| 10(11) | 47 | 27(28) | 73 | 46(47) | 59 |
| 11(12) | 50 | 28 (29) | 44 | 47(48) | 65 |
| 12(13) | 54 | 29(30) | 67 | 48(49) | 99 |
| 13(14) | 54 | 30(31) | 89 | 49(50) | 132 |
| 14(15) | 47 | 31(32) | 68 | 50(51) | 70 |
| 15(16) | 82 | 32(33) | 53 | 51(52) | 101 |
| 16(17) | 60 | 33(34) | 80 | 52(53) | 98 |
| 17(18)A | 57 | 34(35) | 70 | 53(54) | 98 |
| 17(18)B | 63 | 35(36) | 57 | 54(55) | 104 |

*The page numbers indicate the first occasion a psalm appears in the Prayer of the Church.*

| PSALM | PAGE | PSALM | PAGE | PSALM | PAGE |
|---|---|---|---|---|---|
| 55(56) | 111 | 75(76) | 87 | 93(94) | 178 |
| 56(57) | 63 | 76(77) | 102 | 94(95) | 24 |
| 57(58) | * | 77(78)A | 185 | 95(96) | 134 |
| 58 (59) | 115 | 77(78)B | 189 | 96(97) | 103 |
| 59(60) | 115 | 78(79) | 154 | 97(98) | 146 |
| 60(61) | 124 | 79(80) | 108 | 98(99) | 152 |
| 61(62) | 105 | 80(81) | 109 | 99(100) | 72 |
| 62(63) | 33 | 81(82) | 168 | 100(101) | 171 |
| 63(64) | 124 | 82(83) | * | 101(102) | 170 |
| 64(65) | 97 | 83(84) | 133 | 102(103) | 176 |
| 65(66) | 163 | 84(85) | 139 | 103(104) | 83 |
| 66(67) | 106 | 85(86) | 145 | 104(105) | 78 |
| 67(68) | 138 | 86(87) | 151 | 105(106) | 120 |
| 68(69) | 155 | 87(88) | 173 | 106(107) | 159 |
| 69(70) | 147 | 88(89)A | 144 | 107(108) | 177 |
| 70(71) | 135 | 88(89)B | 150 | 108(109) | * |
| 71(72) | 111 | 89(90) | 150 | 109(110) | 38 |
| 72(73) | 166 | 90(91) | 193 | 110(111) | 130 |
| 73(74) | 141 | 91(92) | 121 | 111(112) | 164 |
| 74(75) | 147 | 92(93) | 129 | 112(113) | 126 |

*The page numbers indicate the first occasion a psalm appears in the Prayer of the Church.*
*\*These psalms are omitted from the Prayer of the Church because of their imprecatory language; some verses from certain other psalms have also been omitted for the same reason.*

*The page numbers indicate the first occasion a psalm appears in the Prayer of the Church.*

# Appendix 4
# MAPS

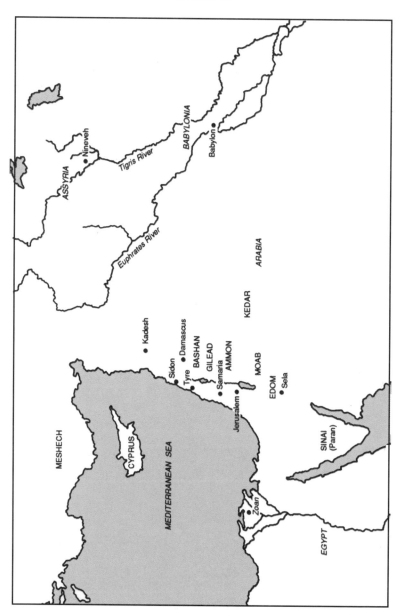

277